U.S. MILITARY SERVICE

A Reference Handbook

Other Titles in ABC-CLIO's
CONTEMPORARY
WORLD ISSUES
Series

Books in the Contemporary World Issues series address vital issues in today's society such as genetic engineering, pollution, and biodiversity. Written by professional writers, scholars, and nonacademic experts, these books are authoritative, clearly written, up-to-date, and objective. They provide a good starting point for research by high school and college students, scholars, and general readers as well as by legislators, businesspeople, activists, and others.

Each book, carefully organized and easy to use, contains an overview of the subject, a detailed chronology, biographical sketches, facts and data and/or documents and other primary-source material, a directory of organizations and agencies, annotated lists of print and nonprint resources, and an index.

Readers of books in the Contemporary World Issues series will find the information they need in order to have a better understanding of the social, political, environmental, and economic issues facing the world today.

U.S. MILITARY SERVICE

A Reference Handbook

Cynthia A. Watson

**CONTEMPORARY
WORLD ISSUES**

A B C  C L I O

Santa Barbara, California
Denver, Colorado
Oxford, England

Copyright 2007 by ABC-CLIO, Inc.

Library of Congress Cataloging-in-Publication Data

Watson, Cynthia Ann.
  U.S. military service : a reference handbook / Cynthia A. Watson.
    p.   cm.—(Contemporary world issues)
  Includes bibliographical references and index.
  ISBN-10: 1-85109-978-6 (hard cover : alk. paper)—
  ISBN-10: 1-85109-979-4 (ebook)
  ISBN-13: 978-1-85109-978-8 (hard cover : alk. paper)—
  ISBN-13: 978-1-85109-979-5 (ebook)
    1. United States—Armed Forces—Recruiting, enlistment, etc.—
Handbooks, manuals, etc.   2. Draft—United States—Handbooks,
manuals, etc.   3. United States—Armed Forces—Minorities—
Handbooks, manuals, etc.   4. United States—Armed Forces—
Women—Handbooks, manuals, etc.   5. United States—Armed
Forces—Gays—Handbooks, manuals, etc.   I. Title.
UB323.W358   2007
355.2'20973—dc22

                                                      2006030997

09   08   07   10 9 8 7 6 5 4 3 2 1

This book is also available on the World Wide Web as an eBook.
Visit abc-clio.com for details.

ABC-CLIO, Inc.
130 Cremona Drive, P.O. Box 1911
Santa Barbara, California 93116–1911

This book is printed on acid-free paper. ∞
Manufactured in the United States of America.

Contents

Preface

believe that joining a national service is an extraordinarily personal decision. The content of this volume, highly biased toward the concept of national military service, is only a portion of the idea, albeit admittedly potentially the most lethal aspect. National service can be federal employment, a private not-for-profit engaging in a "good cause," or many other things. The commitment to that service, however, must entail a strong, personal willingness to do something that we take for granted but is a profound idea: giving up time—an irreplaceable and finite aspect to each and every one of our lives—in exchange for contributing to a cause that is outside of ourselves. Many of us engage in this exchange without giving it much thought at all, because "we need the money" or " everyone else does it," but I recall the years when many people did it because the Constitution of the United States and the legal system forced them to do so. During the war in Southeast Asia, many in the United States protested that war and saw national service not as a commitment but as a requirement that they hated and eventually changed.

As a result of the change, people who engage in national military service in the United States today do so completely voluntarily. The process of getting to the all-volunteer force from a draft was extraordinarily painful for society and evidenced considerable misunderstanding on both sides of a bifurcated society. Many of those who went to Vietnam, did their tours of duty, and came home to bitterness and hostility often could not comprehend the reception they received from their fellow citizens. Others who disagreed with the national decision to go to Vietnam often protested the basic premise of U.S. power, the use of that power in a corner of Southeast Asia, and the idea that those who had served should be acknowledged for their service. This bifurcation of society was ugly, manifesting almost a complete misunderstanding of the other side's views and basic values; I am not sure we have, in fact, progressed a great deal in the third of a century since the war ended or the all-volunteer force replaced the prior system. Indeed, the 2004 presidential election illustrated how deep the divisions remain. The Nixon administration's abolition of the required military draft in 1973 led to the current volunteer force that wages wars, provides defense, and increasingly does nation-building around the world.

That lack of understanding by each side of the great divide bothers me tremendously not only because of the policy disconnects it creates but also because it personalizes misunderstandings about the people on the "other side." The last time I checked, all of us are citizens of the same Republic who have the right—perhaps the obligation—to disagree on policy proscriptions but not to assume such high levels of hostility to those with whom we disagree, especially on the use of national military service in society. I bias this book disproportionately toward trying to bridge that gap by discussing one aspect of national service—national military service. I do not expect anyone else to agree completely with my interpretations or even choices of topics. I seek to be as complete as I can, but I know that any two people looking at this very intricate topic are bound to interpret the material differently. It is those interpretations that form the basis for the much-needed national debate on our policies. If I can get anyone to engage more thoroughly in this policy debate, then my book will have been a success.

I work with senior officers in the U.S. and foreign militaries as a professor of strategy at the National War College. That is an incredible privilege that few share. I did not serve in uniform, but I did grow up heavily imbued with the national service ethos, having come from an Agency for International Development family with extended years overseas. I have learned a great deal about military service by teaching with people who serve the nation in military uniform. I only wish everyone in society had the luxury to engage in a similar national debate about service that characterizes many seminars and coffee discussions at the National War College; I believe we would all be far better off if the kinds of exchanges we have took place more frequently across society.

There are, as ever, many people who helped me with this project. I apologize in advance for probably missing some. Mildred "Mim" Vasan has been my friend for two decades, beginning with her time at Greenwood Publishing when I wrote *U.S. Interest Groups*. I am always intrigued by her suggestions and honored that she thinks of me when she is looking for an author. Dayle Dermatis at ABC-CLIO has been most helpful in this process. Anna Moore was patient and gracious.

Dr. Sharon Murphy has been the closest thing I ever had to a sister over more than twenty-five years, and I know she is always there: thank you. Scott W. and Bonnie L. Nordstrom are the two most patient children in the world. I cannot ever repay them for their patience, tolerance, support, and enthusiasm. As we have discussed, I wish for them the ability to see the work that ignites their passion, regardless of what it is. It is that passion that will carry one on to success and sustainability, regardless of what others may say.

I am extraordinarily lucky to work at an institution that cherishes collegiality. The National War College, celebrating the education of its sixtieth class of national security strategists, is a federal institution where three-quarters of its students are sent by the services and a quarter from civilian agencies, most prominently the Department of State. Generals George Marshall and Dwight Eisenhower, among others, recognized that national security strategy could not be developed or executed without trust between civilians and uniformed officers. The faculty of the institution has always reflected roughly the same representation that exists within the student body. I am privileged to work with some of the most committed individuals of the services and federal agencies as well as academics who have been both practitioners and scholars of national security strategy.

Major General Theresa "Marne" Peterson, USAF, Class of 1993, has brought a breath of fresh air to the college as our new commandant and is an exceptionally successful graduate who excels at national security strategy. Dr. Mark Clodfelter, a retired Air Force officer, took the time to offer significant improvements for which I owe him a great deal of thanks. His generosity and willingness to put other things aside to help me exemplifies the collegiality for which the college faculty is renowned. Colonel J. C. Conner, USAF, and Colonel Mark Tillman, USAF, represented their service chiefs to the students and gave me a couple of answers I had searched for over the weeks. Dr. Geb Schweigler is not only an impeccable analyst of our own and his native European political systems but also one of the most adept users of the

Internet that one can imagine. Susan Sherwood has a steel and a glue that are so valuable for our institution, but more particularly and delightfully for me she is a friend. Susan's patience and ability to invariably find something positive in every discussion we have ever had is truly invaluable. Colonel Victoria Leignadier and Colonel Tom Trobridge, USA, and Colonel Kevin Keith, USAF, all clarified some questions with virtually instant responses, which I appreciated greatly. I thank Dr. Roy Stafford for his long service as a superb, gifted teacher as well as patient administrator at the National War College over his twenty years in uniform and as a civilian; I have rarely met someone who would invariably drop whatever he was doing to help a student or a colleague. Although he loved being the curmudgeon, he has been so much more to the college. Dr. Dave Tretler and I began at the college at the same time. He has subsequently hung up his Air Force uniform for civilian attire but is a passionate, keen defender of the art of teaching national security. He offered a historian's eye for the portions of this volume that he read. Captain Steve Camacho, USN, is the consummate professional who is such an asset because of his unflappability and wry smile when he's amused; thankfully, he is often amused, but his support as my department chairman was important. I regret that the Fairfax County schools lost Colonel Mark Pizzo, USMC Retired, because public education needs teachers like him, but getting him back with the college in 2004 has proved a great gain for the National War College and for me as a colleague. Mark retains the tenacity that earned him his Marine moniker of "bulldog" for a reason: he never forgets nor does he abandon anything that needs to be done, regardless of how many other people have given up. Dr. Lorry Fenner helped me with some questions about women in combat. Dr. Paul Godwin is a superb scholar who remains a dear friend even if he has left us and gone to California. Dr. Bud Cole is my best friend. He teaches me daily about the Navy, national military service, China, and life; I thank him profoundly and look forward to his smile each and every day.

Finally, I note that the views expressed here are personal and do not represent those of the National War College or any agency of the U.S. government.

1

Background and History

In March 2003, after a year of buildup and political debate, George Walker Bush, forty-third president of the United States, asked young men and women in uniform to oust Saddam Hussein, a brutal Iraqi dictator of more than a quarter of a century. The fear was that Iraq's repressive regime was intent upon developing weapons of mass destruction and would use those weapons against anyone in its way, much as Saddam Hussein had brutalized the Kurdish minority in the north with chemical weapons in 1988 and invaded Kuwait in 1991 (on the grounds that the region had historically been an Iraqi province).

Through the actions of Bush's father, George Herbert Walker Bush, the Iraqis were thrown out of Kuwait, but the menace continued for another twelve years, until George W. Bush's 2003 invasion of Iraq, which was taken in the face of much international and domestic criticism and skepticism. Coming eighteen months after the airliner attacks that killed 2,800 people at Shanksville, Pennsylvania, the World Trade Center in Manhattan, and the Pentagon along the Potomac, the rebuttals against this invasion of Iraq were more vocal than were those spoken against invading Afghanistan to oust the Taliban but still proved unsuccessful in dissuading the president from his mission.

Little serious opposition was expected from Iraqi troops, and this expectation proved accurate during the initial days of the invasion. However, conditions deteriorated into a bloodier and more prolonged struggle. Three years later, more than 130,000 officers and enlisted personnel were still in the theater, while more than 2,500 U.S. lives had been lost and tens of thousands more had suffered significant injury. The victory over

Saddam Hussein's forces and his subsequent capture proved easy compared to the mammoth task of rebuilding Iraq and bringing democracy to the country.

The U.S. armed forces have also served as vital problem-solving agents, not only in Iraq but also during the hurricanes that hit the Gulf Coast in late August and early September 2005 and during the tsunami that devastated the Indian Ocean region and killed hundreds of thousands of people in early 2005. The decision to ask men and women to give their lives to free another people, to defend national interests, or to preserve democracy (to name a few) is an awesome one for any president. This decision is particularly serious in situations that are not so clearly linked to protecting the homeland, as was the case during the disaster recovery efforts on the U.S. Gulf Coast and during the Indian Ocean tsunami. One cannot replace the time that a man or woman in uniform gives to the nation nor can we replace those lives lost. President George Walker Bush is not the first man to ask that of his fellow citizens, nor, sadly, is he likely to be the last. But it does not mean that the request or even the willingness to serve is without controversy.

The United States is currently experiencing one of its periodic low-level debates about returning to mandatory national service. The topic is beginning to appear in a number of conversations because of the exhausted state of the armed forces today in light of the deployments to Iraq and Afghanistan. The debate over the merits of obligatory versus volunteer national military service is one that has long created sharp divisions among the public and our political leaders.

A parallel discussion has emerged regarding whether the United States should be using its sons and daughters to solve the world's problems. For some, that argument lost all relevancy on September 11, 2001, when a terrorist plot sent airplanes that ripped into the World Trade Center. For others, however, the blood that has been shed in Iraq is wasting the most precious national resource for the sake of goals that do not seem to warrant the sacrificing of so many lives. This view holds that the world is an imperfect place that will always be peopled with dangerous actors who should be confronted only when necessary rather than be sought out to create conflict. In other words, nations will be nations.

National service describes a commitment by members of society to fulfill an obligation to the rest of society. This does not exclude noncitizens, nor does it require citizens to contribute to a broader societal goal. In the chapters that follow, I will discuss this subject, though I will place less of an emphasis on it than on national military service. National service in the United States has often been characterized by volunteerism or even volunteer activities in the service of less fortunate people outside our own country, and it is often more synonymous with the Peace Corps, VISTA (Volunteers in Service to America), or AmeriCorps than it is with carrying arms. Gorham (1992) and Dionne et al. (2003) examine this approach in detail.

National service is a core principle of the United States, even though focus upon it has been somewhat cyclical. The United States' unique blend of national self-assessment, which emphasizes the individual, and the general preference for individual (as opposed to government) responsibility have long characterized the citizens of this nation. As a generalization, people in this country believe that some sort of national service is part of our self-assessment as caring and compassionate people. In his inaugural address in 1988, President George H.W. Bush talked of "a thousand points of light" as a way of encouraging his fellow citizens to engage in some aspect of national service to help others. Similarly, his son, President George W. Bush, has vigorously supported federal funding for faith-based volunteer activities to enhance citizens' abilities to work for those in need.

The concept of national service is not solely the property of Republicans. President Bill Clinton also promoted volunteer service, even though both he and President Jimmy Carter were perhaps better known for their service activities after they left office. President Clinton has worked in tandem with the elder President Bush on behalf of those in need in the wake of the 2004 Indian Ocean tsunami and Hurricane Katrina (2005), while President Carter has for many years been a visible promoter of health-related, political, and electoral activities around the world through the Carter Center at Emory University in Atlanta. Carter's and Clinton's services as retired presidents have brought prestige to the United States and its citizens in the eyes of the world.

National military service is part of national service and is, arguably, far more controversial and visible in the United States because it may require the ultimate sacrifice of one's life. The citizenry of the United States has had mixed feelings about whether we should worry about the world beyond our borders. George Washington's parting words to the nation cautioned us about foreign entanglements, which by extension might necessitate armed service, and generated a controversy that has endured for more than two centuries. National military service today is each participant's voluntary decision, but that has not always been the case. For example, between 1940 and 1973, all males in the United States were required to sign up for military service (a process called "the draft") when they turned eighteen unless they received certain types of deferments for clear-cut reasons. Women citizens were finally allowed to vote as of August 26, 1920, but they remain excluded from the requirement to register for national military service. In some other countries around the world, both men and women sign up to be available and serve when the nation needs them. The decision to ask men and women to bear arms is very much dependent on a state's history and societal context.

The U.S. Constitution does not grant an absolute right for anyone to engage in national military service; joining the military is a privilege that requires that certain conditions be met. When one signs up to serve the nation as a member of the active-duty military, the individual enters the service as a full-time participant. All men and women, enlisted and officers, report for duty if they meet certain physical and age conditions. No one under seventeen is to serve, and the upper limit for initial entry to the services is thirty-five, although certain conditions can apply to the particular category one is entering. Navy Reservists, for example, are not accepted above the age of thirty-nine, though twenty-eight is the upper limit for active-duty Marines. Others sign up to serve their fellow citizens through the Reserves (now more commonly known as the Reserve component because the Reserves are considered an integral part of the active-duty force) or the National Guard (the title given to the state militias after they were made part of a national patchwork of state groups in 1903). The basic premise for whoever signs up for national military service is the same: all those signing up for national military service offer their lives if society requires it to protect their fellow citizens.

Other conditions that enter into the candidate's acceptability for national military service include drug and/or alcohol abuse, criminal activities, overt homosexuality, mental aptitude, weight standards (at the upper and lower ends), and height standards. In short, participating in national service is not a given, nor does it represent a simple decision to join. It is a conscious choice to serve the nation in one of the armed services.

Military Basics

The top ranks of the military are the officers, running from highest (in contemporary society, this is a four-star general or admiral) to lowest (second lieutenant in the Army/Air Force/Marine Corps and an ensign in the Navy) commissioned officer. Officers' commissions are a commitment by the Congress of the United States; that is, promotions are also granted by Congress. Rank is a pyramid structure, so there are fewer officers at each rank higher along the ladder. In common parlance, officers are known not merely by their formal title, Commander X, but also as an O-5 (officer at the fifth rank from the bottom) in the Navy. Along with the higher rank comes significantly enhanced responsibility for achieving missions assigned and commanding higher numbers of forces.

The period one spends at each rank is completely dependent on one's service record. Promotions take place through a selection board of peers and superiors. Selection board procedures vary from service to service, but they are generally highly subjective to the individuals on the board as much as dependent on the merits of any individual's file. A soldier who earns his promotion earlier than his peers, known as his "year group" according to the year that his cohort earned their commissions, is often called "deep selected," particularly by the Air Force community. There are regulations governing how long one can serve related to the rank that individual has achieved. Someone at the lieutenant colonel or commander rank, for example, must retire at twenty-six years of service if no promotion is on the horizon. Once a promotion selection board selects someone for the next rank, Congress must approve the commission. Although this is virtually automatic, the Congress has the right not to confirm individuals for ranks for which they have been nominated and has chosen not to promote some individuals whom it believes are not representatives of what the United States seeks in its military personnel. Some of these decisions may result from politics, but failures to confirm do occur, as happened to General Gregory Martin, USAF, who withdrew his 2004 nomination as Pacific Command combatant commander when confronted with Arizona Republican senator John McCain's strong resistance.

Each service has both enlisted and noncommissioned officers. Noncommissioned officers (NCOs) are the heart of the armed services and one of the aspects of the U.S. military that makes it so successful because these career officers provide the interface between the officer corps and the enlisted personnel of the services. Many NCOs become the mentors of the young men and women who serve. NCOs supervise the men and women who enlist for a fixed period of time; these men and women are most often extremely young and are often undirected in both their behaviors and goals. NCOs take the strategy, operations, and tactics of the officer leadership on a ship or in any unit, then translate them into specific guidance and supervision to help the bulk of the force—the enlisted—make the operation or campaign happen in the most basic ways.

Enlisted personnel, both men and women, sign on for an enlistment period determined by the law. The overwhelming majority of those enlisted in the services are young and have no distinct sense of how they want to proceed with their lives. Many enlist because they are looking for some structure in their lives, while others sign up because they need the financial benefits that result, whether a job or educational payback for having service. Enlisted personnel attend basic orientation (the famous Marine boot camp, which is a commonly cited term in society meaning lowest level orientation) and then pursue a period in active duty when they carry out that activity.

The military is highly structured and hierarchical. Chain of command is absolute and to be respected to maintain a functioning organization and to prevent problems. Yet it has its oddities in each of the services. Senior officers are addressed formally by rank and surname. Often senior officers address inferior officers by their surnames. As one Navy captain explained, in this way it is easier to get a person's attention in a crisis, since the youngster has been accustomed to hearing a surname but will jerk to attention upon hearing the given name if a crisis arises. Certain terms, procedures, and laws are common across the four services (for example, promotion, retirement, change of command, seniority by date of rank), but each service has its own culture, traditions, and values. Those service-specific cultures are fascinating but also confusing, even to others in uniform. As the services have become increasingly specialized over the past thirty years, even the communities (e.g., aviation, infantry, quartermaster) within a service may not be all that familiar with the other communities. This is particularly true for the Navy, which is spread so far across the globe. For a dated though still valid analysis of these cultural differences within the armed forces, see Builder (1989). Beginning in the mid-twentieth century as the United States acknowledged its global presence and responsibilities, the military became divided into operational units called Unified Combatant Commands. These regional commands are a mixture of at least two services that work under a single unified commander with a title exemplifying the region where it was operating. Pacific Command, headquartered at Camp Smith outside Honolulu and Pearl Harbor, has the area of responsibility from the western coast of the United States to the India-Pakistan border, a region encompassing 1.3 billion Chinese and over 1 billion Indians among millions of others living there. Southern Command, located at Miami, has responsibility for the area from southern Mexico to Tierra del Fuego. European Command (EUCOM) worries about activities from Africa north into Europe and Russia into Central Asia. Central Command has the volatile Middle East into Pakistan, but not Israel, which is part of EUCOM. The newest regional division is Northern Command, which focuses on the homeland of Mexico, the United States, and Canada.

The senior officer is the combatant commander, which was known as the commander-in-chief (CINC) for that command until Secretary of Defense Donald Rumsfeld reminded everyone that the United States has a single commander-in-chief and he serves in the White House. With the Goldwater-Nichols act of 1986, a more concerted effort was made to promote cooperation across the services, hence a sharing of the leadership of the combatant commanders for the regional commands emerged. Testament to this change was the appointment of the Marine commandant, General James L. Jones, as combatant commander for European Command (and its parallel command at the North Atlantic Treaty Organization) in the early 2000s, a post traditionally held by a four-star Army general.

Functional commands are accountable for a technical skill or concern. The Joint Forces Command, in the Tidewater region of southeastern Virginia, worries about promoting cooperation across the services in meaningful operational ways. The Strategic Air Command, located in Omaha, Nebraska, concentrated on nuclear weapons—both bombers and missiles—from the 1950s through its reincarnation as the U.S. Strategic Command (USSTRATCOM) in 1992 at the end of the Cold War. This group shows the amalgamation of strategic weapons from all the services into a single command as Goldwater-Nichols intended. Other functional commands include the U.S. Transportation Command (USTRANSCOM) at Scott Air Force Base on the Illinois side of the St. Louis metropolitan area, or Special Forces Command, headquartered in the Florida panhandle, which concentrates on coordinating special forces across the services. The Reserve component operates through Reserve Affairs Worldwide Support as a command.

The period during which an enlisted person is obligated to serve is called his or her enlistment, while an officer's period of service is his or her commission, as granted by Congress. All officer ranks are approved by Congress, while officers on the ground have the power to promote an enlisted person if they should find this necessary. Flag and general officers retain their rank into retirement unless it is revoked for cause. All military personnel, from the newest buck rifleman to the chairman of the Joint Chiefs of Staff, are governed by the Uniform Code of Military Justice (UCMJ), which supersedes the Constitution for the time in service for the nation. Statutory retirement age for a military personnel member is age sixty-two, although a commissioned officer can be recalled for active duty until age sixty-five.

The Services

The U.S. Congress's moves toward jointness, as promoted through Goldwater-Nichols, revolve around the individual services, which retain a pride and culture all their own. The following notes present just an overview; for more details, please consult each service's extensive Web site, which contains a detailed history and references (which are also found the in the Resources chapter of the present volume); in addition, many "coffee-table" volumes exist on the services for further reference.

The Army, dating to its founding in 1775 as the Continental Army, is the ground service with several branches: the infantry, cavalry, and artillery branches concentrate on fighting activities, while the quartermaster corps (logistics), intelligence, and signals perform support functions. The Army is oriented toward following doctrine and toward a system that allows it to operate across the world. Whether its soldiers are stationed in Iraq or Arizona, the Army operates with a commonality to provide a standard product that serves the nation. Like the Marines and the Air Force, the Army values education and training. The Army homepage is at www.army.mil, and its recruiting page is at www.goarmy.mil.

In contrast, the Navy is a tradition-oriented service, but it has a far more independent role for the captain of the ship. With many historical links to the Royal Navy of the United Kingdom, the Navy is as wide-ranging in its span as are any of the other services. With the United States the only global power in the early twenty-first century, no service exclusively operates within the continental United States, but historically the Navy's communications have not allowed the captain the option (even if he so desired) to verify each and every action he took when deployed on the high seas. As a result, the Navy allows its personnel a greater sense of independence within the widest context of the operations under way. The Navy also retains a set of titles for its personnel that differs from those of other services. Admirals hold the highest rank while ensigns are newly commissioned officers. Noncommissioned officers are petty officers, and enlisted personnel are sailors and seamen/women. As a result, the Navy has warfare specialties in surface, carrier, or air operations, and submarines, as well as the traditional support functions (intelligence, logistics, and such). The Navy values its officers and sailors learning from their experiences "with the fleet," which means operating at sea instead of sitting with books, because the most relevant professional experience comes from sailing with the fleet. The official Web site for the U.S. Navy is www.navy.mil; the Navy Historical Center can be found at www.history.navy.mil.

The Marine Corps is easily the smallest and most tightly knit service, dating to the founding of the Republic but always wary of protecting its role as a "sea service component" (the Marine Corps is considered under the Navy in many situations) and yet with dedicated amphibious, air, and ground-pounding components. The Marine Corps has an incredible commitment to the idea that the Corps is a single unit with parts around the world; on the Marine Corps' "birthday" (November 10), a proclamation by an early twentieth-century commandant, Major General John LeJeune, reminds all Marines of their responsibilities and shared experiences with their peers. Marines allow their leadership to take charge within a firefight to save the lives of unit members but always within the history and tradition of the Corps. The stereotype of a barking, solidly built man with the shortest of crew cuts belies the creativity and ingenuity that characterize most Marine Corps personnel. The Marine Corps extols its long history and current challenges at www.usmc.mil.

The Air Force, formally created by Defense Department reforms in 1947, dates back to the early twentieth century, when the airplane introduced a whole new perspective on warfare. Operating as the Army Air Service from the end of World War I until the eve of Pearl Harbor when it became the Army Air Force, the Air Force as an independent service reflects its relative youth. The Air Force has an extraordinary openness to new technology and firmly believes that technology can change the face of warfare and any specific battle. A joke across the services is that the Air Force believes that bombing is all that is ever necessary in a conflict, leaving anyone else to come in to clean up what the bomber pilots have done. This commonly held view contains more than a little truth. Yet, within the Air Force, the hierarchy starts with fighter pilots whose responsibility it is to fight one-on-one with other pilots in highly skilled operations and tactics that emphasize the skills of a small number of pilots. Interestingly, in the older, more established services, pilots' focus is somewhat more pointed than that of any other warfighters within that service. The official Air Force Web site is www.af.mil.

History and Controversy

The United States underwent a much shorter evolution for its citizens, whose histories initially involved an amalgam of sociohistorical experiences (immigrants) and those who grew up here focused on the future, not the past. Perhaps the size of the nation and the vast resources that have always been available to its citizens, or perhaps because of some other aspect, the United States has had the luxury of debate about many of the issues characterizing the political system over the years.

One of the most enduring controversies in the U.S. experience has been whether the United States needs a standing military. The institution of armed service in this country was founded by the immigrants of the British Isles and north-central

Europe and sustained by people from the rest of the world, and during the first century of U.S. colonization the nation witnessed a tremendous fight over whether it would have a standing army. This concern dated to the colonial period but was heightened by the British army's pernicious behavior during the seventeenth century. Those who feared the standing army, often referred to initially as the radical Whigs (after the particular political view with which adherents were aligned in England), noted that it would become an instrument of tyranny. The radical Whigs' political philosophy, long important in England, came across the ocean along with the waves of colonists, as did the fear that the Crown completely ignored the desires and needs of its people. The English civil war (1642–1645, 1647–1648, and 1649–1651) manifested this struggle in England and ended with the Parliamentary forces tempering the monarchy's implied absolute powers. This hatred for the role of a strong central government, which acted with no clear-cut respect for the desires or rights of the governed, became an enduring cornerstone of political beliefs in some quarters of the evolving United States.

A strong central government backed by an armed force was a source of fear for several reasons. First, the standing army would allow the government to act without consulting those it represented. Second, the crown was likely to ignore completely the desires of a significant portion of the nation. Third, a standing army would be an expensive use of scarce resources. Fourth, a standing army philosophically alienated the society's sense of citizenship by putting power in the hands of those with guns rather than election tools. This view emphasized a commonly held and repetitive concern in U.S. society throughout its history: that a central power did not understand the needs and interests of those existing farther from it.

As the new nation developed, a second school of thought gained support and gradually won the day in the establishment of national service. This school of thought emphasized that individuals could contribute to the formation of this new society but that they could do so only through active involvement. To many, this meant that they would offer their time, whether as officers or enlisted infantrymen, to secure the freedom and prosperity of their lifestyle. This also meant that some members of society were likely to choose the standing army as a career, an alternative that was anathema to the radical Whigs. The nature of armies was, as ever, changing throughout this period, with an emerging requirement for professional soldiers who would guide the service through even further changes or war itself.

Those supporting a standing army often recognized their opponents concerns but saw that opinion shifts were weighted more toward permanent armies. The standing army could evolve with the standards of the military profession around the world, but it would be best for the society if that evolution were linked with people who understood the society as citizen-soldiers and could return to their civilian lives when the military obligation ended. This notion conformed with the idea that people participated in their nation's governance by giving a few years of their time to better the lot of all.

The Debate in the Founding

All too often, the adherents of a particular philosophy begin to believe that they get their guidance from marble tablets handed down to them from some all-knowing being, enabling them to handle questions such as the role of a national military service. The founding of the Republic was neither easy nor quick; rather, it was the culmination of a number of "victories" by one ideological strain over another. In most cases, the "losing" side in any particular political skirmish simply regrouped and reattacked at a later point. As a result, we present repetitive discussions of questions such as whether to have a standing army or merely a state militia system, whether women should be in combat roles, or the issue of whether lesbian and gay members of society should be allowed to serve. The role of defense and national service in those debates cannot be overestimated.

The United States ultimately ended up with a blend of professional military, Reserve, and National Guard forces that works well at times but has had two centuries to grow. Nothing precludes the reopening of the debate at any point, however, since it is all too frequently forgotten how strongly the debate raged throughout the colonial years. Britain, as another example, did not have a standard, uniform belief about the role of military service in the society; the supporters of a strong central government frequently disagreed with those who feared that the central power would allow unfettered use of that power against the average citizen in unwarranted situations, just as the debate sometimes goes in the United States. Many of the authors listed in this chapter's bibliography have recounted this struggle and have elucidated the differences in basic philosophy that endure.

It is often forgotten that British colonists arriving in the United States were developing a national culture on the future of defense and military service at the time of their arrival. The idea that a majority could be repressed by a minority was a fear not far below the surface, and many people believed that the militia or a standing army could be used to accomplish this antidemocratic move. When civil war ended in Great Britain and constitutional government returned to London, others feared that the military legitimized the government and added to concerns that the military had to take a partisan political position.

The questions of British governmental institution-building coincided with the need for similar answers in the colonies. Although the militia was initially created in individual colonies to protect colonists from attacks by Native American, the expansion of colonies into the interior required additional help, since British colonies came into contact with French and Spanish colonies where competing interests led to opposing claims and challenges. The British colonists may have had a military advantage over the Native Americans, but the military balance between the French and British colonials meant that a protective device for land claims was necessary. In this circumstance, the standing Army proved more effective in providing defense against the foreigners. But using the standing army incurred other costs for society and raised fears that the state was infringing on the rights of the individual. Questions also arose about whether citizen-soldiers were more efficient and committed to defending their lands or whether having standing military was a better choice. To a great extent, the answer depended on who was answering the question rather than on the possibility of a simple, straightforward response.

In the United States, national military service has always been central to the national concept of citizenship. The thinking is that one cannot be a fully functional citizen without being willing to put down the plow and take up the rifle to defend one's home, standard of living, and life. Not everyone, however, has agreed with this perspective. For some, national service has always been a voluntary aspect to life in a democracy or in the republic that is our form of governance. For these adherents, national service is a right and a privilege but not a responsibility. This fundamentally different view of obligation raises questions.

As is true of all things in a democracy, debate far outshines decision-making, since people get the opportunity to voice their opinions while lawmakers in Congress must seek a compromise position that is most workable for the entire society.

National service also raised other questions that cut to the heart of the political debate during the founding of the nation and still resonate today. Would citizen-soldiers be quartered in the homes of their friends and neighbors under a forced program, or would they go elsewhere if they were not welcomed? How would that affect the nature of the endeavor to protect their lands? Was the military becoming a defined profession with a skill set that went far beyond that of citizen-soldiers? How much did the citizen-soldier concept relate to one's ownership of land? If such ownership was required, that condition significantly decreased the available pool of militiamen (and they were all white freemen), affecting the agricultural economy across the colonial system.

As some colonists leaned toward creating a professional national military, supporters of the voluntary, militia-style defense raised fears that the standing, professional army would undermine the colonial lifestyle. These supporters advocated the use of militia because after serving a fixed term, they would return to their normal positions in society rather than take on a role that would fix their status.

The Articles of Confederation versus the Constitution

Once the nation was founded, the Articles of Confederation only confounded an already complicated national structure by giving a lot of power to the states and little to any national entity. In light of the vast territory of even the original thirteen states of the Union, it remains inexplicable how the supporters of the Articles believed that the United States could provide for an adequate defense in the absence of a strong, federal government. That lesson soon became apparent, with the Articles lasting less than a decade as the governing authority for the nation. However, the fundamental questions this system created remain important today. The evolution of the national political system into a republic with the signing and ratifying of the Constitution in 1787 was earth-shaking, but it also marked a new stage in the debate, since the Constitution was a uniquely balanced system of federal and state controls, including controls over the individual bearing of arms and use of armed forces for a variety of activities.

The ultimate test of the national psyche about the power of the central government versus states became the bloody and wrenching four-year Civil War that cost so many lives and fractured the nation in ways that have not entirely healed. Again, the decisions about the deployment and use of the militia and required military education at land-grant colleges and universities under the Morrill Act of 1862 illustrated that questions about military service arise in many subtle or secondary ways in the United States but with profound effects on the fabric of society.

In the mid-nineteenth century, national military service provided the glue to hold the Union together by defeating ceding brothers from the South, and it further reconstituted the nation as the Army was promoting expansion to the west to achieve the "manifest destiny" that many found ordained. Because the Army was a national institution, it became an option for reintroducing those who had left the Union. This was a difficult societal task, but the national military has long achieved broader goals than simply winning victories on the battlefields, such as President Harry Truman's decision to integrate the military, which broke the color barrier. The Corps of Engineers built much of the West, while units operating on the western frontier involved themselves in nation-building in a fundamental and important way.

Although the Navy had always been a way for young men to flee their landlocked homes to grow up on a ship at sea, the Navy did not come into its own until the administration of Theodore Roosevelt (1901–1909) and his decision to send the Great White Fleet around the globe to show U.S. navy power and presence. Roosevelt was acting upon the theories of one of the most important national military minds to grace a U.S. classroom, Naval War College professor Alfred Thayer Mahan. Mahan espoused the importance of sea power, and his ideas were widely accepted in an era when other states were building their navies for battleship engagements like the 1916 Battle of Jutland. Roosevelt understood that showing the flag around the world was crucial to raising expectations and understanding of the emerging power of the United States beyond its borders, as well as to protect its newly acquired single colony in the Philippine Islands, thousands of miles from the continental states, or even the newly acquired territory of Hawai'i in the mid-Pacific.

In the World War I period, the United States engaged in serious national efforts to broaden military service by establishing camps outside of the control of the traditional services. Important men such as Grenville Clark, a civilian who advocated military camps to broaden citizen preparation for war, and John McAuley Palmer, an Army educator who sought to make the nation—beyond the military academies—best prepared for war, urged the nation to add military education at Ivy League colleges, institutions other than the military academies such as the Citadel or Virginia Military Academy. Neither the leadership of the services nor the Congress entirely bought the arguments, however, so the 1916 Military Reform Act, vast in its scope at the time, did not include the money for these parallel camps.

World War II presented such a clear need for physical national security that debate about military service subsided a bit. Most of the debate that did occur swirled around the full participation of women in the national effort and the service of genuinely conscientious objectors by some method other than the services. In the case of women, few serious compromises to their participation occurred until the needs presented by the war became so intense that women were allowed to fill in the gaps. Similarly, African American men, most notably through the Tuskegee Airmen at the Tuskegee Institute in Alabama, formed a flying unit with impressive results but not without overcoming protests from the "establishment." Japanese Americans, fresh from their incarceration as "loyalty risks," also served with great dignity and pride in the European theater, even in light of the humiliation they had just endured.

The conscientious objector issue remained relatively low-keyed compared to its appearance twenty years later during the Vietnam War. With patriotism running so high during World War II, especially because of the manner by which the war began, the number of objectors was relatively small during this conflict, and so there was no real impact on the readiness of the force. By the late 1960s, however, as opposition to the Vietnam War grew, military leadership had to address the conscientious objection issue in a way that had never been necessary before.

More Recent Debate on Military Service

For a good portion of the twentieth century, the United States required its young men of a certain defined age, from their late teens through their early thirties, to serve the nation in the armed forces unless there was a reason for exemption. Exemptions included legitimately determined health problems such as asthma, a readily communicable disease, or homosexuality. Particularly from the beginning of World War II in 1941 (under President Franklin Delano Roosevelt) through the ending of the draft in 1973 (under President Richard Milhous Nixon) this obligation put millions of men into uniform as they fulfilled their national obligation.

Less than a decade after President Nixon's decision, President Jimmy Carter reimposed the requirement that men between eighteen and twenty-five years of age register with their local Selective Service boards. The impetus for President Carter's action was the Soviet Union's intervention in Afghanistan in December 1979, but the concerns about a Soviet military buildup and the United States' ability to defend itself had begun several years earlier. President Carter assured the public that he did not intend to reinstitute a draft; instead, he said, he merely wanted to have men registered should the unlikely need for their services arise. All the same, the public expressed significant concern that a remilitarization of society was occurring.

A quarter of a century later, young men must still register, but the United States maintains the "all-volunteer force" military that Nixon instituted in the 1970s. Today, with the United States heavily involved in Iraq and Afghanistan, questions have been raised about whether an all-volunteer military can adequately meet the requirements of combat. Women remain excluded from combat, creating an issue that roils many women's groups in their struggle for equality.

As daily reports reach the public about the young men and women who are losing their lives in the Middle Eastern conflicts, their pictures are spread across the pages of local and national newspapers. These pictures show individuals from every ethnic group that has come to America throughout its history. The all-volunteer force does indeed illustrate our diversity, but at the same time it highlights how the military disproportionately attracts minorities who turn to the armed forces as a path out of disadvantaged childhoods.

Some people believe that military service harkens back to feudalism, a system in which the lord could demand obligation by his fiefs regardless of the cause for which service was required. Few in the United States would agree, however, that national military service in the first decade of the twenty-first century represents the service of enlisted and commissioned fiefs (the U.S. military) to President George W. Bush. Democracy simply eradicates the relationship that feudalism implies. Although this is not a widely held perspective, it is one argument offered.

Other nagging debates remain, such as whether national service has become a deadly substitute for well-paying careers for those who are vulnerable, undereducated, and economically disadvantaged. In this formulation, national service uses those who are not as well educated to fight the wars that support the wealthy, who are not willing to sacrifice their sons and daughters. So those who cannot find an option are giving their lives for the nation because they can find no other way than the military to finance their livelihoods. This may be considered a form of modern-day mercenary service for the good of the whole of society. In classical mercenary terms, the men paid to wage war for a state were often from distant lands and headed back out of the country when their service was concluded. In the new view, men and women are fighting for their country's needs but have no voice in the goals being pursued.

During Operations Desert Shield/Desert Storm of 1990–1991, some questioned whether the United States waged war against Saddam Hussein by sacrificing the blood of young people from the United States in exchange for cheap oil. Many cried "No Blood for Oil," but President George H. W. Bush denied this link. He and those in his administration argued that we were supporting democracy while protecting the interests of the United States in the region. During Operation Iraqi Freedom, such queries have become stronger and more persistent—and remain unanswered three years after the war began.

In the minds of most U.S. citizens, military service is not mercenary service but is instead seen as either a noble, patriotic endeavor or something that kills the young in the prime of their lives. The debate between people on opposing sides has not always been calm and rational: the protests against the Vietnam War were some of the most divisive in our history. In the recent past, as the war in Iraq loomed, protests against this war also proliferated. After the invasion, similar protests were launched, shifting to the argument that politicians were continuing the conflict on the backs of young men and women in the armed services. What remains unknown in this conflict is whether the public will continue to support a policy that is leading to the death of increasing numbers of military forces.

Democratic congressman Charles Rangel of New York argues that the draft would represent a fairer system than the present one, in which children of the wealthy rarely serve. Not all enlistees, however, are from the lower socioeconomic levels of society. One outstanding individual who gave up a very comfortable life to serve his country was Pat Tillman. He played professional football for the Arizona Cardinals football team until the attacks on September 11, when he gave up a lucrative, multimillion dollar contract to join the Army Rangers. In April 2004, Tillman died as a result of misdirected fire by his unit in Afghanistan. Tillman's death has been a terrible blow to the Army's campaign to recruit a wider range of personnel to serve because it illustrated the dangers of combat. If someone as famous as Pat Tillman could die from "friendly fire," it could happen to anyone.

Tillman seems to be the great exception, however; for the overwhelming number of volunteers, educational opportunity is the reason for enlisting in the national service. Many young men and women study through the Reserve Officer Training Corps (ROTC) programs at many universities; these are throwbacks to the 1862 Morrill Bill at land-grant institutions and subsequent laws to create reserve programs parallel to those of the Academies. Others prefer to serve their time first, and then under the educational benefits known as the GI Bill they enroll in higher education. Under the GI Bill, the benefits are set out by law, by time served, and by other criteria. The quid pro quo is the outcome that may motivate many, but the danger may win out over the desire to serve. Yet another motivation for enlistment is to satisfy an innate sense of adventure that appeals to those with wanderlust.

Societal Effects of Military Service

In the three decades of voluntary military service, U.S. society has become increasingly bifurcated into those who serve and those who have no ties with the men and women who serve. The armed forces are increasingly concentrated among people from the South, who tend to have a stronger religious ties and traditional values than their northern or western counterparts; they believe they share surprisingly few connections with their fellow citizens from other parts of the country, especially the "northern liberals." Some critics fear that the self-selection process, which has been in place for more than thirty years, has created an increasingly conservative and politicized officer corps. In 2001, Richard Kohn, University of North Carolina professor and former chief historian of the Air Force, and Peter Feaver, a political scientist from Duke University and Navy reservist, conducted a survey of officers that concluded that the military is becoming more conservative. Many members of the military, however, believe that Kohn and Feaver's claims were exaggerated.

In many cases, those who serve are the sons and daughters of other officers, a process that further reinforces their self-selection and isolation from the rest of society. Although this is not expected to lead to behavior that would dispute the decisions of the civilian chain of command over military affairs, the United States certainly has a different view of military service than it did two generations ago. For many, particularly in the aftermath of the wrenching societal divisions resulting from Vietnam, military service is a more honorable cause that reinforces some social beliefs. A significant portion of the corps of officers in the United States who were still young children during the Vietnam conflict are still very disturbed that their fathers came home to a country that had not appreciated the sacrifices they made. For many, the "civilians" (a term that is sometimes used too broadly to refer to the majority of the U.S. population) had lesser standards and lower levels of patriotism and duty than did the young men and women who served in the military. For many who have lived the Vietnam experience only through their parents, the choices appear so much more clear-cut than they probably did at the time, as people agonized over the war and the U.S. role in that conflict.

As the debate appears to stretch out on Afghanistan (as the initial success has been challenged by the Taliban resurgence) and especially on Iraq, the questions may provide far fuzzier answers to this generation of women and men than Vietnam did for their parents. The use of the armed forces, regardless of the call, is the last-ditch method for solving troubles in the world arena; as most of us believe, war is what we engage in when every single option disappears and we still confront a terrible foe. We do not generally share the philosopher Carl von Clausewitz's view, which he expressed in *On War* almost two centuries ago, that war is just an extension of policy by other means.

National military service raises other uncomfortable issues about equities in society. If service is obligatory, how does the society handle those who deviate from the norm in their dress, their behavior, their sexual orientation, or their belief systems? For example, the United States has excluded Jews from its shores because of their religion, though such exclusion is prohibited today because freedom of religion is protected by the First Amendment and antidiscrimination laws prohibit actions against another on the basis of that person's religious orientation. During World War II, Japanese Americans were incarcerated and then forced to serve only in Europe as if their ethnic backgrounds were a guarantee of disloyalty. Democratic Senator Daniel Inouye, a Japanese American from Hawai'i, was permanently maimed during the war.

Many homosexual women and men who are vocal about their choices are prohibited from joining the service. The ostensible reasons for their exclusion are that gays and lesbians would detract from unit cohesion, undermine the unit's sense of mission, and generally lead to less than stellar collective unit behavior. In this era of fighting terrorism in the Middle East, even extremely capable translators of languages like Arabic, who are in such short supply, have been terminated by the Army on the grounds of their homosexuality because they have breeched the "don't ask, don't tell" policy instituted in 1993. Gays and lesbians ask why their service is not sought after even though they perform honorably and at the same level as their heterosexual peers. As a result, many people are coming to the conclusion that the military is now self-selecting individuals who look and think alike rather than representing the rest of U.S. society's patchwork of colors, sounds, orientations, and backgrounds.

The negative reaction to gays and lesbians is not exclusive to the military. What if the draft were reinstated? Would gays and lesbians still be excluded? What about those who persist in their desire to fulfill their national obligation? Is the nation shortchanging itself when it excludes these young men and women?

Similar issues have arisen with regard to women serving in combat situations. Under policies argued in the 1990s during the Clinton administration, women were deliberately prevented from serving in combat jobs. Various reasons for this decision were given, but the Gulf War of 1991 showed that the distinctions between combat and noncombat positions were somewhat fuzzy. Army physician Rhonda Cornum was in a noncombat position as a medical officer during the effort to remove Saddam Hussein's forces from Kuwait, and yet she was taken prisoner by the Iraqis and subjected to tremendous harm. Under the artificial distinction between combat and noncombat, she should never have been placed in that position. The question still makes many people uncomfortable, but women are increasingly important in all sectors of the U.S. services, even though they represent only 15 percent of the force.

The resolution of each controversy confronting the nation's services results from a process of compromise that is classic to the U.S. experience. On the one hand, this is a nation whose people have ambitions; on the other hand, it is a land inhabited by humans with foibles, differences, and significant strengths. Those in national military service are just as beset by the good and the bad as anyone else. Women and men who enter service conduct their jobs, often marry, commonly have children, frequently divorce, and eventually die like all their peers. The sense of honor and pride felt by the women and men who wear the uniform of the U.S. armed forces is real and deep, but it would be unfair to expect them to have higher aspirations than anyone else in the society.

Talking Past Each Other

In the past quarter century, the United States has reverted to a pattern that some find extremely troublesome. With the end of the draft in 1973 under President Nixon, the all-volunteer military is now constituted by those who seek to serve rather than by those who have been called on to meet an abstract societal obligation. This is true at the highest socioeconomic levels and among those with the most education; few of them have ever donned a uniform or have the vaguest notion of what military service is. Similarly, few who serve are intimately connected with those who operate at the highest levels of education or industry. The misunderstandings of those with whom each group is not acquainted abound. Perhaps the most egregious stereotyping exists between the higher education community and the military, because there has been virtually no crossover between the groups since a decade prior to the end of the draft.

The Clinton administration, constituted of many senior officials who had protested or worked to avoid military service in the 1960s, was seen as the epitome of nonunderstanding by the majority of men and women in uniform. At the same time, there were perceived biases against the uniformed services by the administration and its staff throughout Clinton's two-term presidency. This lack of common understanding bred suspicions and dislike on both sides.

In addition, few people in the U.S. Congress have served in the armed forces and hence lack credible understanding of military affairs as they affect people and policies. This is not a completely new tendency on the Hill; no congresswoman or senator is intimately familiar with all issues facing lawmakers, but the professionalization and special knowledge of the military as an operating force make lawmakers hesitant to question those in the military with whom they interact to make laws. Although this is not in itself dangerous, the lack of knowledge causes them to abrogate the civilian responsibility to administer their portion of the civil-military equation. Some scholars of military affairs, such as Charles C. Moskos, professor emeritus of sociology at Northwestern University in Evanston, Illinois, have argued that reinstituting the draft would benefit society by, if nothing else, remedying imbalance.

Contemporary World Issues and National Military Service

This volume captures the major debates that have characterized the topic of national military service in the United States from colonial times to the present. Chapter 2 discusses the myriad complicated, often contradictory controversies that have arisen over the course of the nation's history. Along with identifying the controversies, the chapter provides some answers to the debates, although some of the solutions are not likely to find political acceptance that would make them workable. Chapter 3 attempts to give comparative perspective across national boundaries. Because national military service is characteristic of virtually all societies, except post-1948 Costa Rica, a sense of how the issue is handled elsewhere provides some useful information to the United States. Chapter 4 considers the chronology of national military service in the United States. Although the timeline cannot chronicle each and every event, an attempt is made to note the most important turning points in U.S. history. Chapter 5 describes the important personalities who influenced national service. This list illustrates the diversity of views held by those leaders who have helped shape our society. Chapter 6 proved the toughest part of this volume; it displays the documents and speeches that explain various policy decisions. Some of these documents date to the Articles of Confederation period, while the 1986 Goldwater-Nichols Military Reform Act is also crucial. The documents were selected on the basis of range rather than type of documents, but in either case the choice of documents and speeches had to be selective. Chapter 7 lists and describes the organizations involved with national military service. This list contains veterans' groups, policy action groups, and conscientious objector support groups; it includes government, nongovernment, and international institutions, all of which are engaged in the debate about national military service. Finally, Chapter 8 provides an extensive, though not exhaustive, list of resources available on military service. This list encompasses articles, edited volumes, monographs, radio and television shows on military service, and Web sites.

The volume aims to be as complete as possible, but the reader should be warned that this field changes regularly and radically. The chapters offer one view of a field that only benefits from the greater society's study, debate, and resolution to understand the complex interactions involved.

References

Bowden, Mark. *Black Hawk Down.* New York: Atlantic Monthly Press, 1999.

Builder, Carl. *The Masks of War: American Military Styles in Strategy and Analysis: A RAND Corporation Research Study.* Santa Monica, CA: RAND, 1989.

Chambers, John Whiteclay II, and G. Kurt Piehler, eds. *Major Problems in American Military History: Documents and Essays.* Boston: Houghton Mifflin, 1999.

Clausewitz, Carl von. *On War.* Trans. Michael Howard and Peter Paret. Princeton, NJ: Princeton University Press, 1989.

Cress, Lawrence Delbert. *Citizens in Arms.* Chapel Hill: University of North Carolina Press, 1982.

Danopoulos, Constantine, and Cynthia Watson, editors, *Political Role of the Military.* Westport, CT: Greenwood Publishing, 1996.

Dionne, E. J., K. M. Drogosz, and R. Litan, eds. *United We Serve.* Washington, DC: Brookings Institution, 2003.

Dole, Robert. *One Soldier's Story: A Memoir.* New York: HarperCollins, 2005.

Gorham, Eric B. *National Service, Citizenship and Political Education.* Albany: State University of New York Press, 1992.

Higginbotham, Don. *The War for American Independence.* Boston: Northeastern University Press, 1983.

Huntington, Samuel. *The Soldier and the State: The Theory and Politics of Civil-Military Relations.* Cambridge, MA: Belknap Press, 2005.

Janowitz, Morris. *The Professional Soldier: A Social and Political Portrait.* New York: Free Press, 1971.

Kohn, Richard H. *Eagle and Sword.* New York: Free Press, 1975.

Kohn, Richard H., and Peter Feaver. *Soldiers and Civilians: The Civil-Military Gap and American National Security.* Cambridge, MA: MIT Press, 2001.

Locher, James R., III. *Victory on the Potomac: The Goldwater-Nichols Act Unifies the Pentagon.* College Station: Texas A & M Press, 2002.

Moore, Harold, and Joseph Galloway. *We Were Soldiers Once and Young: Ia-Drang—The Battle Which Changed the Vietnam War.* New York: Random House, 1992.

Shapiro, Peter, ed. *A History of National Service in America.* New York: Center for Political Leadership and Participation, 1994.

Umansky, Eric. "Explainer: Army Reserve vs. National Guard." *Slate Online Magazine,* January 7, 2005. http://slate.msn.com/toolbar.aspx?action-print&id–2112001

2

Problems, Controversies, and Solutions

ational service has been one of the more controversial issues
in the U.S. public policy debate. It cuts across the age, gender, and political lines of society. Although the controversies
discussed in this chapter are the major ones, the list is not exhaustive.

The men and women in uniform today discuss controversial
subjects solely in private conversations because by law, specifically the Uniform Code of Military Justice, those serving in our
armed forces cannot challenge the chain of command as long as
the orders being promulgated are legal. Hence, they are often
highly unlikely to introduce these questions either in public settings or in writing. Their concerns are voiced in educational settings, which offers a cover for them to voice their concerns in hy-
pothetical terms.

Obligatory versus Voluntary Service

For much of its history, the United States used its armed forces
for purely domestic issues such as "opening the West" rather
than in foreign actions (as the Europeans did). In the first 125
years of its history, the United States fought "foreign" wars only
three times: the War for Independence, the War of 1812, and the
War of 1848, although its forces did engage in skirmishes with
the Barbary pirates along the coast of North Africa early in the
nineteenth century. Since there were infrequent challenges to the

survival of the Republic, the military that the new nation developed was relatively small.

The United States also developed a different view of warfare than virtually any other state in the world: it viewed warfare as an unnatural act and believed that upon its conclusion the society could return to "normalcy." In contrast, Europeans tended to see warfare as Baron Carl von Clausewitz viewed it: as "a continuation of politics by other means." The late Temple University historian Russell Weigley, in his work *The American Way of War,* illustrates the U.S. view of exceptionalism in military affairs.

This difference between the U.S. and European perspective produced a fundamentally different approach on how to develop the military. The United States has never found the idea of a professional military, set apart from its citizenry, to be acceptable. Instead, the U.S. concept of a "citizen-soldier" cropped up early in the colonial period and became part of the basis of George Washington's forces during the War for Independence. This citizen-soldier was not intended to be a professional who could be hired out by various sides to fight ongoing conflicts. Instead, he was intended to resolve a conflict and then could return to his former traditional job as a farmer or small-business operator (Cress, 1982: 61–62). This desire to raise a military to answer only when called upon was the natural outgrowth of the American people's innate fear of an overly strong head of state or any political mechanism that might oppress the minority within society. It was thought that citizen-soldiers would protect their land but not overreach as professionals would be tempted to do.

Most of the rest of the world did not regard the military man as a citizen-soldier. Because warfare was becoming a more highly specialized activity, it required a more highly trained individual who became a military professional. The irony associated with the growing U.S. ability to provide much better and more thorough professional education than other world states cannot have escaped the attention of the military establishment in other parts of the world.

As the nature of the U.S. role in the world changed, however, the type of military changed to address national security requirements. As early as the 1780s, as the nation was beginning to wrestle with institution-building and was developing a coherent political ideology, George Washington, Alexander Hamilton, and Baron von Steuben argued for the creation of a standing army to defend the new nation. Nor did the need for an institution of national armed forces preclude the individual states' desire for a militia (Cress, 1982: 62). The result, as this volume indicates, was the complex patchwork of active-duty Marine, Navy, Air Force, and Army forces, along with the National Guard and Reservists. As the small-enclave groups discovered in the pre-9/11 environment of the 1990s, small militia groups still existed until the last decade of the twentieth century. The existence of these groups was an argument against the need for a standing military that could impose the will of an overly powerful central government.

Can Something Else Be Substituted for National Service?

The United States has long had a national ethos of service to the community as well as a streak of pacifism. Many have raised the question of whether national military service is the key component of our society or whether something else could be substituted for it. They maintain that the key is service and not necessarily the type of service (Moskos, 1988). In the debate about whether national service must entail a military obligation, organizations such as the Friends National Committee and the War Resisters League have argued passionately against the armed portion of service. Many of their members have even been willing to risk imprisonment and public disapproval by their fellow citizens to stand up for their beliefs that what is important is the principle rather than the specific instance.

Three prominent examples of alternatives to national military service are the Peace Corps, VISTA, and AmeriCorps (Shapiro, 1994). The Peace Corps began under President John F. Kennedy in 1961. It sends U.S. citizens (most of whom were very young in the initial years but later even included elderly volunteers) abroad to teach and help develop basic infrastructure in the newly independent states of Africa and Southeast Asia as well as the less developed Latin American nations. Funded by the U.S. government, the Peace Corps was seen by many of its participants as a way to make a long-term difference in these societies while promoting positive, peaceful values at a time when U.S. power was feared in much of the Third World. Not all commentators, however, saw the Peace Corps as an altruistic organization; instead they assigned it a more nefarious role—that of promoting the goals of the United States in the Cold War under the mantle of social justice, thereby enabling the organization to push U.S. interests less visibly. The participants' volunteer role, however, has always been important and has been seen as giving citizens the opportunity to participate in a meaningful way.

VISTA grew out of the social activism of the 1960s; it came on the heels of the Peace Corps, but it had a decidedly domestic commitment. It was begun formally after President Lyndon Johnson signed the 1964 "War on Poverty" legislation to remedy widespread inequalities in the nation. Participants worked to eliminate all the sources of poverty in the United States. As opposed to the Peace Corps' multiple-year commitment overseas, VISTA required only a one-year obligation in the United States, but like the Peace Corps it involved a fairly small salary paid by the government. VISTA has gradually receded into the background in the debate about national service, but it played a fundamental role in the 1960s.

AmeriCorps, a much more recent organization, began in 1994 as an alternative to military service; in it, young teachers go into the inner-city schools, older citizens could share their experience with younger people in community programs, faith-based organizations target illiteracy and lack of public housing, and various other community-based activities serve the nation while helping communities. AmeriCorps, along with Senior Corps and Learn and Serve America, are all part of the Corporation for National and Community Service, a federal corporation that encourages citizens to use their skills as a payback to their communities.

Notably, the only portion of the national budget relating to national service that has been growing is the military. Over the past twenty-five years, the emphasis on the military tool of statecraft has increased dramatically as Congress (especially through members such as former North Carolina Republican senator Jesse Helms) and the executive branch have chosen to pursue national security goals through that instrument rather than nonmilitary tools such as the Peace Corps. Similarly, private, nongovernmental organizations have pushed for nontraditional military service commitments; perhaps the best-known example is the George H. W. Bush administration's repeated discussions of "a thousand points of light." This encouragement of private rather than government activities in helping those unable to help themselves generated much frustration and debate during the early 1990s. President George W. Bush's support for faith-based organizations engaging in these activities instead of VISTA or AmeriCorps has not been missed by those who fear the society is turning to religious organizations in violation of Thomas Jefferson's "wall of separation" between church and state.

Nonmilitary volunteer activities have not received universal approval. During the 1960s, for example, when the conscription system was still in place, many saw these alternative national service options as merely ways to avoid the draft or to get out of national service. These opponents simply rejected the level of equivalence of nonmilitary volunteerism. Now that no draft exists, this issue has become a moot one. Should the draft be resurrected, the charge that some do not uphold an appropriate level of citizenship would undoubtedly arise again.

What Is the Acceptable Role of Conscientious Objecting?

The United States has a long history of conscientious objection, beginning with Richard Keene, a Maryland colonist who refused to respond to the summons to join the colonial militia. Better known were the Quakers who left Europe to settle in current-day Pennsylvania in the late seventeenth century. The Quakers, also known as the Society of Friends, do not believe that violence can or should be used to settle conflict.

Throughout the nation's history, but particularly in the twentieth and twenty-first centuries, Quakers and others have taken the position that conscientious objection is acceptable in the face of military service. The Selective Service System Web site (http://www.sss.gov/FSconsobj.htm) defines a conscientious objector as "one who is opposed to serving in the armed forces and/or bearing arms on the grounds of moral or religious principles." It goes on to note that this does not have to be a religious belief, but it cannot "be based on politics, expediency, or self-interest." The Selective Service allows two types of alternate service for COs, as they are known: alternative service for those whose objection is based on rejecting any sort of military service, while noncombatant capacity goes to those who believe they can serve but do not want to carry or use a weapon.

People with pacifist views opposed U.S. entry into World War I and World War II (to a lesser extent, since this conflict was seen as more directly relevant to the nation's survival). Pacifists tended to combine with the traditional isolationist strain of the U.S. public, which opposed foreign entanglements. Unlike the isolationists, pacifists believed that war did not solve conflict—only negotiations and understanding did. If those holding pacifist views were called for national service, they were handled on a case-by-case basis, with little discussion in society at large (Shapiro, 1994).

During the Vietnam War, a large number of young men chose CO status. But war supporters in particular maintained that many of these COs had neither religious nor conscientious objection to the conflict but were actually claiming exemption out of fear or simply their unwillingness to put their lives on the line for their country. A good deal more of those who rejected the war on political grounds, however, either went "underground" or fled overseas, primarily to Canada or Sweden. Many Americans strongly disapproved of their decisions to flee rather than be drafted, to the point that today, more than thirty years later, the topic continues to be a tense one.

In a highly controversial act, President Jimmy Carter declared amnesty for those who had fled abroad during the Vietnam War. That decision, issued through a presidential proclamation, preceded Carter's decision to reinstitute registration for national service for young men between eighteen and twenty-five years of age. Carter's decision to reinstate Selective Service registration alienated the left, though it also infuriated the right because he took back "traitors." His actions are said to have contributed to his defeat as he stood for reelection in 1980.

During both the Vietnam and Iraq wars, some individuals become conscientious objectors after entering the armed services. This has led some to flee abroad rather than return to their units, while others have initiated lawsuits to gain release from their voluntary service commitment. Questions over CO status have again arisen because the conflict in Iraq is far less clear-cut than wars such as World War II.

Should Women Be Allowed to Participate in National Service?

According to scholar Jeanne Holm, women have been engaged in national military service in the United States since World War I, when they served as "yeomanettes." Although women have only been involved in combat missions over the past generation, they have found that noncombat roles often put them into harm's way during their national service. A small number of women volunteered to assist in various capacities with U.S. involvement in World War I, but women participated in a significant and widespread way in World War II, when millions of men were called to service in the Pacific and Atlantic theaters.

Women also served in Korea and Vietnam, though primarily in support functions. With the end of Vietnam, women's general role in society dramatically broadened, and the first significant number of women prisoners of war occurred during the first Gulf War (1991). As noted earlier, a woman physician, Rhonda Cornum of the U.S. Army, became one of the first women prisoners of war; she was captured, abused, and subsequently released that same year. Cornum remained in the Army despite the experience and told her story in the book *She Went to War: The Rhonda Cornum Story.*

The crux of the issue is not one of women serving in the armed forces; rather, the question centers on how women serve. Women first served in notable numbers in World War I, but their participation accelerated during World War II and even more in Vietnam. With the changes in female roles in society in the 1960s and 1970s, some women demanded a greater role in all aspects of national service: many women wanted to participate in combat. Without being involved in combat, some women felt they were not serving their nation as fully as their male counterparts. Other women argued that it was degrading to assume that women could not serve in combat as well as or as faithfully as men. Still others believed that the prohibition again women in combat was a method of keeping women out of the more prestigious and sought-after positions in the various services. Finally, some believed that women were discriminated against and belittled by the men in the services, attitudes that would disappear if women were treated equally as they pursued the services' career paths. Still others had no interest in participating in combat.

Critics charged that it was inhumane for women to participate in armed service positions that might involve combat. It was also feared that women would not be as reliable as men and that women did not have the stamina or skill, particularly as pilots and naval aviators, required for the various positions. Others were adamant that women's presence in units would degrade discipline and morale and would lead to romantic relationships.

After decades of debate, women today are gradually taking positions as senior U.S. military officers. No woman has yet made chairwoman of the Joint Chiefs of Staff or chief of service, nor are there many women in the aviation community of any of the services. Nonetheless, as Colonel Jeffrey Conners, chief of staff of the Air Force chair at the National War College, and Colonel Mark Tillman, chief of staff of the Army chair at the National War College, explained to the author in August 2006, women are gradually appearing in positions that were historically held by men and have aroused little public comment upon assumption of those positions. Women are allowed in various aircraft and on surface vessels but not in jobs that are inevitably going to put them into direct combat with the enemy.

Arguably, the subtle distinction between being in proximity to conflict versus being in combat missions is affecting the broader picture of the debate on women in the services. Women today are routinely trained for positions that bring them into dangerous situations, and so women are no longer separated from combat. Army urologist Rhonda Cornum is a perfect example: when her role as physician required that she be present in combat areas so that she could perform her needed services, the line between a woman and combat soon disappeared. By simply carrying out her job she became a prisoner. The increased numbers of women in those fields will automatically wear down the division between combat and noncombat. As war has evolved, the importance of keeping a woman "out of harm's way" has come into conflict with the concept of gender equality.

Should National Service Expedite an Immigrant's Citizenship?

The United States is, as the expression goes, a nation of immigrants. Many immigrants have served in uniform as resident aliens or as something less than full citizens. The need for fluent linguists and the role of the all-volunteer force, however, have raised questions about speeding up the citizenship process as a means of rewarding those who offer their lives for this country. The percentage will never be huge, but as immigration questions become more and more heated, the issue of providing a shorter route to full citizenship will persist.

In the aftermath of the 9/11 experience, two divergent trends have emerged with regard to giving immigrants a shorter path to citizenship. The long-held belief in some quarters that the nation should tighten up its borders through much stricter immigration laws was dramatically reinforced by the events of 9/11. Indeed, Mexico was the nation whose bilateral relationship with the United States was most hurt by September 2001. During the week prior to the catastrophe, Mexican president Vicente Fox Quesada had completed a successful visit to Washington, and there appeared to be a genuine movement within the U.S. Congress to reconsider the previous reduction in immigration requirements between Washington and Mexico City. The ability to send more immigrants, even temporary ones, to the United States is crucial for any Mexican leader in light of Mexico's economic needs. Once the Twin Towers fell, however, there was absolutely no chance that any Mexican or U.S. leader could increase the northward flow of people. Indeed, Fox Quesada actually witnessed increased barriers against immigration; this was an extremely disappointing development for Mexico but an utterly predictable one for the United States as it sought to prevent another 9/11.

The Iraq war marks the United States' first sustained military engagement since the all-volunteer force came into being in 1973. The drawn-out nature of the war and repeated Army and Marine deployments to Iraq have affected some recruiting (generally the Army). Individuals who hold a green card and put their lives on the line for the nation are sometimes given the opportunity to accelerate the citizenship process. In several cases this expedited process has offered individuals serving in Afghanistan or Iraq earlier U.S. citizenship. To this point, a relatively small number of cases have been accelerated, but the entire basis of the expedited acquisition of citizenship is connected to a willingness to engage in national military service for the United States.

Does the United States Desire a Military That Is De Facto Separated from the Rest of Society?

Civil-military relations present one of the most contentious balances in any society. The United States has probably experienced fewer such tensions (and certainly never undergoing a military coup is one measure of such) than most other countries in the world. At the same time, in the post-Vietnam period, when so much healing has been needed to bind the nation's societal wounds produced by that conflict, questions have arisen about whether the military is in fact representative of the country or increasingly separate from the people it represents.

Public debate was particularly intense during the 1960s and early 1970s when the mandatory draft was still in place. Those who considered themselves conscientious objectors or simply avoided the draft argued that the armed forces were neither part of nor representative of society because the acts that the armed forces committed, in the name of the state, were immoral acts. The generation who entered the armed forces in the immediate aftermath of this period—after 1974—tended to have certain characteristics and values that set them apart from their peer group by age: they tended to be southern, were often at least a second-generation military child ("brat"), and had conservative politics. In addition, they often but not exclusively shared a view that U.S. social and cultural mores had shifted away from their beliefs.

The controversy reared its head again in 1992 when the first "baby boomer" president, who was seen as having avoided the draft, was elected president in a close election. This period coincided with the end of the Cold War, a period when military men and women knew their job; however, the post–Cold War world was increasingly asking them not to be citizen-soldiers fighting for the survival of the nation against communism and nuclear destruction. Instead, they were being sent to the beaches of Mogadishu, Somalia, to dole out foodstuffs to starving people in the midst of a civil war ten thousand miles away. Many in national service thought their skills were being frittered away and that they were being taken from their primary duties in a way that could hurt the nation in a conflict. Many of them also resented being asked to engage in social reengineering abroad or to do something that did not conform to their understanding of military service. That debate died down somewhat with the end of the Clinton administration, when the Bush administration proclaimed its commitment to traditional patriotism and respect for those in uniform. Ironically, however, Bush's administration has become involved in more nontraditional military actions than the Clinton administration.

Researchers at the Triangle Institute for Security Studies, the University of North Carolina, and Duke University maintain that during the 1990s, members of the military adopted some views that set them apart from those who served in the past. This belief is far from universally accepted, but the debate about whether the United States needs a citizen-soldier corps or a national service built primarily on multigenerational soldiers, sailors, airmen, and Marines is still open (Kohn and Feaver, 2001).

Anecdotal evidence shows that some individuals serving in the military see themselves as separated from their fellow citizens for reasons relating to an amorphous sense of higher morality. During the Clinton administration, when complaints and embarrassment about the commander-in-chief's personal behavior became more widespread than for any president in recent memory, a number of military personnel opined that they were glad they were part of a group in society that retained its own morality and sense of personal ethics beyond those of society at large. These may have been outlying perceptions; that is, perceptions that would have proved abnormal if a random, statistically valid poll had been conducted across the military. But the self-selection promoted by the voluntary nature of the force may have led some to view the armed services as an escape from the "bad" aspects of U.S. society, since the military requires its personnel to adhere to the Uniform Code of Military Justice.

Does a Voluntary Force Rely Disproportionately on Minorities?

With the introduction of the all-volunteer force in 1973, people have asked whether minorities, notably African Americans, Hispanic Americans, Asian Americans, and Native Americans, are disproportionately represented in national service. In particular, because the all-volunteer force has historically seen its recruitment levels rise and fall in relation to the state of the domestic economy, many have wondered whether the lower socioeconomic groups in society (especially African Americans and Hispanic Americans) are subject to these fluctuations because of their socioeconomic levels, which makes them enter the military at higher levels than they represent in the population at large (Rangel, 2003). In addition, because these two groups have lower college enrollment and graduation rates, they tend to enter the armed services at the enlisted level. In fact, many have repeatedly asked this question in view of the conflicts that are part of the Operations Enduring Freedom and Iraqi Freedom, where an ever higher number of personnel are being attacked on the ground.

For some, the military is a jobs program that offers a steady, reliable source of income. Because levels of unemployment are higher among minorities, it would not be surprising that employment might be the chief motivator for them to join the armed forces in numbers disproportionate to their share of the population. Few U.S. politicians, however, would dare to acknowledge that the United States relies disproportionately on minorities' willingness to become soldiers. Instead, participation in the military by minorities is seen as a greater opportunity to serve the nation as well as a manifestation of patriotism.

Is National Service a Valid Manner for Furthering Social Causes?

Many citizens are concerned that the federal leadership is using national service to further social policies that cannot be accomplished in any other way since there are few ways that men and women under arms can escape direct orders. These critics cite President Harry S Truman's use of the armed services to begin integration during the late 1940s and 1950s in the United States. As the Army, in particular, seemed to drag its feet in accomplishing the command, Truman responded by pushing harder until segregation became a less desirable approach for the Army. Today, six decades later, the U.S. military is completely (if not perfectly) integrated.

In more recent years, critics have feared that accepting gays and lesbians into the military would lead to increased rights for gays and lesbians throughout society. Similarly, people have argued that putting women in combat positions has nothing to do with equality of compensation or equality of opportunity; instead, it is a method of pushing women into the traditionally all-male environments of a ship or an army unit. Furthermore, when the military ordered its personnel to take anthrax vaccine, many people feared that the military was treating human beings like guinea pigs.

The military is sometimes able to accomplish things—like integration—that are harder for society to do. It is also true, however, that the military can become a method for accomplishing some societal changes because it operates through a hierarchical system that responds directly to orders. When former chairman of the joint chiefs of staff and retired general Colin L. Powell became secretary of state in 2001, people often joked that the general would pull his hair out when he told the State Department staff to do something, because bureaucracies do not generally move in response to individual orders. (As a general, Powell had been accustomed to ordering the Army officers and enlisted men below him to do something.) It is quite plausible that those seeking to make societal changes simply believe the armed services provide a more efficient method of accomplishing things than the bureaucracy or society as a whole, which is made up of individuals who seldom have a common goal.

How Do the Reserves and the National Guard Relate to the Active-Duty Force?

Active-duty personnel are full-time servicemen and -women whose job focuses on national security as part of national service. These people are active regardless of whether the United States is engaged in an ongoing conflict that could lead to their deployment or keeping them home (where they continue to train) because nothing immediately threatens the nation.

The Reserves are individuals in each of the four services (Air Force, Army, Marines, and Navy) who have agreed to be part-timers in their national service. These individuals generally train one weekend monthly and for two weeks each year, with the goal of keeping up their readiness. The Reservist receives pay for the time he or she puts into the reserve commitment. The individual has the same rank structure as that of the active-duty force. Anyone with a Reserve position (officer or enlisted) is subject to being called up by the president for active duty in case the president deems it necessary.

The National Guard is a state-based structure with a direct chain of command to the governor of the state in which the individual resides. The governor can call up a person for emergencies, such as Hurricane Katrina, which utterly devastated the Gulf Coast, or the governor can release the Guard for national deployment—abroad or domestically. In that case, the Guard is federalized for service and then under federal government control. The National Guard was built on the state militia systems that were the basis of the U.S. defense experience and was the genesis of the "civilian-soldier" concept that is so fundamental to the U.S. view of warfare and defense. The Dick Act of 1903 converted state militias into the National Guard, and the Guard has representation, at the senior level, on the Joint Chiefs of Staff.

Many women and men who leave active-duty status become members of the Reserve component. The same statutory conditions exist for the Reserves: members can serve to age 62, they are governed by the Uniform Code of Military Justice, and they can be called to serve their nation by the president. The difference is that Reservists do not train daily, nor are they paid full-time by the Department of Defense; yet they are still members of the all-volunteer force. These Reservists can be called up for active-duty service in a crisis. According to Dr. Mark Clodfelter, Air Force historian at the National War College and retired Air Force officer, Reserve and Guard pilots made up 50 percent of the Air Force's airlift (transportation) and tanker pilots in today's operations.

Can Active and Reserve Components Mesh?

This is an exceptionally controversial issue dividing the active-duty force and the Guard and Reserves. The active-duty force almost invariably believes it serves the nation better, more effectively, and with less stress because a full-time job is needed to engage in national service. These individuals train regularly, they are given the newer equipment at roughly the same time across the service (rather than from dates of resupply or upgrading varying from state to state), and (in theory, at least) they do not have any chance of split concerns since this is their full-time work.

Reservists and National Guard personnel, however, hotly dispute the active-duty force's supposition. These individuals commit to their monthly preparations, along with the annual two weeks of full-time training, so that they can be adequately prepared to integrate with the active-duty force as intended under current designs for national service. In the 1980s, they were often derisively called Weekend Warriors; today, however, they are serving in the war theater in vast numbers. There is an unspoken sense of frustration that the active-duty component might feel a sense of superiority over its Reserve component and Guard brethren. It is clear, however, that the Reserves and the National Guard are important to the states in which they operate, since these individuals may be called up for emergency requirements. Congress has continued funding them as a major portion of the U.S. force.

One important lesson learned from the Southeast Asian conflict of the 1950s, 1960s, and 1970s was that the nation is far more supportive of a war that involves the entire nation. According to military historian Dr. Mark Clodfelter, this belief led Army Chief of Staff Creighton Abrams to put some essential components of the Army, such as civil affairs, in the reserves to guarantee mobilization of the nation's "citizen-soldier" force in the event of war, thus (Abrams believed) securing popular support for the effort. As a result, the leadership who came of age during the Vietnam experience—including Generals Colin Powell and Barry McCaffrey of the Army—believes that the United States must continue to call up both the Reserves and active-duty forces for the wars in Afghanistan and Iraq. Using both components will help ensure that the nation supports the current wars more than they did in the late 1960s and early 1970s, when many families felt isolated from war efforts. The danger, of course, is that by doing this more families will lose loved ones to war and criticism of war will heighten.

Does the Sexual Orientation of Some Military Personnel Affect Overall Unit Effectiveness and Cohesion?

President Truman was successful in integrating African Americans into the national service structure in the late 1940s and 1950s, but no one has managed to do the same thing with openly gay and lesbian personnel. Indeed, the discussions on accepting gays and lesbians that President William J. Clinton initiated in the 1992 presidential campaign led to some of the most heated, contentious arguments in the history of the U.S. military service.

Little direct attention had been given to the topic until the administration of Ronald Reagan (1981–1989) when many members of his conservative movement sought to fight the social deterioration that they believed had occurred in the prior decade. A policy of nontolerance for homosexuality was imposed, though this provoked a great deal of protest from the gay and lesbian communities. Clinton's suggestion that he would try to overturn the ban would have met with some opposition under any circumstances, but the anger and hostility to the suggestion was exacerbated by Clinton's personal avoidance of military service during the Vietnam era and allegations that a range of his views and behaviors disrespected the values held important by many in the military.

Matters were only made worse by a widely circulated story that supposedly occurred in the initial weeks after Clinton took office. It involved a young political appointee who supposedly said that men in uniform were not welcomed in the White House. This story only reinforced the belief that the president disrespected those who put their lives on the line through national service. Additionally, many in uniform conflated their disapproval of Clinton's personal behavior with their assumptions about his actions. In January 1993, when Clinton announced that he would study the idea of overturning the Reagan ban for six months, the entire idea was doomed: giving a specific amount of time only gave his opponents time to rally their forces to defeat the move.

Aside from the many religious overtones in the debate, opponents argued that the change would undercut unit cohesion and effectiveness. Though subjective, this interpretation was a persuasive one for many people who feared that heterosexual soldiers would feel uncomfortable around homosexual soldiers, a situation that could become dangerous on the battlefield. U.S. military leaders argued against the change, at least partially because they knew the men serving below them were so opposed to the change.

In the summer of 1993, Charles C. Moskos proposed a policy that would soon take effect: the "don't ask, don't tell" policy. Under this policy, the military leadership does not inquire about one's sexual preferences unless the individual engages in flagrantly gay behavior. At the same time, homosexuals must not proposition or in any other way manifest their sexual preferences to their peers.

During the wars in Afganistan and Iraq, a significant number of individuals, particularly in language specialization billets, have been ousted from the military because of their sexual preference. Although the armed services claim that expulsions have occurred because unit cohesion is suffering, others, especially members of the lesbian and gay communities, say this has nothing to do with unit cohesion but is strictly bigotry and an attempt to ignore changes that are happening elsewhere in society.

What Is the Relationship between Sexual Orientation and the Military?

Another question that is being asked is whether the armed services ought to be used as a social engineering tool for society. Critics of homosexuality believe that open admission of gays into the services would destroy the military, while supporters of the change argue that no harm could come from legalizing what must for now at least remain unsaid. For those who are lesbian or gay, this is not a relevant inquiry, because the issue is willingness and effectiveness in combat, not sexual orientation. This remains a tremendous divide within U.S. society.

What Is the Power of the Federal Government over State Militias?

At the core of the U.S. governmental system is the relationship between federal and state governments known as federalism whereby states have control/responsibility over some functions and the government in Washington has others. Historically, however, there have always been tensions about this balance. Along with those tensions, there is the specific question about whether state Guard forces, which have historically been under the control of the state governors, can be called upon to serve by the president. In the earlier years of the country, governors rejected calling up the militia (during the War of 1812 a number of governors refused to use their state forces for a proposed invasion of Canada). Even in the twentieth century, controversy arose about using the Guard for foreign escapades. During the 1980s and 1990s when presidents tried to use the Guard to engage in activities overseas, such as rebuilding Central America after hurricane damage, governors refused to allow their prerogatives to be undercut by federal authority.

As public doubts have grown about U.S. involvement in Iraq in particular, calls have been issued to restrict the use of Guard forces by not surrendering them to federal control. Governors have sought to maintain their power over the National Guard units in their states, but few governors ever deny presidents the ultimate decision to choose how to deploy U.S. forces in case of conflict.

This issue is bound to resurrect controversy, especially when we consider that the Gulf Coast states found their National Guard troops deployed in Iraq and Afghanistan instead of available for the massive relief requirements raised by Hurricane Katrina. According to some accounts, the lack of immediate response to the hurricane-induced damage in New Orleans in late August and early September 2005 resulted from the Bush administration's attempts to persuade Louisiana governor Kathleen Bianco to federalize the Louisiana National Guard. If Louisiana had bowed to federal pressures, the state's response to the disaster would almost certainly have been even more inadequate.

Who Should Decide Where Soldiers Are Sent?

One of the perennial issues that individuals in national service face is the question of whether they are better off under purely military decision-making or whether civilians, as head of the chain of command in the United States, ought to be dictating some level of policy in a conflict. Although anyone in the U.S. uniform is bound to observe and execute the orders given by a superior in the chain of command, the broader question of whether civilians or military ought to be making the decisions has been a burning one going back at least to Vietnam. Many serving and retired national service personnel bluntly blame civilian interference in the military's affairs for the outcome in Vietnam, for example. This debate about the relevance or appropriateness of civilian input and the amount of that input becomes all the more heated in direct correlation to the controversial nature of the conflict.

As the United States entered the third year of war in Iraq and the fifth year in Afghanistan, increasingly it was asked whether the military leadership in those two campaigns were being given all the resources they needed to accomplish their missions. The chief concern has focused on whether the campaigns require more troops on the ground. Some critics have suggested that the defense leadership, such as the president or Secretary of Defense Donald Rumsfeld, has shortchanged the commanders on the ground by not providing the troop levels they need. Others, however, have wondered whether these uniformed leaders have not asked for adequate troop levels for fear they would be punished for their requests. President Bush and Secretary Rumsfeld have strongly disagreed with this line of argument, saying that the transformation of the U.S. force has given commanders such a level of confidence that they can handle the challenge with a more technologically sophisticated and smaller force.

A particular subset of the questions has come from retired senior military officers, some of whom served in the decision-making relating to Iraq and Afghanistan. These veterans became particularly vocal in March and April 2006. Particularly prominent among them was retired Central Command Marine General Tony Zinni. These officers, no longer governed by the Uniform Code of Military Justice (which prohibits speaking against the chain of command), argued that the war had been poorly conceived and executed. They argued, to varying degrees, that Secretary of Defense Rumsfeld was not serving the president well and should resign. These critics were, in turn, strongly chastised for undercutting the president during the war as well as for politicizing themselves as retired military men. This debate appears far from concluded as the war in Iraq has no obvious end in sight.

Others have asked whether the military has convinced the civilian leadership of the need for adequate body armor for the war in Iraq and Afghanistan. The final issue that has led to questions relates to what the civilian leadership meant to do with the captives in the prisons at Abu Ghraib near Baghdad and at Bagram Air Force Base in Afghanistan. As the treatment of detainees became public beginning in 2004, both civilian and military leadership steadfastly held that they never suggested any inappropriate or illegal form of behavior or interrogation. Both enlisted and noncommissioned personnel disagreed, however, reporting that they were carrying out the orders handed down to them from above. As of this point, the enlisted and noncommissioned views have not been proven correct, but the question remains unresolved.

Should the Armed Forces Be Used as Peacekeepers or as Warfighters?

Many members of the national service see their role as that of "warfighters" who are dedicated to defending the American people's freedom and way of life. They believe that their preparation for this work, along with understanding and committing to using the "pointy end of the stick" (as they refer to lethal weapons in some conversations), separates them from people carrying out other missions for the country's national security. In the post–Cold War era, however, much debate about whether either nation-building or humanitarian assistance is an appropriate use of the military has arisen. It is not just in the post-1989 period, however, that the armed forces have been involved in such activities. The rescue of thousands of Vietnamese citizens from Saigon and other cities in South Vietnam as the North Vietnamese closed in on Saigon in April 1975 was an example of humanitarian assistance even if it was veiled by the emotions of the time.

In the post-Soviet era, when U.S. dominance originally seemed to lessen chances of armed conflict, those engaging in national service believed that their specialty of waging war would not be needed again in the same way. Yet, these forces found themselves deployed to places like Somalia, Haiti, Bosnia, and Liberia to rescue people—many of them not even U.S. citizens— or to distribute humanitarian assistance. The very use of U.S. forces for these activities became controversial because those elements in national service who saw their role as "warriors" asked why they were being used to perform this nonwarrior activity, and they also wondered whether humanitarian aid-giving would ultimately weaken their readiness for real war.

Some people thought the answer would come when candidate George W. Bush, in the 2000 election campaign, repeatedly downplayed any use of the U.S. military tool for nonconflict scenarios (Rice, 2000). September 11, 2001, together with the new conceptualization of the world and threats to the United States, altered the practice of using the military "just" for warfighting. That new conceptualization made clear that national security meant a far broader understanding of defeating the enemy than had been true before. The new uses of the military included returning to many of the nation-building aspects that had been so controversial in the past.

The debate as to whether these missions erode the military's readiness for traditional force-on-force wars has not diminished. The jury is out on whether the world has changed enough that traditional wars are unlikely to occur in the future, but the debate about it—and how to staff, arm, train, and prepare for it— continues at a rapid pace.

Is Military Service a Different Caste from the Rest of Society?

Military service, which during the Southeast Asian conflict was an extraordinarily divisive component of U.S. society, is today regarded with great respect by the overwhelming majority of the society. The military's return from their required service in the early 1970s to be greeted with jeers and humiliation was in starkest contrast to the heroes' parades and accolades that were given those who returned home at the end of the first Gulf War in 1991.

Many who served from the beginning of the all-volunteer force argue that being a warfighter puts one in a different category from those who rejected the war or—worse—rejected the individuals who carried out what the nation asked them to do in war. Some members of the national military, as we have said, are second-generation warfighters who have grown up on military bases, were educated in military schools, and without even realizing it may prefer to isolate themselves from society by keeping the prerogatives and perquisites of military service rather than integrating fully with society as a whole because this is what is required to accomplish their mission.

This continuation of the warfighting tradition from one generation to another is not inherently bad but may be a shift from the U.S. experience of the citizen-soldier. Professional soldiers, handed down from one generation to another, may create an extremely effective and efficient warrior class within society, but this may not be the path the United States seeks to pursue.

Should National Service Be Replaced by Private Firms?

The view that war is the ultimate instrument of statecraft, and is only to be used when all other tools fail, has been a pervasive one in the United States throughout our history. At the same time, the view that limited government is superior because private, nongovernmental organizations are more efficient at virtually any activity has led to a strange phenomenon of private security carrying out portions of the national service mission. This state of affairs derives specifically from the desire to "outsource" or privatize some "support" (noncombat) functions of the military on the grounds that the private firms are more efficient than a large government bureaucracy and because it does not increase the budget necessary to accomplish these tasks.

This turn of events has given rise to two major questions. First, at Abu Ghraib prison prisoners of war were not being interrogated exclusively by military police who are governed by certain codes of conduct, are required to follow certain procedures, and have direct accountability to the public through Congress and its oversight function. Private contractors do not have this same accountability and, particularly overseas, simply cannot be forced to behave in accordance with international treaties and norms of behavior. The private firms' behavior may be regulated somewhat by the U.S. government through indirect means such as public humiliation or fines, but the situation is far different from the military service of the United States being held accountable in any particular instance.

Second, the United States does not have a tradition of hiring mercenaries ("hired guns") for security purposes. The citizen-soldier tradition flies in the face of mercenary service. Yet, the idea of private security firms engaging in the traditional role of national service is a deeply troubling one for some.

What Is the Minimum Age for National Service?

In the all-volunteer force, recruiting young men and women to join the national service is important. Under the current system, the military has two ways of bolstering its ranks: it can recruit soldiers, sailors, air personnel, and marines, and it can accept volunteers from the civilian population.

Questions about the minimum age for joining the force are longstanding. The military's recruiting programs in high schools have long been controversial and are no less so now. Many critics note that seventeen- or eighteen-year-olds are not allowed to drink alcohol anywhere in the United States, yet they can be encouraged to sign up to carry guns. Those who support the current system retort that anyone eighteen or older can vote; thus, that is the de facto age of citizenship.

No one in the United States supports allowing children younger than seventeen to join national service, but the debate about whether people between seventeen and twenty-one should be eligible to join will continue.

Is It Worth Using National Service for Humanitarian Intervention?

This issue originally emerged during the Clinton administration when the United States deployed its forces to address humanitarian crises in Somalia (actually, the original mission began under President George H. W. Bush, but it expanded into a broader one under Clinton), Bosnia, Kosovo, and other places that did not seem critical to U.S. national interests. These concerns have resurfaced under the present Bush administration whose avowed goal is to spread democracy around the world.

The Bush administration's decision to use the military to oust nondemocratic regimes, as was done in Iraq, is especially interesting in light of the positions taken by presidential candidate George W. Bush of Texas in 2000. At that time, Bush, along with his secretary of state in the second term, Dr. Condoleezza Rice, argued that the military ought not to engage in nation-building but should concentrate on what it did best: defending the nation against external threats. Rice voiced what was thought to be the governor's position in an early 2000 *Foreign Affairs* article that was heavily critical of the policies of the outgoing Clinton administration.

More recently, however, as the U.S. leadership has made clear its willingness to "stay the course" until Iraq is delivered from a myriad of possible threats to democratic rule (Shi'ite rule through a *Shar'ia* state, civil war among the three major factions in Iraq, Iranian intervention in Iraq, Syrian intervention in Iraq, and others), some at home have begun questioning whether the armed forces are suited or trained to accomplish this mission. These critics fear that the military is being asked to accomplish what takes other nations years to do. These critics believe that the excellence of U.S. national service revolves around fighting wars, not in rebuilding the institutions—brick and mortar or political—of states. President Bush has staunchly voiced his determination to stay the course, but the questions are likely to persist as long as U.S. forces are deployed in the war theater.

Does Having a National Military Make a State More Likely to Use It?

Few states around the world have abandoned having a military: Costa Rica did so in 1948 because the population got tired of the military seeking to take control over government and to spend the budget elsewhere. No one in the United States seriously believes that the country would ever do away with the armed forces.

The question of whether having the military makes it more likely that the nation will use it is not an idle one, however. During the Clinton administration when the country was wrestling with which international obligations were appropriate for the country and specifically for the armed services, then United Nations ambassador Madeline K. Albright was supposed to have asked then chairman of the Joint Chiefs of Staff, General Colin L. Powell, what purpose such a marvelous military served if the United States could not use it (in this instance for humanitarian reasons in the former Balkans). Although General Powell and most military officers probably choked at the implications of the question, it did raise an issue that society needs to address: if the skilled, paid-for military exists, is it more tempting to use it?

This question relates to the national propensity to see war as a final option when absolutely everything else has failed. Implicit in the question is the possibility that this view of war is changing. Although asking the question does not mean the change has occurred, it does raise the possibility that the social and political views of force are changing.

Does Evangelicalism Have an Effect on National Service?

Evangelicalism and religious fundamentalism are on the rise in the United States, as they are in many other areas of the world. As a country with a wall of separation between the secular government and religious members of society, the U.S. military has never adopted a recognized religion, nor has it promoted one religion over another.

Over the past decade, however, allegations have been made that the Air Force, in particular, has adopted a decidedly evangelical posture in education issues at the Air Force Academy, which may put students of other faiths at a decided disadvantage. In particular, someone serving under an evangelical senior officer, the thought goes, might be disadvantaged, if not reprimanded, by disagreeing with a senior officer. Furthermore, some critics have argued that by tacitly welcoming evangelicalism, the foreign and defense policies of the United States might be altered in a manner that is dangerous for the country.

In 2005, the Air Force Academy took steps to stop such allegations, but the debate is far from over. The number of evangelical and fundamentalist chaplains in national service is growing far faster than the diminishing number of "mainline" Protestant and Catholic chaplains (as is true in society as a whole).

Similarly, in the eyes of some the propensity for evangelical military personnel to promote their faith may cloud their vision on policy. The case of Army Lieutenant General William "Jerry" Boykin, deputy undersecretary of defense for intelligence, who gave a talk to a religious audience in which he identified Islamic people and the religion as a whole with terrorism, comes immediately to mind. Although General Boykin was investigated by the Army for the incident, he retained his position for a full term.

References

Cable News Network (CNN). "Rangel Promotes Plan to Reinstitute the Draft." January 27, 2003. http://www.cnn.com/2003/ALLPOLITICS/01/27/rangel.draft/.

Cornum, Rhonda. *She Went to War: The Rhonda Cornum Story.* Novato, CA: Presidio Press, 1993.

Cress, Lawrence Delbert. *Citizens in Arms.* Chapel Hill: University of North Carolina Press, 1982.

Danopoulos, Constantine, and Cynthia Watson, eds. *Political Role of the Military.* Westport, CT: Greenwood Publishing, 1996.

"Generals Speak Out on Iraq." *NewsHour Online.* April 13, 2006. Public Broadcasting Service. http://www.pbs.org/newshour/bb/military/jan-june06/iraq_4-13.html.

Holm, Jeanne. *Women in the Military: An Unfinished Revolution.* Novato, CA: Presidio Press, 1993.

Kohn, Richard H. *Eagle and Sword.* New York: Free Press, 1975.

Kohn, Richard H., and Peter Feaver. *Soldiers and Civilians: The Civil-Military Gap and American National Security.* Cambridge, MA: MIT Press, 2001.

Moskos, Charles C. *A Call to Civic Service: National Service for Country and Community.* New York: Free Press, 1988.

Rice, Condoleezza. "Promoting the National Interest." *Foreign Affairs* 75, no. 1 (January/February 2000). http://www.foreignaffairs.org/200 00101faessay5/condoleezza-rice/campaign–2000-promoting-the-national-interest.html (accessed August 24, 2006).

Shapiro, Peter, ed. *A History of National Service in America.* New York: Center for Political Leadership and Participation, 1994.

Weigley, Russell Frank. *The American Way of War: A History of United States Military Strategy and Policy.* Bloomington: Indiana University Press, 1977.

3

Worldwide Perspective

ational service is one of the items most specialized to the peculiar culture, history, civil-military relationship, and strategic context of each state. Covering this phenomenon in a single chapter is difficult because of the large, varied array of states,
histories, and thus experiences. This chapter will appear somewhat superficial considering the almost two hundred nation-
states existing in the international system today, but it is intended to illustrate the range of approaches to national service.
Each country has its twists on why and how it calls upon citizens
to serve, but there are a number of common items that are fundamental to understanding military service around the world.

Standing Military Forces

A most basic measure of national service can relate to whether a
state has a permanent national military. In today's world, many
people do not realize that this phenomenon generally dates back
only two hundred years. Almost all states have a military; even
neutral Switzerland, which believes that a military is crucial to
maintaining its neutral status. A few entities—mostly island
states—have no standing armies, including Dominica (in the
Caribbean) and Tuvalu (in the southwest Pacific). Both Germany
and Japan, the two major states defeated in World War II, have
armed forces, although Japan's military operates under the eu-
phemistic title Japan Defense Agency. Andorra, Lichtenstein, and
Monaco are city-states in Europe without standing forces, but the
understanding is that nearby neighbors would provide for their

security in a crisis situation. Panama lost its military with the U.S. invasion to overthrow General Manuel Noriega in December 1989; U.S. forces demilitarized Panama, and subsequent democratic regimes have retained only a police force for the republic. Costa Rica, a Central American republic, decided in 1948 to dissolve the military to invest in other aspects of society. The Costa Rican state's decision was related to the situation in the country whereby military rule often supplanted elected governments because each thought it had the best interests of society in mind. With the armed element in society, the military sought to uphold its national responsibilities by seizing power when necessary. To prevent future such occurrences, a conscious decision was made to end the military since there was no easily identifiable threat to consider.

Most countries have reached a consensus that the armed services are an important actor with a specific, easily determined task: to defend the nation against (generally external) threats. Most militaries are written into constitutions with explicit national responsibilities and limitations on their actions. The devil is often in the details for states, however, as the different groups in society negotiate the actual use, limitations, and role of the armed forces. Most societies, however, believe that the national military obligation to achieve a standing military is necessary and should continue.

Professional Service versus the Citizen-Soldier

Napoleon Bonaparte is often credited—incorrectly—with developing the concept of a national army. It was Lazare Nicolas Marguerite Carnot who recognized that a developed, sustaining corps of fighters could be trained to a much higher proficiency if they were paid a decent wage by the state as increasingly necessary to engage in increasingly complex warfare. In addition, this professional army would be more likely to develop a sense of national patriotism or respect and love for the government for which they might be asked to make the ultimate sacrifice. Prior military service had been more personally committed to a king as a mercenary force paid on a war-by-war basis; the colonial experience in the United States saw many characters who had fought their way across Europe on the payroll of many different rulers before they came to the new world.

Bonaparte's radical view of this instrument of statecraft was one of the truly revolutionary shifts in world history. At the same time, however, the role of the professional military officer was becoming more separate from that of the forced laborers, who became known as the enlisted personnel. Professional military officers began to receive specialized training, while the enlisted personnel were given far less specialized training.

Few countries around the world harbor as deep a respect for the citizen-soldier, or nonmilitary professional, as the United States. Europe, where military professionalism developed over the nineteenth century, has always had a tradition of someone carrying out the military tasks, but prior to the late eighteenth and early nineteenth centuries many were mercenaries hired by one government or another because of the inadequate supply of citizens committed to the regime or its cause. Many men in Europe (and during the wars for independence in both North and South America) fought on one side or another from war to war throughout their lives, giving little thought to the idea of commitment as citizens of a state or the long-term implications of their actions.

National Service Obligation

Conscription mandates that citizens provide involuntary service to the nation. Most nations restrict this service to their male citizens, although a substantial number allow women to volunteer, and Israel requires all women citizens to participate in the military. No other state shares quite the U.S. view of a citizen-soldier—a part-time soldier who has a regular career outside the military—as the norm. Still, this concept is much diminished even in the United States, where only members of the National Guard and Reservists are now considered citizen-soldiers.

The concept of conscription or levy or forced service to the nation harkens back to the French Revolution (1789–1800) when the French Republic, which replaced the monarchical government overthrown by the masses, needed help defending the nation against other European monarchies. The Grand Armée began with a government act of September 1798 calling for Frenchmen to defend their nation as part of their historic experience and as proof of their support for their heritage. Napoleon, France's best military strategist during this period, shaped this Grand Armée into an institution of tremendous professionalism. The French military was to support the basic aspects of the nation rather than rely on mercenaries to do the "dirty work" of defense. In return, soldiers would receive monetary compensation.

Since the French Revolution, each society has debated the advantages and disadvantages of national service as an obligation. Israel probably offers the most clear-cut example of the need for required service; there is a widely held national view that the state and society are under constant threat of attack. The manner of applying this national obligation across the society is the crux of the debate in Israel. As Israeli society has changed, some are particularly uncomfortable with religious exemptions from military service. As a general rule, however, mandatory national military service is a requirement in the Jewish state for people of both sexes when they reach the age of seventeen and until they reach forty-nine years of age. The mandatory conscription period is thirty-six months for men and twenty-four for women.

Other societies have a wider range of discussion about national service, even though some of them face obvious threats that are not all that different from Israel's situation. Taiwan, the island a hundred miles off of China's southeast coast, is an example of a state that has an interesting and evolving approach to obligatory national service. Recognized diplomatically by only two dozen nation-states around the world (because the People's Republic of China [PRC] refuses to acknowledge it as an independent, sovereign state), Taiwan has survived for fifty-five years as an entity with a stable government (which has been democratic for the past two decades), a prosperous economy, and a relatively high standard of living. For much of the past six decades, Taiwan's government has required military service to defend the country against expected Chinese actions to reunify the island with the mainland. Over the past decade, however, as China's confidence has increased, and as Taiwan suffered its first serious recession in many years, the society has evidenced a decreasing willingness to pay for a military infrastructure. As a result, the country is apparently moving to an all-volunteer force. This strikes many people as odd because it is occurring as China is both improving its military and expressing growing impatience with Taiwan's moves toward independence. Many analysts ask why Taiwan would move away from required national service when the threat to its survival seems increasingly at risk.

If Taiwan and Israel are important studies in national obligation, the remainder of the world falls somewhere in between—few states share the survival dilemma confronting these two states. Many states have the luxury of choosing between conscription and some alternative approach to providing defense. In recent years, particularly after the Soviet Union's collapse and the end of the Cold War (1947–1989), a growing number of states have decided that they would be better off with a nonobligatory system that allows but does not require citizens to participate in national defense. This is often done to prevent the military from assuming so much power that it takes over governance, as occurred in Argentina for much of the period between 1930 and 1994 (when voluntary service began). Other states, such as Costa Rica as noted, have opted against a standing force to avoid the recurring problems of an armed portion of society trying to seize power when it disagrees with civilian rule.

One other important note is a semantic one. Japan, under its U.S.-drawn constitution, does not have a military but has "Self-Defense Forces" for the various services. This is truly only a name change from a traditional military, however, as the Japanese Self-Defense Forces are quite competent to defend the nation.

The text that follows presents the various categories of military service together with the states that belong to these categories. This is not a complete list of the world's nations; instead it is a selective look at the larger states across the various regions and their current state of national military service. This data comes from the online version of the 2005 *CIA World Factbook*, accessible at http://www.cia.gov/publications/factbook.

No Standing National Military Obligations

Costa Rica: The nation dissolved its armed forces in 1948 to prevent the repeated *golpes del estado* (equivalent to coups d'etat) that had characterized so much of the nation's history.

Iceland: The nation's defense is considerably easier than that of most states of the world owing to its geographic isolation. There are no standing military forces, although Iceland operates a Coast Guard and a National Police. Its role in the North Atlantic Treaty Organization is actually performed by U.S. forces.

Panama: The 1989 U.S.-led invasion wiped out the military as an actor in the society. A police force now administers security in the country.

States Lacking Conscription

Argentina (1994): Young men eighteen or older can volunteer for the Argentine Army, Air Force, or Navy (containing the naval and Marine Corps elements).

Australia (2001): Young men can participate in military service as of age sixteen, but it is a purely voluntary participation in any of the Australian Defense Force components (Royal Navy, Army, Royal Air Force, and Special Forces).

Bahrain: Eighteen is the eligible age for voluntary service in the National Guard, Army, Air Force, and Navy.

Bangladesh: Without conscription, voluntary service is open at age eighteen to men in the Army, Air Force, and Navy.

Belgium: Women and men are eligible to volunteer at age sixteen, with women constituting 7 percent of the national military.

Burma: Both sexes are eligible for voluntary service in the Army, Air Force, or Navy at age eighteen.

Cameroon: Men are eligible for voluntary service at age eighteen in the Army, Air Force, or Navy.

Canada: At age sixteen, men or women may volunteer to serve in the Royal Canadian Land Forces, Maritime Command, Air Command, or newly instituted in 2006 Canada Command for Homeland Security. Women constitute 11 percent of the force.

Czech Republic: Voluntary service is open to men between eighteen and fifty as the Czech military began evolving in 2004 to an all-volunteer force, which will be done by 2007.

France: Voluntary service in the Army, Navy, Gendarmerie, or Air Force is open at age seventeen.

The Gambia: Voluntary service is open at age eighteen for the National Guard, Presidential Guard, National Army, or Navy.

Hungary: With conscription ended in 2004, voluntary service applies at age eighteen for the Ground or Air Forces.

India: Voluntary service applies for those at sixteen seeking to participate in the Ground Forces, Air Forces, Navy, and paramilitary groups.

Ireland: The lowest age for volunteers is seventeen unless the volunteer possesses a special skill to serve in the Irish Army.

Japan: The Maritime Self-Defense Forces, Ground Self-Defense Forces, and Air Self-Defense Forces accept volunteers at age eighteen.

Jordan: Conscription ended in 1999, but all men under thirty-seven must register for military service while volunteers are welcome at age seventeen. The Royal Jordanian Army, Royal Jordanian Navy, Royal Jordanian Air Force, and Special Forces Command are available to volunteers.

Liberia: Voluntary service applies at age eighteen for the Army, Air Force, or Navy.

Malawi: Volunteer service takes place after age eighteen in the Army or Police.

Malaysia: Volunteers can serve as of age eighteen in the Royal Malaysian Air Force, Army, or Royal Navy.

Namibia: Voluntary service is open at age eighteen for the Army, Navy, and Police.

Nepal: Age eighteen opens the door to voluntary service in the Royal Nepalese Army and Royal Nepalese Police.

The Netherlands: Volunteer service begins at the age of twenty for the Royal Netherlands Army, Royal Netherlands Air Force, Royal Netherlands Navy, Royal Netherlands Constabulary, and Defense Interservice Command.

New Zealand: Voluntary service opens at age seventeen, but deployment cannot occur until age twenty. The services open to the volunteers include the Royal New Zealand Air Force, Royal New Zealand Navy, and Royal New Zealand Army.

Nicaragua: Volunteers arrive at age seventeen for the Army.

Nigeria: Eighteen is the minimum age for voluntary service in the Army, Air Force, and Navy.

Oman: Voluntary service in the Royal Omani Army, Royal Omani Air Force, or Royal Omani Navy begins at age eighteen.

Pakistan: Volunteer service opens at sixteen, but volunteers cannot be deployed before age twenty-one. Service is in the Navy, Air Force, and Army.

Portugal: Conscription ended in 2005, and voluntary service applies at age eighteen in the Navy, Army, Air Force, and National Republican Guard.

Qatar: Voluntary service is available to those eighteen or older, but the majority of the Land Force is nonprofessional military enlisted personnel from abroad. The Qatari Amiri Land Force, Qatari Amiri Air Force, and Qatari Amiri Navy constitute the military of the country.

Rwanda: Voluntary service applies at age sixteen for the Army and Air Force.

Saudi Arabia: No conscription exists, so volunteers, at age eighteen or above, may participate in the National Guard, Land Forces, Air Force, Air Defense Force, Ministry of Interior troops, or Navy.

Sierra Leone: Voluntary service applies to citizens at age eighteen for the Army.

Slovenia: Conscription ended in 2003, while volunteers participate as of age seventeen for the Army and Navy.

South Africa: Women, participating in noncombat roles as far back as World War I, and men may volunteer at age eighteen for the Army, Navy, Air Force, Joint Support, Joint Operations, Military Health, and Military Intelligence.

Sri Lanka: Volunteer age is eighteen for service in the Navy, Air Force, Police, or Army.

United Arab Emirates: No conscription still exists, so voluntary service for the Army, Air and Air Defense, Navy, and Paramilitary forces is at age eighteen.

United Kingdom: Voluntary service for the Royal Navy, Royal Air Force, and Her Majesty's Army begins at age sixteen.

United States: President Richard M. Nixon abolished conscription in 1973, but President Jimmy Carter partially reinstated it with the requirement that men between eighteen and thirty-five register with the Selective Service should a national military call-up occur.

Mandatory Participation in Military Service

Afghanistan: At twenty-two, men incur a four-year commitment to the Army or national Militia.

Albania: At nineteen, men may be conscripted for the General Staff, the Army, the Navy, or a number of military commands.

Algeria: Between nineteen and thirty, men serve a twelve-month mandatory service commitment in the People's National Army, People's National Navy, Air Force, or Territorial Air Defense.

Angola: Men must serve a compulsory term of national service of two years' duration (plus time training) upon reaching seventeen years of age. Their options are the Navy, Army, and Air Force.

Armenia: Men can volunteer for military service at age eighteen, but between eighteen and twenty-seven, men incur a twelve-month national service obligation to be served in the Army, Air Force, or Navy.

Austria: Eighteen-year-olds must serve compulsory obligations of eight months, but volunteers are welcome at age sixteen. In 2007, the service obligation will drop to six months' duration. The Land Forces and the Air Forces are the options for service.

Azerbaijan: Voluntary and mandatory conscription attach to men aged eighteen, while the upper limit for mandatory service is now thirty-five. The options for service include Army, Navy, Air Defense, and Air Forces.

Belarus: An eighteen-month obligation is held by all men upon reaching eighteen years of age with eligibility to serve in the Army, Air Force, or Air Defense Force.

Benin: Men and women are eligible to volunteer at twenty-one when they will also reach the age for compulsory service for eighteen months. Volunteers may appear, as early as age eighteen, however. The options include the Army, Air Force, and Navy.

Bolivia: Men must register for the Navy (including the Marines), Army, or Air Force when the number of volunteers, welcomed at age eighteen, does not meet the national defense recruitment goals for a year. If conscription is required, eligibility for conscription drops to fourteen years of age. Conscription is a twelve-month commitment.

Bosnia and Herzegovina: With its recent circumstances, Bosnia-Herzegovina has a complicated set of obligations. In times of peace, the compulsory service age is eighteen but two years earlier in times of war. The four-month obligation affects healthy men and women between eighteen and sixty for service in the subordinate commands of the Army.

Brazil: Men must enroll for mandatory service at age nineteen but are welcomed to volunteer at age seventeen. Conscription is a twelve-month obligation for the Navy, Army, or Air Force.

Bulgaria: Conscription applies to men at age eighteen for a nine-month period of obligation. In 2006, Air Force and Navy conscription will end as the services professionalize, while the following year it will end in the Army.

Burkina Faso: Compulsory service attaches at age eighteen, while voluntary service is open to those interested at age twenty. Service is in the National Gendarmerie, Army, or Air Force.

Burundi: Compulsory or voluntary military service occurs at age eighteen in the Army or the National Gendarmerie.

Cambodia: Compulsory service for men is between ages eighteen and thirty for an eighteen-month period in the Royal Khmer Army, Royal Khmer Navy, or Royal Khmer Air Force.

Central African Republic: Voluntary or compulsory service begins at age eighteen. Time in conscripted service is two years. The options include the Republican Guard, Directorate of Gendarmerie Inspection, or the Land Forces.

Chad: Voluntary service, with a guardian's consent, is open at age eighteen, while a three-year conscription period goes into effect at twenty. The Army, Air Force, and the Gendarmerie are the service options.

Chile: All men must register between the ages of eighteen and forty-five for military service with twelve months' obligation to the Army and twenty-four months to the Air Force and Navy.

China (PRC): Compulsory service is between ages eighteen and twenty-two with a twenty-four-month obligation. There is no age limit for males seeking to volunteer, while women are welcome at age seventeen for specific jobs. Military service can be done in the People's Liberation Army, People's Liberation Army-Navy, People's Liberation Army-Air Force, II Artillery, People's Armed Police, and the Militia.

Colombia: A two-year obligation is incurred by all volunteers or conscripts, each of whom has reached the age of eighteen. The opportunities to serve fall in the Army, Navy, and Air Force.

Cote d'Ivoire: Eighteen-year-olds are eligible to volunteer or do their conscription service, the latter lasting for eighteen months in the Air Force, Army, or Navy.

Croatia: Sixteen years is the age for voluntary service, while conscription takes effect at age eighteen, for a six-month obligation. The Police Force, one of the options for the obligation, is ending conscription in 2006, while the Army, Navy, and Air Forces will continue to require service.

Cuba: Both sexes may be eligible for military service as of age seventeen in the Revolutionary Army, Navy, Air Force, Air Defense Force, Territorial Troops, or Youth Army.

Denmark: Voluntary service or conscription occurs at age eighteen, with the initial conscription period of four to twelve months to determine specialization in the Royal Army, Royal Air Force, Royal Navy, or Home Guard. Conscripts go into the Reserves upon completing their obligatory service.

Ecuador: A twelve-month service obligation pertains to all men at age twenty, with the choice of the Army, Navy, or Air Force.

Egypt: Three years' service is the requirement for men upon reaching age eighteen. Service can be in the Air Force, Air Defense Force, Army, or Navy.

El Salvador: Men may volunteer at sixteen, but compulsory service attaches at eighteen for twelve months in the Army, Navy or Air Force.

Eritrea: Voluntary or conscription service is available to men at age eighteen, with the conscription period of sixteen months in the Army, Navy, or Air Force.

Estonia: Men at age eighteen are required to serve an eight-month obligation for conscripts along with an eleven-month commitment for sergeants and reservists. Voluntary service is open to anyone at age seventeen. The Republic does not intend to end conscription through at least 2010. Reserve requirements last until age sixty. The service can be fulfilled in the Ground Forces, Security Forces (homeland security), Maritime Border Guard, Coast Guard, or Volunteer Defense League.

Ethiopia: Conscription or voluntary service applies at age eighteen, with service opportunities in the Ground or Air Forces.

Finland: Men at eighteen are eligible for voluntary service or conscription in the Army, Navy, or Air Force.

Gabon: Voluntary or compulsory service is open at age eighteen to the National Police, Gendarmerie, Army, Air Force, or Navy.

Georgia: National service is open between ages eighteen and twenty-four, through voluntary or compulsory service. Compulsory time requires an eighteen-month commitment to the National Guard, Army, Air and Air Defense Forces, Interior Forces, and Maritime Forces.

Germany: Men serve at eighteen for a nine-month compulsory service requirement in the Army, Air Forces, Navy, or associated commands.

Ghana: Compulsory and voluntary service goes into effect for eighteen-year-old men to serve in the Army, Air Force, and Navy.

Greece: Conscription goes into effect the January of the year the enlistee reaches his eighteenth birthday (including some seventeen-year-olds, as a result) for a twelve-month Army and Air Force service versus a slightly longer Navy service. Volunteers are welcomed at age seventeen.

Guatemala: Men between eighteen and fifty may be conscripted for periods ranging from twelve to twenty-four months in the Army, Air Force, or Navy.

Guinea-Bissau: Eighteen is the age for voluntary or conscript service in the Revolutionary Army or paramilitaries.

Honduras: At eighteen, men must serve for three years in the Navy, Air Force, or Army.

Indonesia: Conscription applies at age eighteen for a two-year commitment. Voluntary service also applies at that age. Service may be applied in the Army, Air Force, or Marines.

Iran: Sixteen is the age for volunteering, while eighteen is the age for conscription to the Iranian Revolutionary Guard and the Iranian Regular Forces. Conscription is for an eighteen-month period.

Iraq: The new provisional government reports that men between eighteen and forty would serve as a conscripted force in the Navy, Army, or Air Force.

Israel: At age seventeen, Jews and Druze must serve regardless of gender, while Christians, Muslims, and Circassians can volunteer at the same point. Mandatory service is thirty-six months for men versus twenty-one months for women, all serving in the Israeli Defense Forces.

Italy: Compulsory service ended in 2005, and voluntary service is divided into the Army, Air Force, Navy, and Caribinieri or border forces.

Kazakhstan: Obligatory service applies at age eighteen for a conscription period of two years in the Air and Air Defense Force, Army, Navy, and Republican Guard.

Kuwait: Obligatory and volunteer service applies at age eighteen in the Land Forces, National Guard, Navy, and Air Force.

Kyrgyzstan: Eighteen is the age for compulsory service in the Army, National Guard, and Air Force.

Laos: Compulsory military service is for a minimum period of eighteen months and begins at age seventeen in the Lao People's Army and Air Force.

Latvia: Volunteering applies at age eighteen, while compulsory service goes into effect for men at eighteen for a period of twelve months. Latvia will have an entirely professional force, however, by the end of 2007.

Lithuania: While voluntary service applies at age eighteen, all men between nineteen and forty-five must serve a military obligation of twelve months in the Ground Forces, Navy, Air Force and Defense Forces.

Macedonia: Conscription is ending, although a six-month conscription period must be served as yet. Volunteers are welcome at age eighteen. The services for obligation include the branches of the Army.

Mali: Volunteer and required service occur as of age eighteen with conscription for two years' endurance. The options for service include the Army, Air Force, and National Guard.

Mauritania: Volunteers alone staff the Navy and Air Force. Army conscription pertains at age eighteen for two years' duration. Most personnel are thought to be volunteers in the Air Force, Army, and Navy.

Mexico: Sixteen-year-old men may enlist with parental consent. Obligatory service pertains to all eighteen-year-old men for twelve months in either the Naval Secretariat (Marines and Navy) or National Defense Secretariat (Air Force and Army).

Moldova: Required service applies at age eighteen for twelve months in the Army or Air Force.

Mongolia: Compulsory service applies between ages eighteen and twenty-five for twelve months in the Mongolian People's Army and Mongolian People's Air Force.

Morocco: Volunteer and compulsory service applies at eighteen, with an eighteen-month conscription period in the Royal Moroccan Army, Royal Moroccan Air Force, and Royal Moroccan Navy.

Niger: Compulsory service of two years is required of all men eighteen or older in the Army or National Air Force.

Norway: For the Home Guard, men may volunteer at age sixteen. For the Royal Norwegian Army, Royal Norwegian Air Force, or Royal Norwegian Navy, men may volunteer at age seventeen and women a year later. Conscription applies at age eighteen for a twelve-month period. In wartime, conscription age drops to sixteen.

Peru: All men must serve their military obligation as of eighteen years of age in either the Navy, Army, or Air Force.

Philippines: Eighteen is the minimum age for volunteer or compulsory service in the Army, Navy, or Air Force.

Poland: Compulsory service applies at age seventeen after January 1 in the year the individual is turning eighteen. Seventeen is the age for voluntary service. Women can serve only as commissioned or noncommissioned officers. Service takes place in the Land Forces, Navy, or Air Force. Poland has shortened its conscription service period from twelve to nine months. By 2007, 60 percent of the Polish military force will be professional; the primary members will be individuals who have already served their obligation (rather than new volunteers).

Romania: Voluntary service opens at age eighteen. Compulsory service is required at age twenty, except in wartime when the age drops to eighteen, for a period of twelve months' obligation in the Civil Defense, Special Operations, Air and Air Defense Forces, Land Force, and Navy.

Russia: Men must register for national service at age seventeen, but service age is between eighteen and twenty-seven for the required two years' obligation, which will drop to a single year in 2008. In 2005, fully 30 percent of the servicemen in Russia were contract personnel, with expectations to raise that to 70 percent in 2010. The forces open to participation include the Space Troops, Air Forces, Airborne Forces, Strategic Rocket Forces, Ground Forces, and Navy.

Senegal: Volunteer and compulsory service applies at age eighteen. The conscription service obligation is two years in the Army, Navy, or Air Force.

Serbia and Montenegro: Compulsory service applies at age nineteen for a nine-month period in the Ground Forces, Air and Air Defense Forces, and Navy.

Singapore: Volunteers may join at sixteen, but obligatory service, for twenty-four months' service, applies to those eighteen and older. Singapore has an Air Force, Army, Navy, and Air Defense Force.

Slovakia: Eighteen is the age for compulsory service, but the nation moves to a completely volunteer military in 2007, with more than 80 percent already volunteers. Women are part of the volunteer component, having reached the age of seventeen. The Slovak military contains an Air Force, Army, and Training/Support Forces.

South Korea: Men between tweny and thirty years of age have obligations to serve for twenty-four–twenty-eight months' duration (depending on the branch of the armed forces), while volunteers are welcome at age eighteen. Four thousand women are in the commissioned and noncommissioned officer corps constituting roughly 3.2 percent of the South Korean military where they began serving in 1950, although they are not in the "combat arms." Korean service is available in the Army, Air Force, Navy, Marine Corps, and National Maritime Police.

Spain: Compulsory service begins at age twenty. The military is composed of the Army, Air Force, and Navy.

Sudan: Mandatory service is for men between eighteen and thirty years of age for three years' duration in the People's Army, People's Navy, Air Force, and Popular Defense Force.

Sweden: Compulsory service is for those nineteen years of age for a period of seven to seventeen months, depending on the task.

Once compulsory service ends, the citizen becomes a member of the Reserves until age forty-seven. Service may be in the Royal Swedish Army, Royal Swedish Navy, or Royal Swedish Air Force.

Switzerland: Women may volunteer but are not expected to do compulsory service as are all men nineteen years of age. Swiss men may volunteer at seventeen. Compulsory service must be for at least 260 days' service, although conscripts receive fifteen weeks' training, followed with ten shorter training periods over the next twenty-two years. Switzerland has Land Forces and an Air Force.

Syria: Men must serve at age eighteen for thirty months' obligation in the Army, Navy, Air Force, Police, and Security Forces.

Taiwan: Citizens between nineteen and thirty-five must serve in the armed forces for sixteen months, a term that will be reduced to twelve months in 2008. Women can hold only noncombat jobs. The Taiwan military has its citizens serve in the Army, Air Force, Navy, Coast Guard, Armed Forces Reserve, and Armed Forces Police Forces.

Tajikistan: Two years' obligation is required for all men of at least eighteen years of age in the Mobile Troops, Air Troops, and Land Troops.

Tanzania: Voluntary service is open to those fifteen years of age. Compulsory service applies at eighteen once the individual graduates from secondary school. Two years is the period of obligation in the National Service, Army, Air Defense, and Navy.

Thailand: Voluntary service begins at age eighteen when men also must register for military service, which becomes obligatory at age twenty-one. The conscription period is two years. The service options are the Royal Thai Air Force, Royal Thai Navy, and Royal Thai Army.

Togo: Both compulsory and voluntary service begin at age eighteen for the Army, Air Force, Navy, and Gendarmerie.

Tunisia: Voluntary service applies at age eighteen, but compulsory service is age twenty, with conscription obligation running for twelve months in the Army, Navy, and Air Force.

Turkmenistan: Obligatory service applies at age eighteen for two years' endurance in the Ground Forces and Air and Air Defense Forces.

Uganda: While the law calls for voluntary and compulsory service at age eighteen, the government in Kampala also states it may call people no younger than thirteen to service in the Army, Marine Unit, and Air Wing.

Ukraine: Compulsory and voluntary service are for men between eighteen and twenty-seven, with compulsory endurance of eighteen months for the Army and Air Force and twenty-four months for the Navy.

Uzbekistan: The compulsory service age is eighteen for a service commitment of twelve months in the Army, Air and Air Defense, and National Guard.

Venezuela: Men are eligible to volunteer or receive mandatory service notices at eighteen for a thirty-month required period of obligation. The options include the Army, Navy, National Guard, or Air Force.

Vietnam: Two years' compulsory service applies to men over the age of eighteen with service in the People's Army, People's Navy, Coast Guard, and People's Air Force.

Yemen: Compulsory service applies as of age eighteen with a two-year responsibility to serve in the Army, Navy, Coastal Forces, Air Force, and Republican Guard.

Problems in Other Societies Arising from Military Service

Gender Questions

The long-running national debate about the role of women in the nation's armed forces is hardly a new one in the United States. Women participated in auxiliary service functions during World War I, but the more substantial influx of women into the armed forces occurred during World War II and the Vietnam War. The establishment of the all-volunteer force in 1973 meant women had the option to join the service in greater numbers because their participation was needed.

As the women's participation became gradually accepted but women's roles in society as a whole became more debated, so did their role in combat functions, the heart of military service. The concerns boiled over during the Clinton administration. Women had been a cornerstone in his 1992 victory over incumbent George H. W. Bush. While Clinton did not make women in the military the key issue that he made gay and lesbian service, during the life of his administration he did gradually promote the growth of women's role in the services. Clinton thought he resolved the issue in the 1990s by gradually lifting the prohibitions against women's participation in "combat jobs," such as flying combat air missions or serving with frontline units in battle. In this way he confronted key issues of women's fitness for equal status in society. Today, a decade after many of the restrictions on women's service options have been gradually lifted, many traditionalists still see the jobs taken by women pilots, tank drivers, and ship personnel as putting them unnecessarily in the line of danger and thus wrongly assigned to those risky jobs.

Some nation-states do require women to serve in the armed forces, albeit in gender-segregated combat situations. Along with Israel, these states include Eritrea, Taiwan, North Korea, Malaysia, Libya, the People's Republic of China, and Peru. Peru, as a predominantly Roman Catholic nation, along with Malaysia and Libya, with their deep Islamic roots, are all interesting additions to this list because neither of these religions allows women the same absolute rights in all aspects of society, especially where religious affairs pertain.

In the People's Republic of China and the Democratic People's Republic of Korea, this application of strict Marxist-Leninist ideological equality is not surprising. Chinese women officers serve in noncombat capacities and are given little serious opportunity to achieve higher ranks; they are given tasks such as translation services at memorials and serving tea. Taiwan, as noted, is more like Israel, where in the interest of the basic survival of the state itself all citizens participate equally in life and defense. The overwhelming majority of states around the world, however, do not make national service mandatory for women, nor do many even want women in uniform as volunteers.

Conscientious Objectors and Draft Evasion in non-U.S. National Military Service

The major reason citizens anywhere refuse to serve in their countries' national service is religious orientation. Sects such as the Mennonites or Quakers (Society of Friends) do not believe military solutions to conflict are acceptable remedies. By extension, members of these religions do not serve; neither do Jehovah's Witnesses. They are sometimes given conscientious objector status, and sometimes the national service simply ignores them. Depending on conditions in the particular state, the steps the conscientious objector must take to get approval for CO status may be quite detailed, such as going through a hearing before a magistrate, or it may mean filing paperwork alone. It may also mean working in an alternative work facility.

In Britain, conscientious objectors became a major issue in both World Wars I and II. While COs had long existed in Britain, until the twentieth century no conflict was significant enough to bring attention to their numbers. In these two conflicts, government moves became more stringent to preclude growing numbers from taking that route. Conscientious objectors were hauled before tribunals, which were able to grant them exemption or put them in jail or initiate some action in between. Over the course of the two conflicts, more people announced their conscientious-objector status, and it spawned a tremendous movement that became important during the 1950s as the basis for the Campaign for Nuclear Disarmament and subsequent peace activities in the 1980s. These activities were designed to eliminate the stationing of modernized NATO medium-range missiles in Britain during President Ronald Reagan's administration. With the end of conscription in Britain and the country's decreased militarization, the numbers of those objecting to military service decreased until the Iraq war. Many in Britain have deeply and vocally opposed Prime Minister Tony Blair's support of President George W. Bush's decision to oust Saddam Hussein.

In other parts of the world, such as Spain or Israel, conscientious objectors also exist as a sizable portion of the society. In Spain, many young men have taken up the 1978 Constitution's opportunity to do alternative service rather than wearing a uniform for a fixed period of time.

Israel, with its defense imperative, offers an interesting example of conscientious objectors challenging a society. The objectors on the left morally reject the existing reasons to wear a uniform, while the objectors on the right tend to be ultrareligious and have a government exemption so that they can pursue Talmudic studies. The 1982 Israeli move into Lebanon and subsequent issues in Israel's evolving position in the Middle East presented serious challenges to the society. Since national service has been fairly universal in the past, the rising number of people condemning the government's actions and rejecting their need to uphold that government by enhancing its security capability has become a tough issue.

The conflict between Israel and Hezbollah in July and August 2006, however, caused the increase in public support because of fear that Hezbollah's activities need curtailing. Over the initial four weeks of the conflict, the challenges of defeating Hezbollah to achieve a relatively vague charge set forth by Prime Minister Olmert became increasingly obvious. Whether popular support for the conflict will dwindle should it become a prolonged event remains to be seen, but in that circumstance the possibility of increased conscientious objection to the incursion could grow.

Canada has also had a large community of conscientious objectors, many of whom came from the United States during the Vietnam War. Canada, with its tradition of relative societal openness, was a place where U.S. youth who did not want to go to jail but passionately objected to the use of U.S. forces in Southeast Asia fled to escape U.S. justice authorities. As noted earlier, President Jimmy Carter ultimately pardoned those who fled north, though some decided not to return home.

Conscientious objection is primarily a North American phenomenon. Russia has a serious problem with draft evasion and with meeting conscription obligations, but this is not strictly speaking a matter of conscientious objection. Few Asian, African, Latin American, or Middle Eastern states ever confront this issue, largely because the collective goals of these societies always outweigh individual desires.

Many other issues are important in national service systems, but since this volume focuses on the U.S. national service system, we have only sought to present an introduction to the topic. The comparisons are interesting, but, ultimately, national military service is custom-tailored to the needs, history, culture, threats, economics, and biases of each society. This is as true today as it was a hundred years ago.

References

CIA World Fact Book 2005. Washington, DC: Central Intelligence Agency, 2005; accessible at http://www.cia.gov/cia/publications/factbook

Danopoulos, Constantine, and Cynthia Watson, eds. *Political Role of the Military.* Westport, CT: Greenwood Publishing, 1996.

Weigley, Russell K. *The American Way of War: A History of United States Military Strategy and Policy.* Bloomington: Indiana University Press, 1977.

4

Chronology

1607   Colonists begin arriving from England expecting to form militias for self-protection but with colonial populations containing many pacifists, such as Brethren, Quakers, and Mennonites, which led to objection to bearing arms.

1620s   Virginia colony requires all free white men to participate with their own weapons in militia preparations.

1630s   Plymouth and Massachusetts Bay colonists also require all free white men to participate with local militia organizations.

1637   The Army National Guard, the predecessor of the state militias, dates its history to this year when the first of the colonies constituted its standing militia, beginning the period of citizen-soldiers.

1658   Richard Keene is the first recorded conscientious objector in the territory known as Maryland. Subjected to public ridicule for refusing the carry out an obligation, Keene is fined for his actions.

1670s   The last militia actions on the East Coast colonies are along the Chesapeake and Massachusetts Bay areas against the dwindling Native American populations.

1690s   The Virginia House of Burgesses agrees to a "standing army" to protect the frontier from incursions. The

1690's burgesses take a direct role in deciding which local com-
cont. munity's militia forces will provide protection in any
specific area.

New York volunteers deal with French incursions in the
region surrounding Albany on the upper Hudson River.
Bounties to provide sufficient enlistments become common practice.

1776 To achieve independence, the first professional army is
raised in the colonies to wage war of independence
against British rule. George Washington leads this group
under the authority of the Continental Congress in
Philadelphia.

1783 Horatio Gates, a War of Independence general, and a
group of others seek to overthrow the "moderate" government being implemented by General George Washington and the bulk of the newly successful independent
government. The Newburgh Conspiracy, as it becomes
known for the place where Washington responded to the
charges, reinforces long-existing fears of the political ideology characterizing colonial America (called Radical
Whiggism by Lawrence Cress) that an individual could
seize a standing federal armed force to repress the majority. This fear of the power of a standing army rings
true throughout the national experience of the United
States.

New York governor George Clinton proposes that each
state identify a college in its boundaries where some students receive military training. This would create citizen-soldiers as well as provide necessary military experience.

1785 Officers in the Army are stationed exclusively at Fort Pitt
(the present-day Pittsburgh, Pennsylvania) on the frontier and at West Point in upstate New York to circum-
scribe their presence across the new nation. At the same
time, virtually all naval vessels are sold off to preclude
their use by nefarious interests.

1786   In Shay's Rebellion, in western Massachusetts, armed men shut down the court system and gain the support of the militia, which ought to have defended the legitimate government. Governor James Bowdoin, in conjunction with the Massachusetts House and Senate, raises a professional army to address this failure of the legitimate government. This incident provides grist for those who believed the need for a national military was paramount to preclude a militia from engaging in this parochial behavior. Local militia who swear allegiance to the government in Boston work in conjunction with regular troops from the eastern part of the state to end the rebellion the following year. This incident plays a part in reformulating the role of the military in the Constitutional Convention discussions in Philadelphia.

1792   The Uniform Militia Act specifically gives the president of the United States the authority to call out the militia in cases he deems necessary. This is a fundamental moment in the formation of national service procedures for the new nation. The law calls for a standardization of enrollment in the militia by all freemen (males and nonslaves) between the ages of eighteen and forty-five across the states, to create uniformity, as well as a requirement regardless of the state. In effect, the federal government has no enforcement capability, but the principle of universal military commitment is in place.

1794   The Whiskey Rebellion in western Pennsylvania represents the first serious challenge to national government. Communities believe they are being overtaxed, underrepresented, put at a disadvantage to reach the court system near Philadelphia, lack security because of Native American attacks, and other conditions that led the settlers to believe they did not have to cooperate with the existing political officials. President George Washington calls upon more than 12,000 national troops to put down the revolt in maintaining national sovereignty over the region around Washington, Pennsylvania. The federal troops prove successful, forcing the chief rebel to flee to the Spanish Caribbean.

1792–
1814

The states have militia commitments on the books, but they are applied to varying degrees while a small national army is formally in place to protect the nascent Republic.

1802

The United States Military Academy at West Point, New York, opens its doors, beginning an enduring tradition of military education leading to service in the Army.

1814

The defense of the nation's capital by militiamen proves unsuccessful as they flee their posts in August upon the arrival of British troops. The British sack the city in their campaign to move north up the East Coast. Part of the problem is the strained chain-of-command relationship between the militia leadership, Brigadier General William Winder, and the secretary of war, John Armstrong. After the defeat at Washington, Armstrong is replaced by the secretary of state, James Monroe, thus giving him dual cabinet appointments but allowing coordination on policy.

Congress rejects the idea of a compulsory draft encouraged by James Monroe, instituting a "cash bounty" incentive system instead. This financial incentive increasingly drives militia participation in the coming decades before the Civil War.

1819

The American Literary, Scientific, and Military Academy in Vermont begins an innovative program with a military service commitment as well as liberal arts education. This is the first college of this type in the nation. Today that institution is Norwich University, retaining its Corps of Cadets, which opened to women in 1974, for military service as well as general education.

1820

Former president Thomas Jefferson directs the University of Virginia in Charlottesville to offer some military education for students to prepare them for their role as citizen-soldiers.

1820s Reform at the Army Academy at West Point is intended to make the academy the primary source of the Army's officers.

1840 Indiana University and the University of Tennessee begin offering training for service in the armed forces.

1845 The United States Naval Academy at Annapolis, Maryland, begins providing education to the Corps of cadets who go on to careers in the Navy and Marine Corps.

1861– During the Civil War, the formal status of conscientious
1865 objector is conveyed on those whose religious beliefs prohibited bearing arms: Mennonites, Brethren, Seventh Day Adventists, and Quakers.

1862 The Congress authorizes the Militia Act of 1862 to increase the militia levels in the states while also guaranteeing a supply of troops for the Union Army as the war drags on.

Draft bounties become more lucrative as a manner of attracting more participants.

Morrill Land-Grant Bill passes, guaranteeing that young men enrolled at land-grant agricultural colleges receive military training. This remains in effect until the onset of World War I. The act aims to create 30,000 acres of state colleges (thus creating land-grant schools) to prepare 20,000 officers for the Army through local training instead of a single, set accession point for officers.

The Confederate States of America declares a draft in order to bolster its number of troops. Prior to that, troops had volunteered to defend the Confederacy

The Militia Act of 1862 calls on the militias of the various states to engage in the conflict against the insurrectionist Confederacy and to execute the laws of the Union while allowing African Americans to fight for the Union forces as paid soldiers.

1862 **cont.**	Congress creates the Medal of Honor, the highest national recognition for exemplary action while in uniform. The medal is the highest award the U.S. government confers on anyone who has acted with valor and courage on active duty against the enemy.
1863	The Enrollment Act attempts to make a draft more tolerable through some of its provisions, but President Lincoln declares a draft for the Union to achieve adequate troop strength to fight the Civil War. One provision of the conflict, fraught with unintended consequences, is the "commutation fee," which allowed a draftee to "buy" his way out of military service for $300 or the bounty market rate in his particular city.
	Riots break out in the summer, most prominently in New York City, against bounties that would have forced required military service because bounty hunters often fled with the cash rather than buying someone else's service. New York rioting cost more than a hundred lives.
	Congress creates national cemeteries for those who served in uniform.
1864	Commutations are revoked by Congress after the rioting the prior summer.
1865	James Oakes, often labeled the father of Selective Service, is head of the local draft board in Illinois. He comes up with the first program that would end buyout programs and other options precluding universal service for freemen of the proscribed age. Oakes proposes a system that encouraged civic responsibility by placing the emphasis on the draftee's role, not that of the draft board, for his activities.
1866– 1890	During this period, the War Department originally sends twenty (ultimately a hundred) officers to the land-grant schools nationally to support training, supply equipment, and provide general assistance to the Morrill Act programs.

1866– With the end of conflict, the militia system deteriorates,
1903 consistent with the U.S. historic view of no standing
army because war is such a horrible, extenuating circumstance. Those in the standing professional army
were used primarily to "tame" Indian actions that ham-
pered U.S. efforts to achieve Manifest Destiny. With no
apparent national security threat, the Army's role is
that of what 125 years later becomes known as nation-
building.

1878 The Posse Comitatus Act passes, prohibiting the Army
from engaging in "law enforcement" and civil governance activities within the United States. For those engaged in national service, this has been a benchmark law
against domestic activities, which came into serious
question with Hurricane Katrina in 2005 and President
George W. Bush's desire to use the military for domestic
activities.

1880 State militias first begin their transformation into National Guard units, retaining their chain of command to
the state governors.

1888 Edward Bellamy, a social Utopian, generates considerable social support through his *Looking Backward* for an
"Industrial Army" with required civic service for youth.

1900 At the turn of the twentieth century, forty-two colleges and
universities around the country offer military training.

1903 State militias are converted into the National Guard under the Dick Act, which regulated their role in the national service community of the United States.

1907 The Aeronautical Section of the Army Signal Corps is
created; it is the first move toward an aviation component of the U.S. military.

1910 William James, penning an article entitled "The Moral
Equivalent of War," builds on Edward Bellamy's social
vision to support a nonmilitary compulsory youth commitment to service.

1910   The Boy Scouts organization is created, advocating
cont.   education of young boys in the United States, stressing
that their roles as citizens should include a service component.

General John McAuley Palmer promotes the concept of
universal military training, which, as a West Point
graduate, historian, and veteran of Cuban and China
expeditions of the early twentieth century, he believes
would facilitate the development of the citizen-soldier
concept that had fallen out of favor in the late nineteenth century. Palmer often notes that this was a way
of opening minds because it pushed students to think
beyond the areas they found comfortable. Palmer is an
early advocate of disaggregating the requirement of national military service from national military training,
understanding this would create a different type of society than the one in the past. Palmer's suggestions are
never adopted because many opponents, as is true of
various aspects of the military today, feel it diverts attention and resources from the armed services' primary
goals of defending the nation rather than enforcing
civic service.

1910–   General Leonard Wood, chief of staff of the Army, moves
1914   the military toward citizen military camps that would
widen participation across society to make the military
into more of a citizen-soldier military because young
men would be trained to enter the body of junior officers
available if mass mobilization were required at some
point. Former president Theodore Roosevelt supports
Wood's concept.

1912   The Girls Scouts organization is created and is specifically open to young women as had not been true of
many civic service organizations in the past.

1914   The Aviation Section of the Army Signal Corps increases
the role of developing technology in the military.

1915   The Plattsburgh Movement begins to implement the Citizens Training Military Camps (sometimes called CATCH) advocated forcefully by former chief of staff of the Army General Leonard Wood earlier in the decade. During the summer of that year, the first camp opened at Plattsburgh in upstate New York and subsequently across the nation. By the second summer, well over 10,000 young men have spent their summers (self-financed) in military education and fitness preparation.

1915–   Military education takes on "an extracurricular phase
1930   after the religious and scientific guidance" it had provided from the prior century.

About to scholars Julie Reuben and Michael Neiberg, scientific ideas had won out by 1910 but were not galvanizing enough for a campus environment. Therefore, this education evolved during the 1915–1930 period, becoming more of a supplemental or extracurricular experience (Neiberg, 2000).

1916   Randolph Bourne advocates universal civic service but opposes World War I. His treatise, "A Moral Equivalent for Universal Military Service," appears to support civic service for both sexes for a fixed commitment of time in ways appropriate to society's needs.

The National Defense Act creates the Reserve Officer Training Corps (ROTC), overturning the Morrill Land Grant Act of 1862 in hopes of generating a more stable, predictable education system. The program's beginning is retarded slightly because of World War I. The ROTC concept has been one of the most enduring in the twentieth and twenty-first centuries as graduates earned reserve officer commissions for the active-duty force. In World War II, the Korean War, and Vietnam, ROTC officer accession was crucial to the foundation of the military services. Initial ROTC programs begin at Dartmouth College, Bowdoin College, Williams College, Harvard University, Princeton University, and Yale University.

1916
cont.
Southern University introduces a ROTC unit, one of the few open to African Americans during the era of severe educational segregation in the nation.

The Plattsburgh Movement comes under the control of Grenville Clark, who injects a deliberate, targeted social aspect into the training to promote civic values. He retains the military education aspect but broadens participation, opening a camp for women in Chevy Chase, Maryland, and anticipating a camp for blacks the following year. Instead, the Plattsburgh Movement ends abruptly with U.S. entry into World War I in 1917.

Conscientious objectors are deemed lawfully required to engage in military service but not combat service.

The American Friends Service Committee begins to help those conscientious objectors seeking to prevent their required military service.

The University of Pittsburgh institutes an ROTC-type program without direct support from the War Department.

1917
The Selective Service Act passes, overtly aimed at preventing the social upheaval resulting from the complicated draft requirements created during the Civil War. The act incorporates many of the suggestions of the prior fifty years, such as James Oakes's move to push the burden of registration onto the draftee instead of the draft board, or the elimination of bonuses to preclude equal requirement to serve. Instead, the act forces all men between eighteen and thirty-five to register for national military service.

The Navy Department authorizes women to enlist, prior to the United States entering World War I. The slang for these women is "yeomanettes."

1918
The Army Air Service begins.

1919
Legally, enlistments in the regular army range from one to three years.

A system of universal military training through civilian functions, known as the Civilian Military Training Camps (sometimes called CATCH programs), is proposed, providing another access source for the Officers' Reserve Corps and National Guard.

ROTC programs exist at 135 universities and colleges around the nation.

1920s Pacifists, emboldened by the carnage of World War I, try to oust ROTC programs from schools around the country.

Questions arise about the type of faculty giving instruction in ROTC programs across the country, reinforcing questions about the ultimate purpose of the program.

1920 National Defense Act Amendments (to the 1916 law) create the Total Army concept based on an integrated system composed of the regular army, the National Guard, and the Army Reserve, a concept supported by people such as John McAuley Palmer. This highly respected law creates an Army of three parts that would be regulated for peacetime activities to make it most effective should it be called upon to fulfill national emergency service, requiring a significant education and training component for the regular army. This creates the basis for the professional military education system that now characterizes the armed services, such as the Army Command and General Staff College (name adopted in 1928) at Fort Leavenworth. The legislation attempts to remove any domestic responsibilities that might be given to the regular army for keeping the peace at home. At the same time, the 1920 legislation creates new branches to accompany the traditional units: the Chemical Warfare Service, the Air Service, and the Finance Department. The 1920 law governs the armed services for thirty years, although its significant emphasis on the Navy as the primary defense provider for the nation ebbed and flowed over that period.

1920– Grenville Clark prominently promotes universal mili-
1940 tary training in informal conjunction with John McAuley

1920– Palmer in the face of formal army opposition as well as
1940, from pacifists who had been increasingly agitated at mil-
cont. itarization of U.S. society and participation in the
world's conflicts.

1921 Four more ROTC units open on school campuses for
African American men.

1923 The University of Wisconsin–Madison converts from requiring ROTC participation to making participation
elective without receiving opposition from the Department of War.

1926 The Air Corps Act replaces the Army Air Service with
the Army Air Corps. This establishes the air portion as
an official branch of service, along with the Artillery, Infantry, Corps of Engineers, Signal, and Quartermasters.

The naval ROTC program begins, although it becomes
consolidated under the Holloway Program in the 1940s.
Prior emphasis had been exclusively on the Army.
These programs for the Navy start at Georgia Tech University, Harvard University, Northwestern University,
the University of California, the University of Washington, and Yale University. While they become important
sources for the officer corps, the overwhelming majority
of the officers come from the academies at Annapolis
and West Point.

1927 An auxiliary (female) unit begins at Kansas State
University.

1928 There are ROTC units in more than 300 colleges and universities, enrolling 85,000 officer candidates, less than a
decade after the ROTC program was legalized by the
1916 National Defense Act.

1932 The Army, under Chief of Staff General Douglas
MacArthur, has to respond to civil strife created by the
World War I veterans known as the Bonus Army, who
were requesting congressionally promised bonuses that

they needed due to the depths of the Depression. Majors George Patton and Dwight D. Eisenhower participate in this action, which was requested by President Herbert Hoover.

1933   The Civilian Conservation Corps begins during the early months of the first Franklin Roosevelt administration. It initially provides temporary help with work relief but takes on a permanent cast in 1935. The recruitment for workers is through the Department of Labor. While many of the effects of this program are beyond the scope of this volume, its contribution to the national view of civic duty is crucial. People understand well in the 1930s and 1940s that conservation is basically created through CCC activities. The program has widespread public support because it is a nationwide activity engaged in by many youth in the nation.

The National Guard Mobilization Act officially places the National Guard under the regular army. The act calls for the Guard to mobilize when the president asks for their participation in a congressionally designaed national emergency.

1934   The U.S. Supreme Court rules that conscientious objectors must participate in ROTC programs. This opposes the University of Wisconsin's actions in 1923 but does not put to rest the subject of the mandatory nature of ROTC training.

1935   The National Youth Administration (NYA), a particular interest of First Lady Eleanor Roosevelt, runs until 1943. The NYA, an arm of the Works Progress Administration, focuses on youth of roughly draft age (between eighteen and twenty-four) who were on public assistance or unemployed in the cities of the United States. Two noteworthy aspects of this program are that much controversy existed about its goal since it was quite concerned with providing work instead of civic service to its participants and the administration was far less discriminatory against women or blacks than were most other civic service activities. In addition, because it does provide

1935
cont.
work-relief, the NYA encourages participation by college students needing federal assistance, something unique for that time period before federal educational aid was so important.

The Thomason Act creates a single-year active-duty program for a thousand officers, but only fifty of them are to receive permanent, congressionally commissioned as officers.

1940
The Selective Training and Service Act allows President Franklin Roosevelt to initiate the first peacetime military draft. This precedes the U.S. declaration of war on either Japan or Germany by a year. In this instance, men between twenty-one and thirty-five register for military service but were chosen by a lottery held under the local draft board for a single year of military commitment. Categories for national service first appear: noncombat soldiers, those completely unwilling to participate, and those willing to take alternative positions.

The National Interreligious Service Board for Conscientious Objectors starts for those who cannot serve because of religious convictions.

By this year, ROTC is producing 80 percent of the reserve officer corps and has created 100,000 educated men in its twenty-four years of existence at 220 educational institutions nationally.

The American Council on Education advocates universal youth service for men and women under the American Youth Commission.

Clark and Palmer actively push national military training in Congress.

Camp William James begins in Vermont as an outgrowth of commitments by National Youth Administration and Civilian Conservation Corps graduates and an activist on civic action, immigrant Eugen Rosenstock-Huessy. This camp has a decidedly more civilian bent but does not last long because CCC leadership sees it as a competitor.

Recruits designated I-A-0—not willing to serve because of conscientious objector designation—are assigned to jobs other than military service.

1941–
1945
A total of 6,000 conscientious objectors, predominantly Jehovah's Witnesses, are jailed for not serving in the military. At the same time, thousands of alternativists attend Civilian Public Service camps set up throughout the nation. Many of the camps have ties to the Quaker congregations of the United States, but the government sets up nondenominational camps beginning in 1943 for those preferring nonsectarian commitment. The work done in the Civilian Public Service camps is supervised by and contributes to the missions of either the Department of Agriculture or Interior as part of civic duty.

1941
The Army Air Corps becomes the Army Air Force as General George C. Marshall and Secretary of War Henry Stimson foresee a need for a greater emphasis on this capability within the Army. This predates the attack on Pearl Harbor by six months.

The Tuskegee Institute, established in 1881 with the work of George Washington Carver as a center for African American education in the aftermath of Reconstruction and during racial segregation, opens an ROTC unit for African Americans, leading to the Tuskegee Airmen corps of World War II.

Late in the year, after the attack on Pearl Harbor, Congress shifts to a mandatory draft for the duration of the conflict plus six months. The Selective Service registration reaches 36 million during this period. More than 16 million men and women actually served; this number indicates that 70 percent of the men between eighteen and thirty-eight years of age were enlisted (Moskos, 1988). Of that number, 10 million came in under the draft.

1943
Army Specialization Training and Navy V12 programs start to deal with the challenge of keeping colleges open at the time when men are needed for military service. The Navy and Army projects target certain fields while

1943 creating a corps of individuals with civic commitments,
cont. military backgrounds, and increasingly sophisticated
technical educational bases.

1944 The Servicemen's Readjustment Act became better
known as the GI Bill. It provided educational assistance
and, later, educational incentives to assist in military recruiting, passes. The GI Bill today has two components:
active duty and veterans. The Reserve and Guard are
known as the Montgomery Bill.

1945 The Navy announces steps to begin desegregating the
service during the last months of World War II.

The Truman administration creates a board of three general officers to examine questions about desegregating the
Army of the United States. Headed by Lieutenant General
Alvan C. Gillem, Jr., the review considers not only how
best to use the forces that might be needed for further conflict in response to the emerging concerns about the Soviet
Union but also in response to fears that protests by
African Americans about segregation in the United States
would continue. The board's report is released on March
4, but it does not include specific suggestions on how to
implement its goal of integrating the Army.

Late The Army and Marine Corps, in particular, continue us-
1940s ing parallel units instead of racially integrated units to
work on various tasks, obviating the goal of encouraging
racial integration.

1946 The Navy Reserve Officer Training Program, equivalent
to that of the Army, initiates units at larger land-grant
universities around the country.

In February, the Navy publishes Circular Letter 48-46 ordering that African American sailors receive the same
opportunity to serve in all types of assignments and elements of naval service while ending segregation in mess
halls, accommodations, and other aspects of the service
life. Critics charge, however, that there are no high-rank-
ing naval officers who are African American.

In mid-April, the Army tries to exclude African Americans from its critical needs billets, based on War Department Circular 105. Eventually, this statement is revised to include African American participation.

1947   The Tuskegee Airfield in Alabama, home to Tuskegee Airmen and the African American contribution to Army aviation, closes. In the future, aviation training occurs in integrated units at Randolph Air Force Base near San Antonio. Closing Tuskegee also represents the termination of the last segregated officer training in the U.S. military.

The National Security Act fundamentally alters the national service component of the United States, creating the Department of the Air Force for that separate service while also transforming the War Department into the Defense Department.

The Compton Commission report endorses universal military training of six months' duration for eighteen-year-old men, followed by an obligation to serve in the reserves for a fixed period. The Compton provisions suggested eliminating racial segregation in the process, along with requiring even conscientious objectors to do some minimal service. The commission's suggestions are not, however, formally adopted.

The Selective Service Act expires, terminating the push for citizen-soldiers in the first half of the twentieth century.

The Officer Personnel Act rationalizes promotion based on merit in the armed services.

1948   In January, President Harry S Truman adheres to suggestions from the Gillem Commission to desegregate the armed services of the United States through issuing a presidential directive rather than sending it through the Congress where it was bound to be highly contentious. In mid-1948, Presidential Directive 9981 calls for the desegregation of the U.S. military. For the remainder of the year, various groups—African Americans supporting the president's decision, southern

1948
cont.

politicians vehemently opposed, northern politicians seeing this as an opportunity to open broader doors for the nation, and General Omar Bradley, the chief of staff of the Army—all advocate differing interpretations of President Truman's January decision as well as subsequent clarifications. President Truman decidedly states in 1949, before the Fahy Committee, that he wants this accomplished as soon as possible.

In December, the Navy's claim of working toward a desegregated service comes under scrutiny when it becomes known that 62 percent of those in the service are assigned to the nonwhite Steward's Branch.

Under the leadership of Lieutenant General Idwal Edwards, the Air Force begins developing its own racial integration objectives on the grounds that many officers resent the approach, but this is less dangerous than an overall inefficient use of available resources.

On June 30, the Army heralds compliance with Circular 124 on racial integration by noting that it has increased its level of African American officers from 41 in April to 1,000 along with 5 warrant officers and 67 nurses to serve along with 67,000 enlisted personnel.

In May, Marine officers John E. Rudder and Frederick Branch break the color barrier in the Marines. Born in Paducah, Kentucky, Rudder earns his commission after graduating from a Reserve Officer Training Corps. Rudder resigns a year later, citing personal reasons, but many observers fear the anti-integration climate of the Corps is a major part of his decision to abandon his commission.

The Central Committee for Conscientious Objectors is created as a centralized location to assist those whose religious convictions keep them from serving under arms.

A Truman policy notes that women should not make up more than 2 percent of the auxiliary permanent corps in the Women's Army Corps, Women's Air Force, and WAVES.

1948- Regardless of peace or war, a draft of eligible men goes
1973 into effect when volunteers are insufficient to fill the vacancies that exist in meeting the force levels required for national security.

1949 The Personnel Policy Board, a Department of Defense function, writes a policy that eliminates all racial quotas while implementing uniform draft standards.

The Fahy Committee, including seven prominent figures under Chairman Charles Fahy, holds a range of hearings on how the services will each formally and de facto desegregate their ranks. The Air Force and Navy prove relatively easy, but continuous plans by the Army are initially deemed incompatible with President Truman's presidential directive to do so. The committee continues to challenge the Army's program until late 1950 when the Army abolishes its 10 percent recruitment goal for African Americans in favor of recruitment that will fill the Army's increasingly dwindling needs during the Korean War.

1949– The Marine Corps attempts to hold on to segregated
1950 policies by establishing a quota of 1,500 blacks in the service.

1950s ROTC units with significant African American enrollments begin to appear more frequently in the southern region of the United States than in the Northeast.

1950 The Army institutes Special Regulation 600-629-1 on Utilization of Negro Manpower in the Army.

1951 The Universal Military and Training Act becomes law, allowing conscientious objectors to take alternative roles in national service.

1953 The Army acknowledges that 95 percent of African American recruits are serving in integrated units.

1955 The Air Force Academy, located in Colorado Springs, Colorado, opens its doors to Air Force cadets.

1957 Naval ROTC units begin using civilian education credits to add to the lecture program for its students, but the military is uncomfortable with this approach, deeming it too broad for the cadets' use.

Ohio State University begins to use civilian professors instead of military officers to teach ROTC cadets.

The Air Force Academy begins to allow elective courses rather than requiring an absolutely bound curriculum. Civilians outside the program herald the change while Air Force officers do not.

The Association of Naval ROTC Colleges and University Schools with naval ROTC units begins using civilians to augment the lectures and to add academic rigor, but the military officers of ROTC consider this to be counterproductive to the program. This sparks an enduring debate about the composition of the naval ROTC academic direction. The same year, the Air Force begins to allow "substitution" courses from the regular university curricula to augment ROTC. Again, civilians basically support this evolution of ROTC programs while the military does not.

1958 The National Defense Education Act is passed.

Late 1950s The Ted Wright cartoon character begins appearing in national publications, illustrating the life of an average student in preparation for defending his nation through national service.

1960s F. Edward Hébert pushes for ROTC reforms.

1961 In his January farewell address to the nation, President Dwight D. Eisenhower warns of the development of a "military-industrial complex" that is threatening to put the nation on a perpetual and expensive permanent war footing because of the linkage between these aspects of society.

The Peace Corps is announced by President Kennedy during a visit to the University of Michigan in Ann Arbor. The program is a major alternative to national military service during the Vietnam War (1961–1975).

1964   The ROTC Vitalization Act is passed to update ROTC but almost immediately begins to run into the growing societal questions about ROTC-produced officers being sent to Vietnam. By the late 1950s and 1960s, questions arise about the length of ROTC programs. Some advocate two-year programs, while others see four as more appropriate and useful for the graduates who were becoming an ever-increasing source of the officers sent to Vietnam.

By this year, the ROTC's substitution program ends. ROTC students had used it to enroll in traditional civilian courses from their universities in place of ROTC-taught military service courses. In its place, contact hours within the ROTC program decline from five to three, which many critics believed made them technical instead of academic in nature.

The Ford Foundation sets aside $100 million for five of the top six schools administering ROTC programs to be converted to two-year programs.

VISTA (Volunteers in Service to America), an urban program aimed at helping the poor, is introduced as another alternative to national military service.

The ROTC Vitalization Act is passed. The act ends the mandatory military training at state land-grant universities and colleges as established by the Morill Act of 1862. This 1964 act, coming in the early debate about growing involvement in Southeast Asia, establishes both two-year and four-year scholarship programs based on a more general curriculum and leadership, instead of emphasizing military education, at universities and colleges across the country. This law creates the junior ROTC program and sets the Air Force down the path to its ROTC program.

1965   *U.S. v. Seeger* allows the Supreme Court to rule unanimously that conscientious objectors may have nonreligious beliefs that form the basis for their objector status.

The ROTC institutes a new national curriculum, but professors around the country challenge its academic rigor.

1966   There are 113 schools across the nation with women in ROTC programs. Public Law 90–130 prohibits a formal ceiling on the number of women recruited for ROTC, but there is no obligation to take this action.

1967   Burke Marshall chairs the Advisory Commission on Selective Service, which generates a report entitled *In Pursuit of Equity: Who Serves When Not all Serve?* The report validates those who charged that military service was not equaled by civilian service, but it leaves open the door to the idea that more thought needs to be given to finding equivalence to the types of national service training.

ROTC programs across the nation are producing more officers than their quotas require.

The practice of granting exemptions, based on certain categories of conditions, to some young men rather than forcing them to participate in the burgeoning war in Vietnam receives considerable criticism from a growing number of national politicians. Many advocate replacing the existing system with a lottery, which is anticipated to be fairer to all men under the Selective Service program.

1968   On March 16, Army troops conduct a massacre at a small village in Vietnam called My Lai. Under the command of Lieutenant William Calley, the unit was on a "search and destroy" mission in a heavily Vietcong area. More than 300 villagers are killed in this incident. Greeted by sheer shock by many in the public when its details gradually come out, those involved in My Lai argue that they were following orders. The incident leads to considerable public debate about the nature and conduct of the war. Calley, an Officer Candidate School graduate, is convicted and serves his sentence under house arrest before receiving a pardon in 1974.

1969 A lottery for military service begins, eliminating blanket exemptions that contribute to the growing perception that national service unduly protects some communities in the United States while overburdening others.

In September, the Benson Report advocating reforms of the ROTC program appears. The participants who helped craft the report include officials from John Jay College, Stanford University, Purdue University, the University of Illinois at Urbana–Champaign, and Tulane University, who serve as representatives of the national educational community. President Nixon responds favorably to these reforms.

Questions arise in some quarters about whether ROTC units should engage in their drill, or military unit preparation, on campus.

The National Strategy Information Center, a private think tank and advocacy organization with a national security focus, begins offering civilian lectures in place of ROTC topics for the unit at New York University. This substitution, somewhat more acceptable than the military science roundly attacked by many critics, becomes known as the New York Plan, introducing nonmilitary into the ROTC training program.

The Civilian School Plan begins, allowing officers two years of full training in traditional civilian education settings in place of three years in ROTC training. Admiral Elmo Zumwalt, chief of naval operations, especially encourages this program because he believes it will lead to a higher number of naval officers with advanced degrees.

1969– Attacks begin on ROTC buildings on college campuses
1970 in various locations around the country. For example, protestors against the war firebomb the ROTC facility at the University of Colorado in Boulder.

Late

1960s Women are increasingly enrolled in ROTC units.

1970s Wearing ROTC uniforms on campus becomes a politically charged issue in many areas.

Many argue that ROTC units are one of the best ways to ensure racial integration of the armed servces.

The military faces tremendous internal turmoil problems as drug consumption, racial divisiveness, and general breakdown in military discipline are common occurrences in the aftermath of the national upheaval over the Vietnam War. The midlevel service leadership, particularly in the Army under Colin Powell, Barry McCaffrey, and Norman Schwartzkopf (all three of whom would go on to lead the war in the Gulf in 1991), institutes a tightening of discipline in the interest of restoring the traditions of the services. Along with the all-volunteer force, this leads to self-selection by many who treasure the hard-core traditional values that they sense are missing in society as a whole.

1970 Ohio National Guard troops shoot and kill four students protesting the expansion of the war in Southeast Asia from Vietnam into Cambodia, on the campus at Kent State University in eastern Ohio. This event sends a chill throughout the country as National Guardsmen are seen to have attacked their own since they are not much older than the kids protesting. It also leads to a fundamental debate about the role of the National Guard in U.S. society. Ten days later, student protestors at Jackson State University are shot and two killed by combined Mississippi National Guard troops and Jackson police.

A bomb destroys the Army Mathematics Research Center in the physics building at the University of Wisconsin in Madison, resulting in the death of a physics researcher and damage to more than two dozen campus buildings.

The Youth Conservation Corps, instituted by the U.S. Congress, which was originally an eight-week public service environmental activity for students, is eventually extended into a broader project across the country.

A National Service act is proposed but not adopted. It was a noteworthy attempt because it suggested three kinds of activities through a National Service Agency: participation in civilian service, registration for the traditional lottery draft, and enlistment in the service.

The Gates Commission supports the concept of an all-volunteer force (AVF), meaning the end of the government's mandatory draft of the military. The commission advises that this new format for filling the force will require higher defense budgets to keep a greater percentage of those who join. In addition, the commission acknowledges that the new force would have an impact on ROTC. This comes at the height of student protests against the draft and during the same calendar year as the Kent State and Jackson State universities shootings. The Gates Commission move meant that military service became identified as a path toward a job, not merely serving in the armed forces.

Welsh v. U.S. expands the concept of conscientious objector status to include people with "ethical and moral beliefs" rather than mentioning a specific religious orientation.

1971   The Department of Defense Race Relations Institute begins at Patrick Air Force Base in Florida as the U.S. military begins to come to grips with growing racial tension within its ranks.

1972   The Marine Corps bans race as a criterion for determining housing allocations at its bases.

The first woman is admitted to Army or Navy ROTC.

1973   President Richard Nixon announces the end of the military draft in the United States.

1973 Congress passes the War Powers Resolution with a veto-
cont. proof majority. While no president has ever agreed to the
law, it has never been invoked and so its constitutional-
ity is unclear. The act requires the president to achieve
the constitutional requirement of consulting with the
Congress by notifying both bodies of his decision to deploy U.S. forces to a conflict or hostility zone. The deployment can thus be only for a ninety-day period.

The Total Force becomes the policy of the land, seeking
to create the national defense force for the United States.
This major shift signals the decision to use all available
portions of the military community—active duty, Reserves, retired military, federal civilians, service auxil-
iaries, and contractors—to achieve national security
goals. This additionally opens the door to the all volunteer force rather than one of forced service under the
conscription system. The decision also indicates the desire to integrate the whole of society into defense since
the Reserve component is the bridge to the rest of the
population that was not drafted. With the policy change,
the ROTC units across the country see enrollments sag.

1975 Draft registration ends in the United States.

The Defense Appropriation Act, Title 8, includes nuclear
power to facilitate greater retention of serving forces.

1976 Service academies open their doors to women cadets.

1977 President Jimmy Carter pardons those who evaded the
draft, on the premise that no national healing can occur
until those who had disagreed with national service are
allowed to reenter society.

University of Pittsburgh academic William King sug-
gests that the country would benefit tremendously by
instituting a strong nationwide commitment to national
service. *Achieving America's Goals: National Service or the
All Volunteer Armed Force* subtly goes against the popular opinion of the day by suggesting mandatory regis-

tration for the military and a gradual national service requirement.

Eighty percent of the naval ROTC majors have science and engineering majors even though the program began in 1947 with a policy to allow a range of degree concentrations.

1978   The Young Adult Conservation Corps works as a national service in states across the country to encourage environmental protection. Its target audience (until it is eliminated by President Ronald Reagan four years later) is young adults without jobs between sixteen and twenty-three years of age.

The Office of the Secretary of Defense issues an initial report on the all-volunteer force (AVF). While quantitative evidence disputed the report's suggestion that the AVF was reaching higher levels of high school graduates and desired groups for the military, the report did show the government's willingness to stick with the program as it was being carried out in the most difficult years after the end of the Vietnam-era draft.

1979   The McCloskey proposal on national service is one of a series from the late 1970s into the late 1990s. Only one, in 1984, receives congressional approval, but President Ronald Reagan vetoes it.

1980   In the wake of the late 1979 Soviet invasion of Afghanistan, President Carter creates the Selective Service System, which requires men between eighteen and twenty-five years of age to register in the event the draft needs to be reconstituted.

1981   The Posse Comitatus Act of 1878 is amended to allow U.S. military forces and the Coast Guard (of the Department of Transportation, not the Department of Defense) to stop drug trafficking in the United States.

The American Conservation Corps is intended to unite national service with conservation in the Interior Department

1981
cont.
and Forest Service, for examples, but the program is never implemented.

1983
The statistics on the military appear in Department of Labor statistics on employment.

The Alternative Service Program is covered in the *Federal Register* for the first time, bringing it to a higher level of prominence.

1984
The Voluntary National Service Act is introduced in Congress; it is reintroduced three years later but does not pass.

The Montgomery GI Bill is passed.

1985
The U.S. military is increasingly called up to deal with counterdrug operations, which many charge is not the mission of the service and challenges the Posse Comitatus Act proscribing the armed forces from domestic law enforcement actions. Many of the antidrug activities are carried out overseas such as in Bolivia or Peru.

1986
The idea that the military would work as a joint service is codified in the Goldwater-Nichols act. Passed in the aftermath of tremendous difficulties in the 1970s and the invasion of Grenada in October 1983, Goldwater-Nichols transformed the methods by which the U.S. military educated its personnel, viewed the requirements for reaching general or flag officer rank, and tried to incorporate the Navy into all the aspects of participation in the "joint force" while concentrating the responsibility for advising the president in the person of the chairman of the Joint Chiefs of Staff.

1988
The secretary of defense issues a "risk rule" asking the services to evaluate the chances of direct exposure to hostile fire or capture when choosing whether an assignment should be open to women, if they were qualified.

1989
Congress raises the obligation for those who earned their commissions through studying at the service academies

from a commitment of five year to six years' service to the nation.

1990   President George H. W. Bush implements the first stop loss policy that prevents active-duty personnel and Reservists from ending their tours of service on the grounds that they are needed to retain force levels for the nation's security. This policy is repeated under President Bill Clinton and especially under President George W. Bush during the Iraq and Afghanistan actions.

1990-   The United States and coalition partners deploy forces
1991   and invade Iraq to oust it from occupying Kuwait. Twenty-four thousand Army women serve in the conflict, with fourteen dying and two seized as prisoners of war.

1991   The ban on women flying in potential combat situations is lifted in the services, and a blue ribbon commission begins studying the question. This issue had long been debated, and the discussion began anew, along with the consideration of gays/lesbians in the armed forces at the beginning of the Clinton administration in 1993.

1992   Arkansas governor Bill Clinton defeats President George H. W. Bush, who was running for a second term. During the campaign, Clinton's evasion of military service during the Vietnam years becomes a highly controversial topic and leads many in the military to question his fitness to be commander-in-chief.

The National Defense Authorization Act of 1992 deems that all officers receiving their commissions after September 30, 1996, will receive Reserve rather than active-duty commissions.

The Herres Commission on Women in Combat, named after Air Force General Robert T. Herres, recommends women be allowed to serve on some combat ships but not fly on combat planes or participate in ground combat that could engage with the enemy in a conflict.

1993   Immediately prior to taking the oath of office as president, Clinton announces that he will seek to integrate gays and lesbians into the military, fulfilling a campaign promise. These groups have been deliberately excluded for more than a decade, on the grounds that their inclusion would affect unit cohesion and could undermine discipline within the services. Recognizing the depth of the uproar his decision produces, Clinton announces a six-month moratorium to find the best way to implement his promise. As a result, his critics mobilize against him instead of seeing his decision as a fait accompli. After considerable public debate and dissatisfaction within the armed services, Clinton announces in a July speech at the National Defense University in Washington that he will institute a compromise known as "don't ask, don't tell." This policy, suggested by military sociologist Dr. Charles C. Moskos, would allow lesbian and gay service personnel to remain in uniform as long as they did not take overt actions that would call their sexual orientation into question. This policy compromise satisfies neither side but remains the policy more than a decade later. Gay and lesbian advocacy groups, as reported in several media outlets in mid-August 2006, have charged that the number of discharges for homosexuality risen by 10 percent in 2005 from 2004 (Files, 2006).

Women are no longer restricted from flying in the armed services on all types of airframes, including helicopters, but they are not allowed in positions of direct combat.

1994   On October 1, the Department of Defense removes the "risk rule," which had previously precluded women from serving in many specialties that were deemed extremely dangerous. This change in procedure aims to conform with the 1993 decision that would allow women greater equality in running military missions.

The Army Chief of Staff, General Gordon Sullivan, begins combined female-male basic training at Fort Leonard Wood, Missouri, and later Fort Jackson, South Carolina.

1996 The National Defense Authorization Act reduces the period of required service from a six-year to a five-year commitment of service in exchange for officers' educational benefits.

2002 "Stop loss" actions become common to prevent the force from dropping to levels that prevent operational effectiveness.

2003 In January New York Representative Charles Rangel reintroduces a bill to reinstitute the draft in the United States

The United States leads a coalition into Iraq. Administration officials anticipate an easy campaign to overthrow dictator Saddam Hussein and to install a subsequent democratic regime. The action receives far from universal support from across the political spectrum.

In January, the Army reiterates "stop loss" rules, prohibiting serving officers and enlisted personnel from ending their prescribed tours of service for fear of inadequate troop strength as a result of conflicts in Iraq and Afghanistan. Orders also bar troops from leaving one assignment for another, thus maintaining adequate force levels in the war theater but causing troops a considerably longer time in the battle area than anticipated.

On June 1, the secretary of the Army institutes a "stop loss" policy for all overseas units involved in Operation Enduring Freedom (Afghanistan) and Operating Iraqi Freedom until further notice. This policy shift means that soldiers may not separate from their units for ninety days after the original anticipated date of departure from the war theater.

In the winter, stories circulate that the National Guard and Reserve forces are unable to achieve recruitment as well as retention goals because of repeated tours in the war theater.

2004   As the campaign in Iraq and Afghanistan deteriorates, increasing calls by politicians and citizens across the nation are issued to prevent the Bush administration from reinstituting a draft (Pope, 2004).

Constant reports surface that the Army is having trouble meeting its monthly recruiting targets, while Reserve units, being recirculated to Iraq and Afghanistan on an increasingly frequent basis, are not meeting retention levels for reenlistment. With the increased *ops tempo* (operational deployment frequency), servicemen and -women face increasingly frequent overseas tours, creating strains for their families and themselves as well.

2005   Pennsylvania Democrat and former Marine John Murtha calls for the Bush administration to pull U.S. troops out of Iraq, arguing that the nation has put U.S. troops in an unwinnable situation. Murtha, a Vietnam veteran, ignites a firestorm. Supporters of his argument note that recruiting and retention rates for soldiers and Marines sent on multiple deployments to Iraq are sagging. Opponents of Murtha's suggestion claim that he is weakening the nation's servicemen and -women. The Bush administration adamantly opposes any date certain for pullout, but the seriously deteriorating conditions in Baghdad in the summer of 2006 lead to redeployment of U.S. forces toward Baghdad.

2006   In congressional testimony in July, chairman of the Joint Chiefs of Staff, Marine General Peter Pace, and Central Command head Army General John Abizaid acknowledge that Iraq may be headed toward civil war, reducing the options to bring home U.S. forces.

References

Files, John. "Military Discharges for Being Gay Rose in '05." *New York Times,* August 16, 2006.

Moskos, Charles C. *A Call to Civic Service: National Service for Country and Community.* New York: Free Press, 1988.

Neiberg, Michael E. *Making Citizen Soldiers*. Cambridge, MA: Harvard University Press, 2000.

Pope, Charles. "No Plans for a Draft, but Rumors Keep Nation Edgy." *Seattle Post-Intelligencer*, October 2, 2004. http://seattlepi.nwsource.com/national/193472_draft02.html.

5

Biographical Sketches

ountless individuals have been engaged in the decision-
making that created the national military service of the
United States. In this list, I have chosen people whose impact
on the system has been enduring or exceptionally controversial.

James Bowdoin (1726–1790)

James Bowdoin was a political philosopher of the colonial and
early independence era. Writing and arguing for various positions in the constitutional development of the United States,
Bowdoin spoke out against the concentration of power resulting
from royalty. As an extension, he opposed developing national
obligatory service for fear it might be used to create a force
against domestic opposition instead of defending the new nation
against external threats. Bowdoin was governor of Massachusetts before his death in 1790. The Brunswick, Maine, institution,
Bowdoin College, is named in his honor.

James Burgh (1714–1775)

Along with John Trenchard of an earlier generation and other
Whig political philosophers, James Burgh, through pamphlets
circulated throughout the thirteen colonies and in England itself,
argued strongly against standing armies as tools of despotism
utilized by corrupt governments. Writing in the mid-eighteenth
century, Burgh represented the opposition to the power of the

monarch or central government to maintain power and achieve its aims instead of deferring to the popular will of the people. Burgh feared that royalty would attempt to retain power at all costs, even if doing so meant turning the army against the people rather than against external threats. These views were the outgrowth of the battle between the Stuart monarchy and Oliver Cromwell a century earlier.

Burgh's writing influenced the early colonists and early Founders in the United States wrestling with the army versus militia controversy. James Monroe and James Madison were especially influenced by Burgh's writings, which were on a broad array of issues, including education, as well as standing army questions. Burgh's most prominent piece, appearing the year he died, was *Political Disquisitions,* which rehashed many of the eighteenth-century arguments against allowing the Crown power to grow because it utilized the army as an extension of itself.

George Walker Bush (b. 1946)

The forty-third president of the United States, George Bush is one of only two men to serve in the presidency after their fathers served; John Quincy Adams was the other. As a young man, Bush did not serve on active duty but as a pilot in the Texas Air National Guard, service that has attracted considerable interest because of unexplained gaps in the service record. President Bush served as the governor of Texas immediately prior to his controversial election in 2000. The controversy resulted from questions about the voting results in Florida. Questions also arose about the president's subsequent reelection in 2004 when issues in Ohio undercut confidence in the election results. President Bush was shocked by the attacks on the twin Trade Towers in New York and the Pentagon on September 11, 2001, when almost 3,000 people died in these attacks. President Bush responded with a campaign against the Taliban in Afghanistan, a hardline religious segment of the Islamic faith that had taken control of the Central Asian state in the 1990s, on the grounds that the Taliban had harbored the architect of the September 11 attacks, Osama Bin Laden. Bin Laden and the terrorist network he constructed, Al Qaeda, had been in Afghanistan or across the line in Pakistan for several years, after the Clinton administration began pursuing them in retaliation for the August 1998 terrorist attacks on U.S.

embassies in Dar-el-Salam, Tanzania, and Nairobi, Kenya. Bin Laden was a bigger than life figure who earlier, between 1980 and 1988, had fought alongside U.S.-supported groups in Afghanistan as the Islamicists sought to oust the Soviet Union from occupying Afghanistan. The president took the extraordinary step, in a June 2002 speech at West Point, of declaring that the United States would protect itself through not only responding to attacks on the nation and its interests but also through *preventing* and *preempting* attacks on the United States by actively pursuing threats against the nation. While some administration officials argued that Bush was not doing anything new, others felt that this doctrine was a radical departure from U.S. historic policy as well as a violation of international law.

The decision to oust, and presumably to prosecute, the Taliban government was a controversial one, but it was not nearly as controversial as the 2003 decision to overthrow Iraqi president and strongman Saddam Hussein. President Bush stated that Saddam Hussein was developing weapons of mass destruction which, if deployed against the United States and its interests, could be far more damaging to the nation than September 11. Additional reasons given for the war included the linkages that the president believed existed between Saddam and terrorists around the world and the need to expand the community of democracies around the world. After a yearlong buildup and debate across the international community, the president ordered U.S. forces to enter Iraq in mid-March 2003, expecting that U.S. forces would receive heroes' welcomes. In a speech on the deck of the aircraft carrier U.S.S. *Abraham Lincoln* on May 1, 2003, President Bush proudly projected that the "major combat operations were over," and, in words that have come to haunt the administration, Bush announced the "mission accomplished." No weapons of mass destruction were found, however. While the initial reaction to the American presence bordered on the anticipated welcome, conditions soon deteriorated as an insurgency was aimed against U.S. forces and the United States' small number of coalition partners. U.S. troop losses began rising as a constant, unrelenting series of attacks—snipers, car bombs, improvised explosive devices along the roadside—began picking off men and women in the U.S. forces, primarily in the Army and Marines. Iraq was now a major battlefield long after the president believed that major combat operations were concluded. Under pressure at home and even from abroad to withdraw U.S. forces from Iraq, President Bush said he would not abandon the people of Iraq until the job of rebuilding Iraq and creating a democratic society was complete. While approval for the president remained relatively high for the first years of the conflict, by mid-2005 public support began to dwindle. One reason for the loss of support was the realization that the war appeared to have an unlimited duration, while others worried about the escalating costs of the war. President Bush continues to stand his ground on Iraq and refuses to withdraw the troops even as it appears that the insurgency is scoring a victory over democratization.

James ("Jimmy") Earl Carter, Jr. (b. 1925)

A man who arguably has been much more prominent and respected as a former president than he was while in the Oval Office, President Carter was president (1976-1980) in the years after the Vietnam War and at a time when concerns about Soviet intentions reemerged. Born in Georgia, Carter spent his childhood in the peanut country of the state. He attended the U.S. Naval Academy, where he graduated as a nuclear engineer and served his national service obligation during the early years of the Cold War. Returning to Georgia where he worked in the peanut business, Carter first entered politics as Democratic legislator, then governor, in the 1960s. He ran for president in 1976 as a virtual unknown in a wide field opposing President Gerald R. Ford who had succeeded to office following President Richard Nixon's resignation from office in 1974. Carter possessed a strong religious conviction and accordingly sought to reorient U.S. foreign policy to include more ethical and moral concerns, especially human rights, while pressures at home increasingly pushed him back to the center or the more traditional side of the political spectrum. When the Soviet Union occupied Afghanistan with a massive force in December 1979, in reaction to the Soviet aggression he prohibited U.S. athletes from participating in the Moscow Olympics in early 1980. Prior to losing his 1980 bid for reelection, Carter decided to reinvigorate the U.S. national service obligation by reimposing the requirement that men between eighteen and forty-five years of age had to register for national service. Denying this was a mandatory service requirement that ended with President Nixon's termination of the draft lottery in 1973, Carter said he wanted young men registered for national service in case of conflict that would require their service. Seen as a sellout to the conservative wing of society, President Carter's decision was greatly criticized by many of his supporters. As of 2006, males are still required to register for national service, but no call-up has occurred.

Grenville Clark (1882–1967)

A wealthy man from New England with railroad and banking ancestors, Grenville Clark was thought to be one of the most influential men of the twentieth century in the United States but with far less visibility than many of his peers. Clark became a Wall Street lawyer with former Secretary of War Elihu Root and Francis Bird, both of whom were friends from their Harvard days, ultimately forming one of the most prominent firms in the city and nation. Involved in a range of national jobs, Clark was instrumental in developing the U.S. war readiness that preceded the country's involvement in World War I, especially after the sinking of the *Lusitania* in 1915. Perhaps his greatest single legacy was the idea behind the Plattsburgh Movement prior to World War I. Intended to prepare nonprofessional soldiers for the possibility of national service, the Plattsburgh Movement created many of the officers who waged World War I for the United States and was the genesis of the selective service that the nation adopted in 1917. Clark was involved in activities later in the century to improve economic conditions in the country after the Great Depression set in, most visibly through the National Economy League, which he used to involve many former Plattsburghers who had gone on to significant positions in the economy. As World War II erupted in Europe, Clark tried to revitalize the Plattsburgh Movement by reinvigorating his colleagues in the National Emergency Committee of Military Training Camps in 1940. Clark was the mind behind the Selective Training and Service Act of September that year, a conscription law for the United States during peacetime. Clark sought to create mandatory civilian military training but never accomplished this as he did not achieve his most important goal: to create a global world government. He did not win the Nobel Prize, although many of his supporters and admirers felt he completely deserved it.

George Clinton (1739–1813)

George Clinton was one of the most important early figures in the United States, though he is little remembered today: he was vice president under two presidents and first governor of New York. Clinton was in national service for the British in the French and Indian War. He came to the colonies in the mid-eighteenth century. Clinton was important to national service because he proposed that each state provide a college in which students would be eligible to receive military training. This proposal was intended both to help provide citizen-soldiers and to make certain that education was developed while a standing army became less necessary. This ultimately evolved into the ROTC program more than 130 years later.

William Jefferson Clinton (b. 1946)

William Jefferson Clinton was one of the most controversial chief executives in the twentieth century. Born to a widow in Arkansas, Clinton grew up in the one of the more depressed parts of the nation. Awarded a Rhodes Scholarship upon graduating from Georgetown University, Clinton studied in the United Kingdom for two years and avoided national service in the Vietnam War. His evasion would later have a negative effect on his service as commander-in-chief.

Clinton next attended Yale Law School, after which he moved back to Arkansas where he ran for governor and won six of seven contests. In 1992, he won the White House as a minority president when entrepreneur H. Ross Perot split the Republican vote with President George H. W. Bush. Almost immediately upon taking the oath of office, Clinton caused upheaval within the services by announcing he would alter existing policy to allow gays and lesbians to serve openly in the armed forces. Opponents of this policy shift maintained that Clinton, with his lack of military service, sought to discredit and disable the military of the United States. Giving his opponents six months to mobilize against the decision, Clinton ultimately was forced to declare a "don't ask, don't tell" policy instead of absolutely allowing the admission of gays and lesbians. His decision to use the military to capture warlord Mohammed Aideed in Somalia in October 1993—an effort that led to the death of eighteen Army Rangers under most degrading circumstances—infuriated most of those in national service in October 1993. The services believed that the administration had shortchanged the needs of the soldiers in the field. The military also grumbled—but complied with the decision of the commander-in-chief—when he used the troops in Bosnia-Herzegovina and Kosovo. Few people initially criticized the president on his decision to ignore genocide in the central African state of Rwanda in 1994 because the operations tempo of the military made it hard to imagine a further deployment; but many later questioned how the United States could have ignored the deaths of a million blacks in Africa when it responded strongly to ethnic cleansing in Bosnia. Later in his administration, Clinton's moral failings in engaging in an affair with a much younger subordinate in the White House caused the armed forces to pull away from him even more and to question his ability as commander-in-chief. Clinton met harsh criticism from the military throughout his terms essentially for putting the forces in harm's way with relative frequency for humanitarian or nation-building activities rather than for traditional warfare. In retirement, Clinton's stock with all sectors of society has risen as the successor Bush administration found nation-building a similar national interest and discovered that engaging in nation-building is not always avoidable.

William Duane (n.d.)

An Irish immigrant in 1796 whose son, William John Duane, became secretary of the treasury in the early 1830s, Duane used his position as editor of the Philadelphia *Aurora* to air his fears that the United States was not able to resolve the question of whether a standing army was preferable to the state militia system. Duane argued that the nation needed to strengthen the militia system rather than rely on a standing military establishment alone to address potential threats. To prevent the populace from contributing to their own protection was ludicrous to Duane, yet he also acknowledged that the nature of warfare was changing and was creating a need for specialized soldiers.

Charles H. Fahy (1892–1979)

Charles Fahy was the chairman of a committee called the President's Committee on Equality of Treatment and Opportunity in the Armed Forces, which became known by Fahy's name—as simply the Fahy Committee. The committee examined the proposals each of the services issued for desegregating their ranks. It came into being following President Truman's Executive Order 9981 on July 26, 1948. None of the services wanted to abolish segregated forces, but the Truman administration's strong moves in that direction in the 1940s made the change absolutely crucial. The Fahy Committee was dogged in its insistence that the Army was trying to preserve segregated units in direct violation of Presidential Directive 9981. The work of the committee ended in 1950. Having served as an Interior Department official in the 1930s and as solicitor general beginning in 1941, Fahy later served as a judge after his committee work.

Horatio Gates (1726–1806)

Horatio Gates was one of the most famous men in the War for Independence. Born in England, Gates came to the colonies to fight the French and Indian War with the British under General Edward Braddock. Gates resigned his commission with British forces as a major in 1769, settling on a plantation in what would become northern Virginia. In 1775, having offered his services to the developing Continental Army under George Washington, Gates received his second commission as a brigadier general and adjutant general of the Army. He ultimately led the Continental forces to victory at Saratoga, New York, but was defeated later at Camden, South Carolina. Gates served the Continental forces in several major battles and at various ranks. In a dangerous role, Gates led the Newburgh Conspiracy in 1783 that unsuccessfully sought to oust George Washington. He was one of the first soldiers of the fledgling United States.

Thomas Gates (1906–1983)

Seventh defense secretary, Thomas Gates was an investment banker born in Germantown, Pennsylvania, who served in the

Navy during World War II. In the early part of the Eisenhower administration, Gates was the Navy secretary and opposed a number of defense reforms proposed in the 1950s. Gates preferred to keep the existing system, maintaining that the defense secretary was receiving the advice needed as the 1947 Military Reform Act stated. Gates, however, did contribute to military reform by supporting the Joint Strategic Target Planning Staff in 1960, which was set up to resolve problems between Strategic Air Command and Navy officers in targeting. Once it was accomplished, the staff put together the first Strategic Inter-Operable Plan (SIOP). Gates was defense secretary when Gary Francis Powers flew the U-2 spy mission over the Soviet Union and was captured by the Soviets. Powers was ultimately returned to the United States but not until after Soviet premier Nikita Khrushchev publicly embarrassed President Eisenhower, who had initially denied the spying allegations. Some considered Gates the most engaged secretary of defense in U.S. history because he was involved in so many crucial decisions during the height of the Cold War.

Truman Kella Gibson, Jr. (1912–2005)

Gibson worked within the governmental structure and advised the Army leadership to terminate racial discrimination in the service. A lawyer by training, Gibson played a prominent role in the administration of President Harry S Truman to encourage Secretary of War Henry Stimson to end legal segregation in the Army. Gibson's actions paralleled much more public actions by others, including the leadership of the National Association for the Advancement of Colored People. The Army was trying desperately to avoid desegregation, but through the work of individuals such as Truman Kella Gibson, President Truman's vision of a nonracially segregated armed forces became reality by the mid-1950s.

Alexander Hamilton (1755–1804)

Killed in a duel with Aaron Burr in Wehawken, New Jersey, Alexander Hamilton exemplified the reasons men came to the colonies in the mid-1700s and was crucial to the debate regarding establishment of many institutions in this nation. Born illegitimate in the Bahamas, Hamilton was a brilliant student educated at King's College, which later became Columbia University in New York City. Studying law, Hamilton was a superb lawyer who took up arms as the Continental Army sought to oust the British from colonial soil. Hamilton was an aide in the American Revolution and sought to hold command, but his patron George Washington was hesitant because of his age and inexperience.

Hamilton became a major player in the public policy decisions that led to the formation of the United States. He was one of the three authors of the *Federalist Papers*, which were fundamental to ratification of the Constitution in the 1780s. Not afraid of concentration of power, a concept that bothered many other independence advocates who feared that Hamilton's vision would transfer power from one tyrant to another potential one, Hamilton sought to create a country with an exquisitely strong executive. He believed the role of the military was to support a strong executive and to provide a powerful national defense, and he saw national service as an obligation.

James Harrington (1611–1677)

James Harrington was a seventeenth-century English political philosopher who lived during the English Civil War period. He hailed from Lincolnshire, north of London, and earned his education at Oxford, a home for English philosophy, after which he served in the military for the Dutch monarchy. Harrington preferred republican (antimonarchical) rule for England and was dismissed from several posts within the government in England at midcentury. His greatest work was *Oceana* (1656) in which he advocated government in which power was not concentrated in the hands of a single person—a king. Harrington's views were fundamental to many of the arriving colonists in the seventeenth century; thus a strain emerged in U.S. political thought as constitutional jurisprudence and political philosophy were developed in the late eighteenth century.

Felix Edward Hébert (1901–1979)

F. Edward Hébert was a New Orleans politician who sought to reform Reserve Officer Training Corps programs across the nation. Initially a journalist in the Crescent City, Hébert eventually won election to the House of Representatives in 1940 where he served for eighteen terms. Upon his retirement in 1976, Hébert was chairman of the Armed Services Committee, holding the post at the time when fundamental reforms were diluting the power of committee chairmen in the aftermath of Vietnam and Watergate. His work on the Reserve Officer Training Program became crucial as the country increasingly needed its officers for the war in Southeast Asia and on the cusp of ending conscription through the draft in 1973.

Thomas Jefferson (1743–1826)

Born in Albermarle County, Virginia, the third president of the United States was a passionate, engaged, inquisitive farmer and thinker. Father of one of the predominant political philosophies of the United States in its formative years, a strain supporting state's rights against a strong central government, Jefferson was a towering figure in the nation. He greatly opposed the idea of a strong military under the control of the central government for fear a wrongheaded individual might seek to use his power for whimsical motives rather than to defend the nation against an external threat. National service issues were not the crux of Jefferson's concerns, but he strongly feared that if the newly independent nation allowed a national army to become too powerful it would be to everyone's detriment. Nonetheless, he endorsed the establishment of the U.S. Military Academy at West Point, which provided the basis for a professional U.S. military force. In his second administration, Jefferson proposed a militia system that would provide national competence for dealing with emergencies but would not concentrate power in Washington's hands to the peril of state's and individual rights. The intent of Jefferson's 1806 proposal regarding military power was to support fewer government prerogatives. Ironically, Jefferson's negotiation of the Louisiana Purchase in 1803 made such a system unworkable because as a consequence of the greatly expanded nation that was a result of that purchase, the need for a standard, centrally controlled military establishment could not be avoided.

Richard Keene (d. 1658)

Richard Keene was the first conscientious objector in the colonies, registering his refusal to serve in 1658. Keene would not take military training as required in the colony of Maryland. The historical documents note his failure to engage in military training, on the grounds of conscientious objection. The sheriff fined him for such an attitude.

Henry Knox (1750–1806)

The first secretary of war in the newly independent nation, Henry Knox was the son of Scots-Irish immigrants who came to Boston via the West Indies. Knox was a bookseller who developed an interest in artillery and military topics. In 1770, he was at the Boston Massacre where the British shot into an unruly crowd that refused to disperse under orders. With the suggestion of conflict against Britain, Knox joined military service in 1772 as part of the Boston Grenadier Corps. He fought at the 1775 Battle of Bunker Hill. He soon came to the attention of General George Washington, who gave him responsibility for moving cannons from Ticonderoga to the area around Boston to relieve the siege. Knox served in some of the most important battles that the independence forces fought in the lead-up to victory. As a result, Washington rewarded Knox with the command of West Point in 1782. Knox was important in the earliest years of the Republic, proposing the construction of a series of fortifications along the coast to protect the nation against outside threats as well as the creation of a Navy. In the early 1790s, he pushed Congress to create the Legion of the United States, which he headed briefly. Knox's vision for a national military would influence generations of military scholars by promoting a sense of a national armed force rather than merely state militias or limited service.

Knox was the namesake for Fort Knox in Tennessee and several counties around the nation. He died in 1806.

Richard H. Kohn (b. 1940)

An academic historian at the University of North Carolina where he long headed the Triangle Institute on Strategic Studies (TISS),

Richard Kohn also was chief of Air Force history during the period 1981–1991. He has also served on more than a dozen major commissions and advisory boards in the United States, emphasizing his concerns about the role of military service in the United States. Along with Dr. Peter Feaver of Duke University, Kohn coauthored the TISS study entitled *Soldiers and Civilians: The Civil-Military Gap and American National Security* (2001), in which Kohn and Feaver spoke of a growing gap between civilians and military personnel. Kohn's article published in *The National Interest* in the spring of 1994, "A Crisis in Civil-Military Relations," had a major impact on national awareness of the role of contemporary armed forces. Kohn posited that General Colin Powell and others within the military had asserted themselves increasingly strongly as a result of frustration with civilian leadership and the repeated nature of weak civilians as the masters of the system. Kohn's argument created a national debate, reinforced by a study he and Feaver conducted a decade later on serving officers and their views of civil society, in *Soldiers and Civilians*. Kohn's most enduring works, however, have probably been his seminal works on the Founders and the development of the civil-military balance in the United States.

James Madison (1751–1836)

One of the towering intellectuals of the early Republic, James Madison was fourth president of the United States and through his suggestions that became the bases for the Constitutional Congress deliberations helped to create the Constitution of 1783. Like Jefferson and Monroe, Madison hailed from Virginia. He penned a number of the arguments for ratifying the Constitution in *The Federalist Papers*. Upon reaching the presidency in 1807, Madison argued for and implemented the expansion of the new nation's armed forces. Confronted with the British invasion of Washington in what became the War of 1812, Madison felt that a strong central government and an accompanying competent military force were essential to sustaining the capacity of the newly independent nation.

Charles Moskos (b. 1934)

A sociologist at Northwestern University in Evanston, Illinois, for four decades, Charles Moskos has become the premier scholar on military and national service issues in the United States. Born in Chicago to a Greek family and educated at Princeton University, Moskos served in the Army as an enlisted soldier during the 1950s when national service was still a legal requirement. Moskos became a specialist in a field that the social science community has generally rejected and viewed as being of less importance or of less scholarly interest. Moskos proved this was not true, and his advice was widely sought by presidents and congressional leaders and staff. Moskos made a point of visiting each and every deployment of U.S. troops beginning in the 1960s to 2005, when he retired. He interviewed troops, analyzed their concerns, and published numerous studies on topics ranging from lesbians and gays in the force to the nature of the all-volunteer force to women engaged in combat. Moskos is generally credited with coining the term "don't ask, don't tell," which became the basis for the Clinton administration's policy on gays and lesbians in the armed forces, a policy that the president enunciated at the National Defense University in July 1993. Moskos also trained a generation of scholars who have continued his work, as illustrated by the Inter-University Seminar on Armed Forces and Society (which he headed from 1992 to 1998) and by his coauthored publications with young scholars to encourage the growth of this field of study.

Richard Milhous Nixon (1913–1994)

While Richard Nixon will always be remembered as the first president to resign the presidency, there are a number of monumental, positive decisions tied to his name. Nixon was a Californian who served in the Navy during World War II, even though he came from a Quaker family. He attended Duke Law School before moving back to California where he ran for the House of Representatives in 1946 as a Republican, then won election to the Senate four years later. A dark horse, he was nonetheless chosen as Dwight David Eisenhower's vice presidential running mate in 1952. The two won election in both 1952 and 1956, but Nixon was unsuccessful in seeking the presidency on his own four years later. In 1968, he finally ascended to the Oval Office in a three-way split against Democratic Vice President Hubert Humphrey and third-party candidate George Wallace, a Southern segregationist from Alabama. Nixon won in part because of his claim that he had a "secret plan" to end the Vietnam War. Once elected, as the conflict dragged on despite the secret plan, public support for the war waned and Nixon decided to negotiate with the communists beginning in the early 1970s. In 1972, as the war against Vietnam and its allies in Beijing and Moscow was winding down, Nixon made historic trips to the People's Republic of China and the Soviet Union, which would fundamentally alter the future of U.S. geostrategic policy. In 1973, the Paris Peace Accords ended the war in Vietnam, codifying U.S. military withdrawal from the region. Two years later, South Vietnam fell to North Vietnam, and the communist forces overwhelmed governments in nearby Vientiane, Laos, and Phnom Penh, Cambodia. Throughout his administration Nixon had faced tremendous opposition to the draft, so much so that in 1973, he announced the end of military conscription and the adoption of an all-volunteer force. Nixon never saw the end of his second term to which he had been reelected in 1972 in a landslide: because of the Watergate scandal and the subsequent complete collapse of congressional support for the president, he was forced to resign the presidency on August 9, 1973. Before his death twenty years later, Nixon miraculously managed to make a partial political comeback and became somewhat of an elder statesman. From the late 1970s into the early 1990s, Nixon frequently discussed geopolitics before various groups involved in foreign policy.

James Otis (d. 1783)

An influential eighteenth-century political pamphleteer who strongly opposed the development of a standing army on economic grounds, Otis, a trained lawyer, originally worked for the Crown in his home colony of Massachusetts. In the 1760s, his political stance shifted and he became a stark critic of Imperial power in the colonies. In 1764, he penned *The Rights of the British Colonies Asserted and Proved*, which argued for the natural rights of the colonists against consolidation of power by London and its minions in the colonies. Otis argued that the British Redcoats were a threat to both Britain itself and to the colonies not merely because they bore arms but also because the maintenance of standing forces was expensive. Furthermore, maintaining these forces, Otis argued, meant that bureaucratic forces were seeking to extend the power of the army. Otis's view reappeared many years later in American history when Dwight D. Eisenhower, in 1961, delivered his farewell speech to the nation warning of the dangerous growing strength of the military-industrial complex, where structural bureaucratic concerns drive societies. Otis was beaten by Crown representatives in the early 1770s, and he died in 1783.

John McAuley Palmer (1870–1955)

The grandson of a namesake who had served in the Civil War, General John McAuley Palmer proved one of the most important thinkers about national military service in the history of the United States. Palmer saw service in Cuba during the Spanish-American War of 1898, participated in the China Expedition of the early twentieth century, and served as district governor in the colonial Philippines. Palmer served in France during World War I. Upon his return, he strongly advocated the cause of national service. His support was critical to passing the National Defense Act of 1920, and he encouraged Congress to enact legislation that would encourage more people to serve as citizen-soldiers. Palmer published a number of books and articles on this point. He returned to active duty after Pearl Harbor and continued serving his nation in advisory capacities upon his retirement.

Franklin Delano Roosevelt (1882–1945)

The president who called up the single biggest commitment of U.S. military personnel in history to prosecute a war against the Axis Powers, Franklin Roosevelt (FDR) was born into money and power in 1882 in Hyde Park, New York. He married a distant cousin, Anna Eleanor Roosevelt, a niece of President Theodore Roosevelt. FDR descended from the largely Democratic Hyde Park branch of the Dutch immigrant family, while his fourth cousin Theodore Roosevelt's family were Republicans from the Oyster Bay. Though he never served in uniform himself, Franklin became assistant secretary of the Navy in 1912. Soon after World War I, Roosevelt contracted polio and was permanently afflicted. Although he was never able to walk again, Roosevelt covered up his disability (which was more feasible in an era when television did not exist and the press had a gentler attitude) and won the presidency in 1932. This would prove the first of an unprecedented four-term victory as president. In 1939, when Germany invaded Poland and soon after when Germany attacked Britain, Roosevelt began working on the means to get armaments to a now weakened Britain. When the Japanese attacked Pearl Harbor and generalized war ensued, the friendship between Roosevelt and Churchill tightened. Roosevelt trusted Generals George Marshall, Dwight D. Eisenhower, and Douglas A. MacArthur to prosecute the war against the Axis powers. Millions of U.S. troops were raised to wage the conflict, and the United States mobilized the greatest force (physical and scientific) ever for this conflict. Roosevelt died just short of the conclusion, in April 1945.

Eugen Rosenstock-Huessy (1888–1973)

Eugen Rosenstock-Huessy taught philosophy at Dartmouth College for decades in the middle part of the twentieth century, espousing the role of "work service" in all states but particularly the United States. This concept argued for voluntary work camps for students, farmers, and others to improve the living standards of those less fortunate. This translated into creating a service ethic consistent with the need to serve as advocated as an alternate to national military service. Born in the late nineteenth century to a Jewish family in Berlin, Rosenstock-Huessy converted to Protestantism in his early youth, yet he retained his ties with Jewish academics in Germany throughout his life. Rosenstock-Huessy received two doctoral degrees, one in law, the other in philosophy, but his passion was philosophy. He was instrumental in the movement in the twentieth century to elevate the importance of national service through voluntary participation in the political culture. During the Great Depression he worked on behalf of President Franklin Delano Roosevelt to create the Civilian Conservation Corps for Harvard, Yale, and Dartmouth (among other schools) to encourage participation in the national need for trained officers and skilled leadership. The Corps ended during World War II, but Rosenstock-Huessy's ideas lived on. Many consider his ideas the basis for President John F. Kennedy's proposal for a Peace Corps, begun in 1961.

Donald Rumsfeld (b. 1932)

The only individual to serve as secretary of defense in two administrations a quarter of a century apart, Donald Rumsfeld has held a number of highly senior positions in Republican administrations of the United States. Born in the Chicago area, Rumsfeld was a naval ROTC boxer at Princeton University before serving in the active-duty Navy from 1954 to 1957. He remained in the Reserves until 1989, even though he had stopped actively drilling in 1975. He first worked in Washington in the 1950s when he was a staff member for a congressman from the Chicago area. Rumsfeld returned to Chicago where he won a seat in Congress in 1962; he served until he left the House to participate in President Nixon's cabinet in 1969. Between 1969 and 1975, Rumsfeld occupied increasingly important domestic and foreign policy positions for Presidents Nixon and Ford. In 1974 President Ford named him chief of staff, and as part of that staff he hired the young Richard B. Cheney (who was on a graduate fellowship at the time). In 1975, President Ford named Rumsfeld the youngest secretary of defense in history. His initial tenure as secretary covered the transition out of the Vietnam War as the United States was adjusting to both its new position in the world and to the new military policy, the all-volunteer force. At the end of the Ford administration, Rumsfeld left government to work as president of Searle, a pharmaceutical company in Chicago. He did not altogether abandon his ties to national security issues, however, for he headed a highly visible commission that evaluated the feasibility of installing a ballistic missile defense system for the nation. In 2000, President-elect George W. Bush nominated Rumsfeld as head of defense again. Rumsfeld was in the Pentagon on the morning of September 11, 2001, when a terrorist-driven airplane attacked the site. Rumsfeld personally aided the rescue effort. In the coming months, he became a highly visible fixture as the media watched the Pentagon leadership for hints as to how the United States would retaliate. Rumsfeld argued strongly for an aggressive response against both the Taliban as protectors of the terrorist leader, Osama Bin Laden, and Saddam Hussein as head of an illegitimate government pursuing weapons of mass destruction. The initial weeks of the Iraqi and Afghan invasions appeared successful, but the subsequent insurgency and governing problems in Iraq would considerably dull the secretary's luster. Rumsfeld was also the key advocate of a policy designed to radically transform the armed forces by making all of the forces more agile, smaller, and more technologically sophisticated to deal with global problems instead of a large force requiring considerable time to deploy and possessing vulnerability to glitches that affect big organizations instead of responding to the nation's needs. Rumsfeld also continued advocating a ballistic missile defense protection for the nation and selected allies.

Isaac Newton "Ike" Skelton IV (b. 1931)

The long-serving congressman from Missouri's fourth district, Democrat Ike Skelton has been the most prominent member of the Congress to advocate better professional military education in the U.S. armed services. Skelton's district, which he began representing in Washington in 1977, includes Whiteman Air Force base (housing B-2 bombers) and Fort Leonard Wood (a major Army facility in the south-central portion of Missouri). Skelton has long been known as a strong advocate of an improved and professionalized military education. Accordingly, he fostered the Skelton Reforms of the late 1980s, which instilled more academic rigor in professional military education at senior-level military schools.

Friedrich Wilhelm Augustus von Steuben (1730–1794)

Born to a Prussian engineer in the Army, Baron von Steuben spent his early years in Russia where he learned a tremendous amount about military operations. Unpaid by the 1770s by the Prussian military which was virtually unfunded, Baron von Steuben offered his services to the fledgling Continental Army in 1777. Von Steuben proved the architect of a coherent force designed to oust the British in the late 1770s. He worked with troops on drills and developed a capable force with discipline. He also brought a basic understanding of the need for sanitation in camp where disease killed many even after awareness of the importance of sanitation arose. Von Steuben proved a keen instructor and organizer, helping forces up and down the Atlantic seaboard. His contributions to the Continental Army have generally been considered some of the most fundamental aspects of the independence struggle. Von Steuben died in New York in 1794.

John Trenchard (1662–1723)

An Englishman from the west country, Trenchard was a staunch critic of monarchical power and was known as a Whig partisan. A scholar as well as a Parliamentarian, Trenchard wrote *A Short History of Standing Armies of England* in the late 1680s, advocating the use of military power for broader interests but not individual aspirations. Trenchard's political philosophy became one of the framing positions for the newly independent United States. His warnings about the dangers of a standing army have remained a touchstone throughout the nation's history.

Emory Upton (1839–1881)

Emory Upton began life in upstate, western New York where he lived until he went to Oberlin College in Ohio. After two years, Upton matriculated at West Point where the discipline and rigor of the Corps of Cadets drove him to excel. Upton served in the Union Army during the Civil War, attaining hero status for his conduct at Spotsylvania Court House and reaching the rank of brigadier general at the youthful age of 28 years. At the end of the Civil War, where Upton had been wounded, he became the influential superintendent at the Military Academy. He introduced greater rigor and substance into the curriculum and wrote a volume on tactics that is still considered fundamental to teaching the field. Upton committed suicide at a young age after a lifetime commitment to the Army. His last book, *The Military Policy of the United States from 1775,* argued for a small army that could augment troops rapidly with "citizen-soldiers" in a crisis and was influential for many reforms Secretary of War Elihu Root implemented in 1903-1904.

George Washington (1732–1799)

The most prominent individual to ever engage in national service in the United States, General George Washington was also important for his philosophical beliefs about the need for a standing, professional army to conduct the defense of the emerging United States. Washington had been a surveyor and a junior officer during the French and Indian War (1763) where he witnessed at first hand the effects of the British Army on the Indian and French enemies. When he was made the commanding general of the Army seeking to achieve independence from the British beginning in the mid-1770s, Washington tested his beliefs that a standing, professional force had a better chance to accomplish national goals. As commanding general he requested that the troops and officers receive half pensions for the remainder of their lives *en lieu* of pay during the dicey period of achieving independence. Instrumental in voicing the need for the national army over the localized militias during the 1780s debate at the Constitutional Convention in Philadelphia, his presidency saw the slow steps taken to constitute that force.

Leonard Wood (1860–1927)

As major general of the U.S. Army, Leonard Wood was an extraordinary officer who influenced virtually all aspects of the Army. Wood was born in New Hampshire and earned a medical degree at Harvard. In his initial years in the Army he served as a surgeon. He participated in the Indian Wars in the western portion of the nation, winning the Congressional Medal of Honor in 1898 for his work as a surgeon in the Apache Campaign over the summer of 1886. During the following decade, he served as President Grover Cleveland's White House physician. At the same time, Wood developed a strong friendship with Theodore Roosevelt who served as his second-in-command when Wood became commander of the Rough Riders, or the First Volunteer Cavalry. Commander at the Battle of Las Guasimas, Wood assumed the rank of brigadier general and led the forces at San Juan Hill. In the aftermath of the Spanish-American War of 1898, Roosevelt named Wood military governor of Cuba until 1902. Wood assumed the governorship of the Philippines in 1902, making major general the following year, where he also met the civilian governor, William Howard Taft. Wood became the Army chief of staff in 1910 during the William Howard Taft presidency, remaining in that position until 1914 when he was replaced by General Hugh L. Scott. During his tenure as chief of staff, Wood promoted the early system, which became the Reserve Officer Training Program and the Preparedness Movement, both of which were important in preparing for the United States' possible involvement in World War I, as were the Mobile Army and General Staff Corps, all of which Wood handled. Wood strongly advocated better preparedness for U.S. forces, running Camp Funston for the 10th and 89th Infantries. After the war, Wood ran unsuccessfully for president in 1920, after which he moved to Manila, Philippines. He returned to the United States in 1927 for medical attention but died in Boston that August while undergoing surgery.

6

Major U.S. Military Service Documents

F ew contemporary issues of the United States have as many documents written about them as does national service. This chapter presents a selected list of important documents and speeches, chosen to be representative of the national debate through which the nation has passed and will continue passing. The selection process, though imperfect, aimed to highlight the range of issues that the nation has had to confront as its views of national service evolved. Most of these documents and speeches have been excerpted due to space limitations.

George Washington, "Sentiments on a Peace Establishment," May 2, 1783

Often forgotten by the postindependence generations, these were George Washington's musings on what should replace the Continental Army in the newly independent United States. The untraditional spelling characterizes eighteenth-century writing.

A Peace Establishment for the United States of America may in my opinion be classed under four different heads Vizt:

First. A regular and standing force, for Garrisoning West Point and such other Posts upon our Northern, Western, and Southern Frontiers, as shall be deemed necessary to awe the Indians, protect our Trade, prevent the encroachment of our Neighbours of Canada and the Florida's, and guard us at least from surprizes; Also for security of our Magazines.

Secondly. A well organized Militia; upon a Plan that will pervade all the States, and introduce similarity in their Establishment Manoeuvres, Exercise and Arms.

Thirdly. Establishing Arsenals of all kinds of Military Stores.

Fourthly. Accademies, one or more for the Instruction of the Art Military; particularly those Branches of it which respect Engineering and Artillery, which are highly essential, and the knowledge of which, is most difficult to obtain. Also Manufactories of some kinds of Military Stores.

Altho' a *large* standing Army in time of Peace hath ever been considered dangerous to the liberties of a Country, yet a few Troops, under certain circumstances, are not only safe, but indispensably necessary. Fortunately for us our relative situation requires but few. The same circumstances which so effectually retarded, and in the end conspired to defeat the attempts of Britain to subdue us, will now powerfully tend to render us secure. Our *distance* from the European States in a great degree frees us of apprehension, from their numerous regular forces and the Insults and dangers which are to be dreaded from their Ambition.

But, if our danger from those powers was more imminent, yet we are too poor to maintain a standing Army adequate to our defence, and was our Country more populous and rich, still it could not be done without great oppression of the people. Besides, as soon as we are able to raise funds more than adequate to the discharge of the Debts incurred by the Revolution, it may become a Question worthy of consideration, whether the surplus should not be applied in preparations for building and equipping a Navy, without which, in case of War we could neither protect our Commerce, nor yield that Assistance to each other, which, on such an extent of Sea-Coast, our mutual Safety would require.

Fortifications on the Sea Board may be considered in two points of view, first as part of the general defence, and next, as securities to Dock Yards, and Arsenals for Ship Building, neither of which shall I take into this plan; because the first would be difficult, if not, under our circumstances, impracticable; at any rate amazingly expensive. The other, because it is a matter out of my line, and to which I am by no means competent, as it requires a consideration of many circumstances, to which I have never paid attention.

The Troops requisite for the Post of West Point, for the Magazines, and for our Northern, Western and Southern Frontiers, ought, in my opinion, to amount to 2631 Officers of all denominations included; besides the Corps of Invalids. If this number should be thought large, I would only observe; that the British Force in Canada is now powerful, and, by report, will be increased; that the frontier is very extensive; that the Tribes of Indians within our Territory are numerous, soured and jealous; that Communications must be established with the exterior Posts; And, that it may be policy and economy, to appear respectable in the Eyes of the Indians, at the Commencement of our National Intercourse and Traffic with them. In a word, that it is better to reduce our force hereafter, by degrees, than to have it to increase after some unfortunate disasters may have happened to the Garrisons; discouraging to us, and an inducement to the Enemy to attempt a repetition of them.

Besides these Considerations, we are not to forget, that altho' by the Treaty, half the Waters, and the free Navigation of the Lakes appertain to us, yet, in Case of a rupture with Great Britain we should in all probability, find little benefits from the Communications with our upper Posts, by the Lakes Erie and Ontario; as it is to be presumed, that the Naval superiority which they now have on those Waters, will be maintained. It follows as a Consequence then, that we should open new or improve the present half explored Communications with Detroit and other Posts on the Lakes, by the Waters of the Susquehannah Potowmack or James River, to the Ohio, from whence, with short Portages several Communications by Water may be opened with Lake Erie. To do which, posts should be established at the most convenient places on the Ohio. This would open several doors for the supply of the Garrisons on the Lakes; and is absolutely necessary for such others as may be tho't advisable to establish upon the Mississippi. The Ohio affording the easiest, as well as the safest Route to the Illinois settlements, and the whole Country below on the Mississippi, quite to our Southern boundary.

To protect the Peltry and Fur Trade, to keep a watch upon our Neighbours, and to prevent their encroaching upon our Territory undiscovered, are all the purposes that can be answered by an extension of our Posts, at this time, beyond Detroit, to the Northward or Westward: but, a strong Post on the Scioto, at the carrying place between it and the River Sandusky, which empties into Lake Erie, mentioned in Hutchins's Description of that Country Page 24, and more plainly pointed out by Evans's Map, is indispensably necessary for the security of the present Settlers, and such as probably, will immediately settle within those Limits. And by giving security to the Country and covering its Inhabitants, will enable them to furnish supplies to the Garrisons Westward and Northward of these settlements, upon moderate and easy Terms.

The 2,631 Men beforementioned, I would have considered to all Intents and purposes as Continental Troops; looking up to Congress for their Orders, their pay, and supplies of every kind.

Not having that particular knowledge of the situation of the Southern and Western Boundaries of the Carolinas and Georgia, which is necessary to decide on the Posts to be established in that District, the allotment of only one Regiment thereto, may be judged inadequate; should that be the case, a greater force may be established and a sufficient allowance made them.

The above establishment differs from our present one, in the following instances Vizt: The exclusion of the light Company and reducing a sergeant and 18 Privates from each of the Poattalion Companies, and giving a Chaplain to each Regiment instead of a Brigade. If it should be asked why the Reduction of Non Commisd. Officers and Privates is made, while the Commissioned Officers remain the same? It may be answered, that the number of Men which compose the Infantry, will be sufficient for my Calculation, and that the situation of our Frontiers renders it convenient to divide them into so many Corps as have been mentioned, for the ease and propriety of Command. I may also say, that in my Opinion, the number of our Commissioned Officers, has always been disproportionate to the Men. And that in the detached State in which these Regiments must be employed, they cannot consistently with the good of Service be reduced.

It may also be observed, that in case of War and a necessity of assembling their Regiments in the Field, nothing more will be necessary, than to recruit 18 Men to each Compy. and give the Regiment its flank Company. Or if we should have occasion to add strength to the Garrisons, or increase the number of our Posts, we may augment 900 Men including Serjeants, without requiring more than the Officers of 4 Companies, or exceeding our present Establishment. In short, it will give us a Number of Officers well skilled in the Theory and Art of War, who will be ready on any occasion, to mix and diffuse their knowledge of Discipline to other Corps, without that lapse of Time, which, without such Provision, would be necessary to bring intire new Corps acquainted with the principles of it.

Besides the 4 Regiments of Infantry, one of Artillery will be indispensably necessary. The Invalid Corps should also be retained. Motives of humanity, Policy and justice will all combine to prevent their being disbanded. The numbers of the last will, from the nature of their composition, be fluctuating and uncertain. . . .

To this Regiment of Artillery should be annexed 50 or 60 Artificers, of the various kinds which will be necessary, who may be distributed in equal numbers into the different Companies and being part of the Regiment, will be under the direction and Command of the Commanding Officer, to be disposed into different services as Circumstances shall require. By thus blending Artificers with Artillery, the expence of Additional Officers will be saved; and they will Answer all the purposes which are to be expected from them, as well as if formed into a distinct Corps.

The Regiment of Artillery, with the Artificers, will furnish all the Posts in which Artillery is placed, in proportionate numbers to the Strength and importance of them. The residue, with the Corps of Invalids, will furnish Guards for the Magazines, and Garrison West Point. The importance of this last mentioned Post, is so great, as justly to have been considered, the key of America; It has been so pre-eminently advantageous to the defence of the United States, and is still so necessary in that view, as well as for the preservation of the Union, that the loss of it might be productive of the most ruinous Consequences. A Naval superiority at Sea and on Lake Champlain, connected by a Chain of Posts on the Hudson River, would effect an entire separation of the States on each side, and render it difficult, if not impracticable for them to co-operate.

Altho' the total of the Troops herein enumerated does not amount to a large number, yet when we consider their detached situation, and the extent of Country they are spread over: the variety of objects that are to be attended to, and the close inspection that will be necessary to prevent abuses or to correct them before they become habitual; not less than two General Officers in my opinion will be competent to the Duties to be required of them. They will take their Instructions from the Secretary at War, or Person acting at the Head of the Military Department, who will also assign them their respective and distinct Districts. Each should twice a Year visit the Posts of his particular District, and notice the Condition they are in, Inspect the Troops, their discipline and Police, Examine into their Wants, and see that strict justice is rendered them and to the Public, they should also direct the Colonels, at what intermediate Times they shall perform the like duties at the Posts occupied by the Detachments of their respective Regiments. The visiting General ought frequently, if not always, to be accompanied by a Skillful Engineer, who should point out such alterations and improvements as he may think necessary from time to time, for the defence of any of the Posts; which, if approved by the General, should be ordered to be carried into execution.

Each Colonel should be responsible for the Administration of his Regiment; and when present, being Commanding Officer of any Post, which is occupied by a Detachment from his Regt., he may give such directions as he may think proper, not inconsistent with the Orders of his Superior Officer, under whose general superintendence the Troops are. He will carefully exact Monthly Returns from all detachments of his Regiment; and be prepared to make a faithful report of all occurrences, when called upon by the General Officer in whose Department he may be placed and whose instructions he is at all times to receive and obey. These Returns and Reports, drawn into a General one, are to be transmitted to the Secretary at War, by the visiting General, with the detail of his own proceedings, remarks and Orders.

The three Years Men now in service will furnish the proposed Establishment, and from these, it is presumed, the Corps must in the first Instance be composed. But as the pay of an American Soldier is much greater than any other we are acquainted with; and as there can be little doubt of our being able to obtain them in time of Peace, upon as good Terms as other Nations, I would suggest the propriety of inlisting those who may come after the present three years Men, upon Terms of similarity with those of the British, or any other the most liberal Nations.

When the Soldiers for the War have frolicked a while among their friends, and find they must have recourse to hard labour for a livelyhood, I am persuaded numbers of them will reinlist upon almost any Terms. Whatever may be adopted with respect to Pay, Clothing and Emoluments, they should be clearly and unequivocally expressed and promulgated, that there may be no deception or mistake. Discontent, Desertion and frequently Mutiny, are the natural consequences of these; and it is not more difficult to know how to punish, than to prevent these inconveniencies, when it is known, that there has been delusion on the part of the Recruiting Officer, or a breach of Compact on the part of the public. The pay of the Battalion Officer's is full low, but those of the Chaplain, Surgeon and Mate are too high; and a proper difference should be made between the Non-Commissioned Officers (serjeants particularly) and Privates, to give them that pride and consequence which is necessary to Command.

At, or before the Time of discharging the Soldiers for the War, the Officers of the Army may signify their wishes either to retire, upon the Half pay, or to continue in the service; from among those who make the latter choice, the number wanted for a Peace Establishment may be selected; and it were to be wished, that they might be so blended together from the Several Lines, as to remove, as much as possible, all Ideas of State distinctions.

No Forage should be allowed in time of Peace to Troops in Garrison, nor in any circumstances, but when actually on a March.

Soldiers should not be inlisted for *less* than three Years, to commence from the date of their attestations; and the more difference there is in the commencement of their terms of Service, the better; this Circumstance will be the means of avoiding the danger and inconvenience of entrusting any important Posts to raw Recruits unacquainted with service. Rum should compose no part of a Soldier's Ration; but Vinegar in large quantities should be issued. Flour or Bread, and a stipulated quantity of the different kinds of fresh or Salted Meat, with Salt, when the former is Issued, is all that should be contracted for.

Vegetables they can, and ought to be compelled to raise. If spruce, or any other kind of small Beer, could be provided, it ought to be given gratis, but not made part of the Compact with them. It might be provided also, that they should receive one or two days fish in a Week, when to be had; this would be a saving to the public, (the Lakes and most of the Waters of the Ohio and Mississippi abounding with Fish) and would be no disservice to the Soldier.

A proper recruiting fund should be established; from which the Regiment may always be kept complete.

The Garrisons should be changed as often as it can be done with convenience; long continuance in the same place is injurious. Acquaintances are made, Connections formed, and habits acquired, which often prove very detrimental to the service. By this means, public duty is made to yield to interested pursuits, and real abuses are the Result. To avoid these Evils, I would propose, that there should be a change made in every Regiment once a Year, and one Regiment with another every two Years.

An Ordinance for the service of Troops in Garrison, should be annexed to our present Regulations for the order and discipline of the Army. The latter should be revised, corrected and enlarged so as to form a Basis of Discipline under all circumstances for Continental Troops, and, as far as they will apply, to the Militia also: that one uniform system may pervade all the States.

As a peace establishment may be considered as a change in, if not the Commencement of our Military system it will be the proper time, to introduce new and beneficial regulations, and to expunge all customs, which from experience have been found unproductive of general good. Among the latter I would ask, if promotion by Seniority is not one? That it is a good general rule admits of no doubt, but that it should be an invariable one, is in my opinion wrong. It cools, if it does not destroy, the incentives to Military Pride and Heroic Actions. On the one hand, the sluggard, who keeps within the verge of his duty, has nothing to fear. On the other hand, the enterprising Spirit has nothing to expect. Whereas, if promotion was the sure reward of Merit, all would contend for Rank and the service would be benefited by their Struggles for Promotion. In establishing a mode by which this is to be done, and from which nothing is to be expected, or apprehended, either from favour or prejudice, lies the difficulty. Perhaps, reserving to Congress the right inherent in Sovereignties, of making all Promotions. A Board of superior Officers, appointed to receive and examine the claims to promotions out of common course, of any Officer, whether founded on particular merit, or extra service, and to report their opinion thereon to Congress; might prove a likely means of doing justice. It would certainly give a Spur to Emulation, without endangering the rights, or just pretentions of the Officers.

Before I close my observations under this head, of a regular force, and the Establishment of Posts, it is necessary for me to observe, that, in fixing a Post at the North End of Lake Champlain I had three things in view. The Absolute Command of the entrance into the Lake from Canada. A cover to the Settlements on the New Hampshire Grants and the prevention of any illicit intercourse thro' that Channel. But, if it is known, or should be found, that the 45th Degree crosses the Lake South of any spot which will command the entrance into it, the primary object fails; And it then becomes a question of whether any place beyond Ticonderoga or Crown Point is eligible.

Altho' it may be somewhat foreign to, and yet not altogether unconnected with the present subject, I must beg leave, from the importance of the object, as it appears to my mind, and for the advantages which I think would result from it to the United States, to hint, the propriety of Congress taking some early steps, by a liberal treatment, to gain the affections of the French settlements of Detroit, those of the Illinois and other back Countries. Such a measure would not only hold out great encouragement to the Inhabitants already on those lands, who will doubtless make very useful and valuable subjects of the United States; but would probably make deep and conciliatory impressions on their friends in the British settlements, and prove a means of drawing thither great numbers of Canadian Emigrants, who, under proper Regulations and establishments of Civil Government, would make a hardy and industruous race of Settlers on that Frontier; and who, by forming a barrier against the Indians, would give great security to the Infant settlement, which, soon after the close of the War, will probably be forming in the back Country.

I come next in the order I have prescribed myself, to treat of the Arrangements necessary for placing the Militia of the Continent on a respectable footing for the defence of the Empire and in speaking of this great Bulwark of our Liberties and independence, I shall claim the indulgence of suggesting whatever general observations may occur from experience and reflection with the greater freedom, from a conviction of the importance of the subject; being persuaded, that the immediate safety and future tranquility of this extensive Continent depend in a great measure upon the peace Establishment now in contemplation; and being convinced at the same time, that the only probable means of preventing insult or hostility for any length of time and from being exempted from the consequent calamities of War, is to put the National Militia in such a condition as that they may appear truly respectable in the Eyes of our Friends and formidable to those who would otherwise become our enemies.

Were it not totally unnecessary and superfluous to adduce arguments to prove what is conceded on all hands the Policy and expediency of resting the protection of the Country on a respectable and well established Militia, we might not only shew the propriety of the measure from our peculiar local situation, but we might have recourse to the Histories of Greece and Rome in their most virtuous and Patriotic ages to demonstrate the Utility of such Establishments. Then passing by the Mercinary Armies, which have at one time or another subverted the liberties of allmost all the Countries they have been raised to defend, we might see, with admiration, the Freedom and Independence of Switzerland supported for Centuries, in the midst of powerful and jealous neighbours, by means of a hardy and well organized Militia. We might also derive useful lessons of a similar kind from other Nations of Europe, but I believe it will be found, the People of this Continent are too well acquainted with the Merits of the subject to require information or example. I shall therefore proceed to point out some general outlines of their duty, and conclude this head with a few particular observations on the regulations which I conceive ought to be immediately adopted by the States at the instance and recommendation of Congress.

It may be laid down as a primary position, and the basis of our system, that every Citizen who enjoys the protection of a free Government, owes not only a proportion of his property, but even of his personal services to the defence of it, and consequently that the Citizens of America (with a few legal and official exceptions) from 18 to 50 Years of Age should be borne on the Militia Rolls, provided with uniform Arms, and so far accustomed to the use of them, that the Total strength of the Country might be called forth at a Short Notice on any very interesting Emergency, for these purposes they ought to be duly organized into Commands of the same formation; (it is not of very great importance, whether the Regiments are large or small, provided a sameness prevails in the strength and composition of them and I do not know that a better establishment, than that under which the Continental Troops now are, can be adopted. They ought to be regularly Mustered and trained, and to have their Arms and Accoutrements inspected at certain appointed times, not less than once or twice in the course of every [year] but as it is obvious, amongst such a Multitude of People (who may indeed be useful for temporary service) there must be a great number, who from domestic Circumstances, bodily defects, natural awkwardness or disinclination, can never acquire the habits of Soldiers; but on the contrary will injure the appearance of any body of Troops to which they are attached, and as there are a sufficient proportion of able bodied young Men, between the Age of 18 and 25, who, from a natural fondness for Military parade (which passion is almost ever prevalent at that period of life) might easily be enlisted or drafted to form a Corps in every State, capable of resisting any sudden impression which might be attempted by a foreign Enemy, while the remainder of the National forces would have time to Assemble and make preparations for the Field. I would wish therefore, that the former, being considered as a *denier resort*, reserved for some great occasion, a judicious system might be adopted for forming and placing the latter on the best possible Establishment. And that while the Men of this description shall be viewed as the Van and flower of the American Forces, ever ready for Action and zealous to be employed whenever it may become necessary in the service of their Country; they should meet with such exemptions, privileges or distinctions, as might tend to keep alive a true Military pride, a nice sense of honour, and a patriotic regard for the public. Such sentiments, indeed, ought to be instilled into our Youth, with their earliest years, to be cherished and inculcated as frequently and forcibly as possible.

It is not for me to decide positively, whether it will be ultimately most interesting to the happiness and safety of the United States, to form this Class of Soldiers into a kind of Continental Militia, selecting every 10th 15th or 20th. Man from the Rolls of each State for the purpose; Organizing, Officering and Commissioning those Corps upon the same principle as is now practiced in the Continental Army. Whether it will be best to comprehend in this body, all the Men fit for service between some given Age and no others, for example between 18 and 25 or some similar description, or whether it will be preferable in every Regiment of the proposed Establishment to have one additional Company inlisted or drafted from the best Men for 3, 5, or 7 years and distinguished by the name of the additional or light Infantry Company, always to be kept complete. These Companies might then be drawn together occasionally and formed into particular Battalions or Regiments under Field Officers appointed for that Service. One or other of these plans I think will be found indispensably necessary, if we are in earnest to have an efficient force ready for Action at a moments Warning. And I cannot conceal my private sentiment, that the formation of additional, or light Companies will be most consistent with the genius of our Countrymen and perhaps in their opinion most consonant to the spirit of our Constitution.

I shall not contend for names or forms, it will be altogether essential, and it will be sufficient that perfect Uniformity should be established throughout the Continent, and pervade, as far as possible, every Corps, whether of standing Troops or Militia, and of whatever denomination they may be. To avoid the confusion of a contrary practice, and to produce the happy consequences which will attend a uniform system of Service, in case Troops from the different parts of the Continent shall ever be brought to Act together again, I would beg leave to propose, that Congress should employ some able hand, to digest a Code of Military Rules and regulations, calculated immediately for the Militia and other Troops of the United States; And as it should seem the present system, by being a little simplified, altered, and improved, might be very well adopted to the purpose; I would take the liberty of recommending, that measures should be immediately taken for the accomplishment of this interesting business, and that an Inspector General should be appointed to superintend the execution of the proposed regulations in the several States.

Congress having fixed upon a proper plan to be established, having caused the Regulations to be compiled, having approved, Printed and distributed them to every General Field Officer, Captain and Adjutant of Militia, will doubtless have taken care, that whenever the system shall be adopted by the States the encouragement on the one hand, and the fines and penalties on the other will occasion an universal and punctual compliance therewith.

Before I close my remarks on the establishment of our National Militia, which is to be the future guardian of those rights and that Independence, which have been maintain'd so gloriously, by the fortitude and perseverance of our Countrymen, I shall descend a little more minutely to the interior arrangements, and sum up what I have to say on this head with the following Positions.

1st. That it appears to me extremely necessary there should be an Adjutant General appointed in each State, with such Assistants as may be necessary for communicating the Orders of the Commander in Chief of the State, making the details, collecting the Returns and performing every other duty incident to that Office. A duplicate of the Annual Returns should always be lodged in the War Office by the 25th of Decr. in every year, for the information of Congress; with any other reports that may be judged expedient. The Adjutant Generals and Assistants to be considered as the deputies of the Inspector General, and to assist him in carrying the system of Discipline into effect.

2d. That every Militia Officer should make himself acquainted with the plan of Discipline, within a limited time, or forfeit his Commission, for it is in vain to expect the improvement of the Men, while the Officers remain ignorant, which many of them will do, unless Government will make and enforce such a Regulation.

3dly. That the formation of the Troops ought to be perfectly simple and entirely uniform, for example each Regiment should be composed of two Battalions, each Battalion to consist of 4 Companies and each Company as at present of 1 Captain, 1 Lieutenant, 1 Ensign, 5 Sergeants, 3 Corporals, 2 Music, 65 Privates.

Two Battalions should form a Regiment four Regts a Brigade and two Brigades a Division. This might be the general formation; but as I before observed, I conceive it will be eligible to select from the district forming a Regiment, the flower of the young Men to compose an additional or light Company to every Regiment, for the purposes before specified, which undoubtedly ought to be the case unless something like a Continental Militia shall be instituted. To each Division two Troops of Cavalry and two Companies of Artillery might also be annexed, but no Independent or Volunteer Companies foreign to the Establishment should be tolerated.

4thly. It is also indispensable that such a proportion of the Militia (under whatever discription they are comprehended) as are always to be held in readiness for service, nearly in the same manner the Minute Men formerly were, should be excercised at least from 12 to 25 days in a year, part of the time in Company, part in Battalion and part in Brigade, in the latter case, by forming a Camp, their Discipline would be greatly promoted, and their Ideas raised, as near as possible, to real service; Twenty five days might be divided thus, ten days for training in squads, half Companies and Companies, ten in Battalion and five in Brigade.

5thly. While in the Field or on actual duty, there should not only be a Compensation for the time thus spent, but a full allowance of Provisions Straw, Camp Equipage &c; it is also of so great consequence that there should be, a perfect similarity in the Arms and Accoutrements, that they ought to be furnished, in the first instance by the public, if they cannot be obtained in any other way, some kind of Regimentals or Uniform Clothing (however cheap or course they may be) are also highly requisite and should be provided for such occasions. Nor is it unimportant that every Article should be stamped with the appearance of regularity; and especially that all the Articles of public property should be numbered, marked or branded with the name of the Regiment or Corps that they may be properly accounted for.

6thly. In addition to the Continental Arsenals, which will be treated of under the next head. Every State ought to Establish

Magazines of its own, containing Arms, Accoutrements, Ammunitions, all kinds of Camp Equipage and Warlike Stores, and from which the Militia or any part of them should be supplied whenever they are call'd into the Field.

7thly. It is likewise much to be wished, that it might be made agreeable to Officers who have served in the Army, to accept Commands in the Militia; that they might be appointed to them so far as can be done without creating uneasiness and jealousy, and that the principle Characters in the Community would give a countenance to Military improvements, by being present at public reviews and Exhibitions, and by bringing into estimation amongst their fellow Citizens, those who appear fond of cultivating Military knowledge and who excel in the Exercise of Arms. By giving such a tone to our Establishment; by making it universally reputable to bear Arms and disgraceful to decline having a share in the performance of Military duties; in fine, by keeping up in Peace "a well regulated, and disciplined Militia;" we shall take the fairest and best method to preserve, for a long time to come, the happiness, dignity and Independence of our Country.

With regard to the third Head in Contemplation, to wit the "Establishment of Arsenals of all kinds of Military Stores." I will only observe, that having some time since seen a plan of the Secretary of War, which went fully into the discussion of this branch of Arrangement, and appeared (as well as I can, at this time recollect) to be in general perfectly well founded, little more need be said on the subject, especially as I have been given to understand the plan has been lately considerably improved and laid before Congress for their approbation; and indeed there is only one or two points in which I could wish to suggest any Alteration.

According to my recollection, five grand Magazines are proposed by the Secretary at War, one of which to be fixed at West Point. Now, as West Point is considered not only by our selves, but by all who have the least knowledge of the Country, as a post of the greatest importance, as it may in time of Peace, from its situation on the Water be somewhat obnoxious to surprise or *Coup de Main* and as it would doubtless be a first object with any Nation which might commence a War against the United States, to seize that Post and occupy or destroy the Stores, it appears to me, that we ought particularly to guard against such an event, so far as may be practicable, and to remove some part of the Allurements to enterprise, by establishing the grand Arsenals in the Interior part of the Country, leaving only to West Point an adequate supply for its defence in almost any extremity.

I take the liberty also to submit to the consideration of the Committee, whether, instead of five great Arsenals, it would not be less expensive and equally convenient and advantageous to fix three general Deposits, one for the Southern, one for the Middle and one for the Eastern States, including New York, in each of which there might be deposited, Arms, Ammunition, Field Artillery, and Camp Equipage for thirty thousand Men, Also one hundred heavy Cannon and Mortars, and all the Apparatus of a Seige, with a sufficiency of Ammunition.

Under the fourth General Division of the subject, it was proposed to consider the Establishment of Military Academies and Manufactures, as the means of preserving that knowledge and being possessed of those Warlike Stores, which are essential to the support of the Sovereignty and Independence of the United States. But as the Baron Steuben has thrown together his Ideas very largely on these Articles, which he had communicated to me previous to their being sent to the secretary at War, and which being now lodged at the War Office, I imagine have also been submitted to the inspection of the Committee, I shall therefore have the less occasion for entering into the detail, and may, without impropriety, be the more concise in my own observations.

That an Institution calculated to keep alive and diffuse the knowledge of the Military Art would be highly expedient, and that some kinds of Military Manufactories and Elaboratories may and ought to be established, will not admit a doubt; but how far we are able at this time to go into great and expensive Arrangements and whether the greater part of the Military Apparatus and Stores which will be wanted can be imported or Manufactured, in the cheapest and best manner: I leave those to whom the observations are to be submitted, to determine, as being more competent, to the decision than I can pretend to be. I must however mention some things, which I think cannot be dispensed with under the present or any other circumstances; Until a more perfect system of Education can be adopted, I would propose that Provision should be made at some Post or Posts where the principle Engineers and Artillerists shall be stationed, for instructing a certain number of young Gentlemen in the Theory of the Art of War, particularly in all those branches of service which belong to the Artillery and Engineering Departments. Which, from the affinity they bear to each other, and the advantages which I think would result from the measure, I would have blended together; And as this species of knowledge will render them much more accomplished and capable of performing the duties of Officers, even in the Infantry or any other Corps whatsoever, I conceive that appointments to vacancies in the Established Regiments, ought to be made from the candidates who shall have completed their course of Military Studies and Exercises. As it does in an essential manner qualify them for the duties of Garrisons, which will be the principal, if not only service in which our Troops can be employed in time of Peace and besides the Regiments of Infantry by this means will become in time a nursery from whence a number of Officers for Artillery and Engineering may be drawn on any great or sudden occasion.

Of so great importance is it to preserve the knowledge which has been acquired thro' the various Stages of a long and arduous service, that I cannot conclude without repeating the necessity of the proposed Institution, unless we intend to let the Science become extinct, and to depend entirely upon the Foreigners for their friendly aid, if ever we should again be involved in Hostility. For it must be understood, that a Corps of able Engineers and expert Artillerists cannot be raised in a day, nor made such by any exertions, in the same time, which it would take to form an excellent body of Infantry from a well regulated Militia.

And as to Manufactories and Elaboratories it is my opinion that if we should not be able to go largely into the business at present, we should nevertheless have a reference to such establishments hereafter, and in the means time that we ought to have such works carried on, wherever our principal Arsenals may be fixed, as will not only be sufficient to repair and keep in good order the Arms, Artillery, Stores &c of the Post, but shall also extend to Founderies and some other essential matters.

Thus have I given my sentiments without reserve on the four different heads into which the subject seemed naturally to divide itself, as amply as my numerous avocations and various duties would permit. Happy shall I be, if any thing I have suggested may be found of use in forming an Establishment which will maintain the lasting Peace, Happiness and Independence of the United States.

Alexander Hamilton, "Report of a Committee to the Continental Congress on a Military Peace Establishment," June 18, 1783

Alexander Hamilton was one of the Founders of the United States whose eloquent writings and stridently centralist ideas could have led the country down a considerably different path had he lived longer than 1804.

The Committee observe with respect to a military peace establishment, that before any plan can with propriety be adopted, it is necessary to inquire what powers exist for that purpose in the confederation. By the 4th. clause of the 6th article it is declared that "no vessels of war shall be kept up by any state in time of peace, except such number only as shall be deemed necessary by the United States in Congress assembled, for the defence of such state or its trade; nor shall any body of forces be kept up by any state in time of peace, except such number only, as in the judgment of the United States in Congress assembled shall be deemed requisite to garrison the forts necessary for the defence of such state."

By the 5th. clause of the 9th article, The United States in Congress assembled are empowered generally (and without mention of peace or war) "to build and equip a navy, to agree upon the number of land forces, and to make requisitions from each state for its quota, in proportion to the number of white inhabitants in each state, which requisition shall be binding, and thereupon the legislature of each state, shall appoint the Regimental officers, raise the men and clothe arm and equip them in a soldier-like manner at the expence of the United States and the officers and men so cloathed armed and equipped shall march to the place appointed and within the time agreed on by the United States in Congress assembled."

By the 4th. clause of the same article the United States are empowered "to appoint all officers of the land forces except regimental officers, to appoint all officers of the naval forces, and to commission all officers whatever in the service of the United States, making rules for the government and regulation of the said land and naval forces and directing their operations."

It appears to the Committee that the terms of the first clause are rather restrictive on the particular states than directory to the United States, intended to prevent any state from keeping up forces land or naval without the approbation and sanction of the Union, which might endanger its tranquillity and harmony, and not to contravene the positive power vested in the United States by the subsequent clauses, or to deprive them of the right of taking such precautions as should appear to them essential to the general security. A distinction that this is to be provided for in time of war, by the forces of the Union, in time of peace, by those of each state would involve, besides other inconveniences, this capital one, that when the forces of the Union should become necessary to defend its rights and repel any attacks upon them, the United States would be obliged to *begin to create* at the very moment they would have occasion *to employ* a fleet and army. They must wait for an actual commencement of hostilities before they would be authorised to prepare for defence, to raise a single regiment or to build a single ship. When it is considered what a length of time is requisite to levy and form an army and still more to build and equip a navy, which is evidently a work of leisure and of peace requiring a gradual preparation of the means—there cannot be presumed so improvident an intention in the Confederation as that of obliging the United States to suspend all provision for the common defence 'till a declaration of war or an invasion. If this is admitted it will follow that they are at liberty to make such establishments in time of peace as they shall judge requisite to the common safety. This is a principle of so much importance in the apprehension of the Committee to the welfare of the union, that if any doubt should exist as to the true meaning of the firstmentioned clause, it will in their opinion be proper to admit such a construction as will leave the general power, vested in the United States by the other clauses, in full force; unless the states respectively or a Majority of them shall declare a different interpretation. The Committee however submit to Congress, (in conformity to that spirit of Candour and to that respect for the sense of their constituents, which ought ever to characterize their proceedings) the propriety of transmitting the plan which they may adopt to the several states to afford an opportunity of signifying their sentiments previous to its final execution.

The Committee, are of opinion, if there is a con[s]titutional power in the United States for that purpose, that there are conclusive reasons in favour of federal in preference to state establishments.

First there are objects for which separate provision cannot conveniently be made; posts within certain districts, the jurisdiction and property of which are not yet constitutionally ascertained—territory appertaining to the United States not within the original claim of any of the states—the navigation of the Missi[issi]ppi and of the lakes—the rights of the fisheries and of foreign commerce; all which belonging to the United States depending on the laws of nations and on treaty, demand the joint protection of the Union, and cannot with propriety be trusted to separate establishments.

Secondly, the fortifications proper to be established ought to be constructed with relation to each other on a general and well-digested system and their defence should be calculated on the same principles. This is equally important in the double view of safety and economy. If this is not done under the direction of the United States, each state following a partial and disjointed plan, it will be found that the posts will have no mutual dependence or support—that they will be improperly distributed, and more numerous than is necessary as well as less efficacious—of course more easily reduced and more expensive both in the construction and defence.

3dly. It happens, that from local circumstances particular states, if left to take care of themselves, would be in possession of the chief part of the standing forces and of the principal fortified places of the union; a circumstance inconvenient to them and to the United States to them, because it would impose a heavy exclusive burthen in a matter the benefit of which will be immediately shared by their neighbours and ultimately by the states at large—to the United States, because it confides the care of the safety of the *whole* to a *part*, which will naturally be unwilling as well as unable to make such effectual provision at its particular expence, as the common welfare requires—because a single state from the peculiarity of its situation, will in a manner keep the keys of the United States—because in time a considerable force in the hands of a few states may have an unfriendly aspect on the confidence and harmony which ought carefully to be maintained between the whole.

4thly. It is probable that a provision by the [Congress] of the forces necessary to be kept up will [be based] upon a more systematic and oeconomical plan than a provision by the states separately; especially as it will be of importance as soon as the situation of affairs will permit, to establish founderies, manufactaries of arms, powder &c; by means of which the labour of a part of the troops applied to this purpose will furnish the United States with those essential articles on easy terms, and contribute to their own support.

5thly. There must be a corps of Artillery and Engineers kept on foot in time of peace, as the officers of this corps require science and long preliminary study, and cannot be formed on an emergency; and as the neglect of this institution would always oblige the United States to have recourse to foreigners in time of war for a supply of officers in this essential branch—an inconvenience which it ought to be the object of every nation to avoid. Nor indeed is it possible to dispense with the service of such a corps in time of peace, as it will be indispensable not only to have posts on the frontier; but to have fortified harbours for the reception and protection of the fleet of the United States. This corps requiring particular institutions for the instruction and formation of the officers cannot exist upon separate establishments without a great increase of expence.

6thly. It appears from the annexed papers No. 1 to 4, to be the concurrent opinion of the Commander in Chief, the Secretary at War, the Inspector General and the Chief Engineer, not only that some militia establishment is indispensable but that it ought in all respects to be under the authority of the United States as well for military as political reasons. The plan hereafter submitted on considerations of economy is less extensive than proposed by either of them.

The Committee upon these principles submit the following plan.

The Military peace establishment of the United States to consist of four regiments of infantry, and, one of Artillery incorporated in a corps of Engineers, with the denomination of the corps of Engineers.

Each Regiment of infantry to consist of two batalions, each batalion of four companies, each company of 64 rank and file, with the following, commissioned and Non commissioned officers, pay, rations and cloathing; to be however recruited to one hundred & twenty eight rank & file in time of war, preserving the proportion of corporals to privates.

Frederick Steuben, "A Letter on the Subject of an Established Militia, and Military Arrangements, Addressed to the Inhabitants of the United States," 1784

The question of whether to establish a militia versus a permanent standing service has permeated U.S. history. Steuben's position was an important one.

Friends and Fellow Citizens,

It is the duty of every member of the community, particularly in a Republic, to be attentive to its welfare, and to exert himself to contribute to its prosperity . . .

The immediate object of my address is to hold up to your calm consideration what I conceive to be the best possible Military Establishment for the United States. Be not alarmed Fellow Citizens at the expression; for no country ever risqued their political existence without one that did not fall a prey to the avarice or ambition of her neighbours. Though America has hitherto been successful, and though no immediate cloud seems to threaten the sunshine of her tranquility, yet it would be idle indeed were we to conclude from thence that she was always to stand exempted from the fortunes and fate of other nations.

The local situation of America, happily removed from Europe and her wranglings, must long continue to make a large army unnecessary—it is not however without its difficulties and its dangers.

On the East an unguarded coast, and a dangerous and formidable Colony planted. On the West a defenceless frontier. Neighbours on the one side who may never be friends; and Savages on the other who are unalterably your enemies. This is your local situation. The security of the former must necessarily be committed in a great measure to a Navy; but a Navy can only grow out of dockyards and arsenals, and the well regulated commerce of your country; and until they begin to operate, for they are the products of industry and time. Your principal ports at least should be raised superior to the fear of injury, or the dishonour of insult.

The latter, *vis.* the protection of your Western frontier, is a subject of perhaps more immediate importance; for upon this rests not only your share of a most lucrative commerce, but closely connects with it the peace, prosperity, and extensions of your Western settlements. These objects are not to be secured but by a chain of well chosen ports, strongly fortified and respectably garrisoned. Hence arises the necessity of an established Continental Corps; and as their services will be lasting and national, their establishment ought to be federal and permanent.

To draught a Militia for such duty, so distant from their homes, and so much more trying to patience than to valour, would be extremely embarrassing and expensive, and fall infinitely short of both the wishes and expectations of Government. But independent of arguments resulting from the nature of the service or general expence, individual embarrassments or eventual disappointments, which must avail every plan for performing it by Militia draughts, there are other and very powerful motives for a small regular establishment.

A Spirit of Providence is one of the strongest assurances of national wisdom, and it may not be improper to lay out your accounts for foreign war or domestic struggle. Where, in an exigency of this kind, without an establishment, would government look up for military talents and experience? Would she call upon her servants who have been engaged in the late controversy? If she did she should find many, if not all of those to whom she could most safely have committed the interest of the Republic, old or disabled—busy or dissatisfied—diffident of themselves—superior to the necessity of hazarding either life, reputation, or care; and totally lost to every military idea and remembrance, except the hardships and the cares. If we examine mankind under the impressions of property and interest, we will find that to make any art a study it should not only be a passion but a business. The Merchant may read Marshal Saxe, the Mathematician Monsieur Vauban, but it is the Soldier alone who regards their lessons and takes up the sword; not as the hasty avenger of a sudden wrong, but as his companion for life, that will study and digest them.

I am conscious in the opinion of many I am undertaking a difficult task in attempting to convince a free people, who have established their liberties by the unparalleled exercise of their virtue, that a permanent Military Establishment is necessary to their happiness, absolutely so to their federal existence. I shall not in this essay address your passions, but I appeal forcibly to your reason. I shall convince you by the statement of a regular and exact calculation, that your present system of Militia draughts recommended by Congress, is not only impracticable in itself, and replete with every inconvenience that can shackle military movements, but it takes a double proportion of every necessary to collect and station them, and more than double the sum to support your frontier in this mode, than by a small regular establishment. Every objection to this system the operations of simple reasoning will fully obviate, by attending to the numbers and materials that shall compose your establishment, and the arrangement that may be made concerning enlistment, reception and muster, sources but too often of much unneccessary expenditure, and of the most flagrant abuse.

Upon a review of all the military of Europe, there does not appear to be a single form which could be safely adopted by the United States; they are unexceptionably different from each other, and like all other human institutions, seem to have started as much out of accident as design. The local situation of the country; the spirit of the government; the character of the nation, and in many instances the character of the Prince, have all had their influence in settling the foundation and discipline of their respective troops, and render it impossible that we should take either as a model. The Legion alone has not been adopted by any, and yet I am confident in asserting, that whether it be examined as applicable to all countries, or as it may more immediately apply to the existing or probable necessity of this, it will be found strikingly superior to any other–1st. Being a compleat and little army of itself, it is ready to begin its operations on the shortest notice or slightest alarm. 2d. Having all the component parts of the largest army of any possible description, it is prepared to meet every species of war that may present itself. And, 3d. As in every case of detachment the first constitutional principle will be preserved, and the embarassments of draughting and detail, which in armies differently framed too often distract the commanding officer, will be avoided.

It may easily suggest itself from this sketch that in forming a Legion the most difficult task is to determine the necessary proportion of each species of soldiers which is to compose it; this must obviously depend upon what will be the theatre, and what the style of the war. On the plains of Poland, whole brigades of cavalry would be necessary against every enemy, but in the forest and among the hills of America, a single regiment would be more than sufficient against any, and as there are but two kinds of war to which we are much exposed, *viz.* an attack from the sea side by an European Power, aided by our sworn enemies settled on our extreme left, and an invasion of our back settlements by an Indian enemy, it follows of course that Musketteers and Light Infantry should make the greatest part of your army; on these principles I should propose the following draught. That a Legion consist, 1st. Of a Legionary Brigade and Regimental Staff. 2d. Of two Brigades of Musketteers, each Brigade of two Regiments, each Regiment of eight Companies forming two Battalions, each Company of a Captain, Lieutenant, Ensign, six Sergeants, one Drum, one Fife, sixty Privates, and four Supernumeraries. 3d. Of a Battalion of Rifle-men of four Companies, each Company to have a Captain, three Lieutenants, six Sergeants, a Bugle-horn and Drum, sixty Privates, and four Supernumeraries. 4th. A Division of Field Artillery consisting of two Companies, each to have a Captain, Captain-Lieutenant, three Lieutenants, six Sergeants, twenty Artificers, forty Matrosses, Drum, Fife, and four Supernumeraries. 5th. A Squadron of Cavalry consisting of two Troops, each Troop to have a Captain, two Lieutenants, a Cornet, six Sergeants, one Farrier, one Saddler, one Trumpeter, sixty Dragoons, and four Supernumeraries. 6th. Of a Train of Artillery and Equipage, to consist of one Quarter-Master, one Clothing and Pay-Master, five Conductors, twenty Artificers, and seventy Waggoners and Drivers.

The principal Staff and Regimental Staff Officers, will be named by Congress—the subordinate Staff by Head of Departments—both to be commissioned by Congress, and subject to their orders alone. The men will be enlisted for eight years, and supported at the common expence of the United States, who after the expiration of their enlistment will accommodate each man with a given quantity of land. The most exact uniformity should be established throughout the component parts of this Corps. The distinction of States should be carefully avoided, and their service as well as their recompense be entirely dependent upon Congress. The Corps of Artillery, though not a part of the Legion (excepting the Field Artillery), bears an immediate relation to it, and it cannot be more properly considered than at this moment. It is not necessary to say more upon it, than, that it shall be under the immediate command of its own General, and that the subordinate Officers shall be composed of field Engineers, Geographers, and Artillerists, men who have and will make military mathematics their study. Their obvious employment will be designing and constructing magazines and dockyards, superintending military manufactures, surveying high-ways, bays, harbours, etc., etc., while the Soldiers will be employed in garrisoning the forts, and guarding the naval and military stores and places of deposit, and Artificers in such manufactures and works as shall be added to them. The Corps of Horse may be of much service; divided into detachments it may be usefully engaged in keeping up a ready communication between the different posts, and with proper arrangements will be much less expensive than expresses. But as the whole Corps will not exceed one hundred and twenty, rank and file, they may with great propriety be employed in guarding the residence of Congress, the public offices, papers, etc. Congress and their executive officers should never be exposed to the mad proceedings of a mob. Guards are necessary, and always proper at the seat of government.

In looking back upon what I have written, I am so happy as to find that much of what I have proposed to say on the uses of this Establishment, has been anticipated in the course of my Introduction; I will close the sketch however with this summary view of them. The American army at present should consist of neither more nor less than one compleat Legion of 3000 men permanent and Continental; a Corps of Artillery, Sappers, Miners, Artificers, etc., of 1000, permanent and Continental also; and seven Legions of well disciplined Militia of 3000 men each, subject to the call of their country, and ready to act on the shortest notice. Agreeable to this your standing force in time of peace will be but 4000 men, and your effective force in case of invasion 25,000 well disciplined troops.

To your established Corps you will commit the security of your docks and arsenals, the defence of those forts which already exist, and such others as may hereafter be constructed. From them you will derive all necessary assurance relative to your dependent settlements, and effectually preserve that important water communication which has fallen to you by treaty. In times of peace they will operate as a principle of discipline and formation to your established Militia, and in those of war become a ready barrier against the designs of avarice and the assaults of ambition; and finally, they will serve as a nursery to those talents which it must ever be your wisdom to encourage, and which in the course of fortune it may become your interest to employ.

In treating the latter part of this subject, *viz.* the established Militia, it may be previously necessary, to take a view of your present system. It is a flattering but I believe a mistaken idea that every Citizen should be a soldier. It would be as sensible and consistent to say every Citizen should be a Sailor. An apprenticeship must necessarily precede the acquisition of any trade, and the use of arms is as really a trade as shoe or boot making. Were courage the only qualification requisite in a Soldier, it would be otherwise, but galantry alone leaves the character very incomplete; to this must be added youth, size, temperance and inclination, docility of temper, and adroitness in the exercise of the field, and a patience under every vicissitude of fortune. Some of these are no easy lesson to a mind filled with ideas of equality and freedom; and in many instances are only to be learned with industry and pains. I have but one inference to draw from these remarks, i.e., that however gallant your Militia may be (and I know them to be brave) they must necessarily want much of the true military character. It may now be asked what are the sources of this defect? I will venture to suggest them: a want of uniformity in their discipline and in their arms-the inadequacy of the several laws under which they exist—the imperfect execution of those laws, such as they are—and the indifference with which every man must regard a business not in some degree pleasing or professional. Hence has arisen that uncertainty of temper—that want of confidence in themselves, that reluctancy to come out, that impatience to get home, and that waste of public and destruction of private property—which has ever marked an operation merely Militia.

These are characteristics that cannot be denied, and which must be as lasting as your belief and declaration, "That every Citizen without exception, must be a Soldier." But when we add the expence of such establishment to the probable disappointment which must follow its operations, it will appear ruinous indeed.

Pennsylvania, it is said, enrols by its Militia Law, about sixty thousand men—and I suppose, that in the article of expence it does not differ widely from those of the other States; these men are obliged to assemble six times in a year at some given place of rendezvous; four days of the six are employed in exercise and two in reviews.

For non-attendence on reviews, each delinquent pays ten shillings per day, and for non-attendance upon exercise five shillings per day; therefore the man who absents himself from all will pay forty shillings per annum, and he who attends all must necessarily lose six days labour, while some, from their distance from the place of rendezvous, will lose ten or twelve. But taking eight as an average, and calculating the expence of each man at six shillings per day, it will amount to forty-eight shillings per man per annum; it then follows, that if the whole Militia should assemble six days in the year, the aggregate expence will amount to 386,666 dollars per annum—if on the other hand they neglect this service and pay the fines, they will amount to 320,000 dollars per annum. View it in any point of light, how imposing and vexatious must this be to the people. For by attendance do they promote the interest of the State? Or does the individual return to his home satisfied, that the information and instruction he has received is any compensation for the loss he sustains? And what is the obvious consequence of non-attendance? Are the fines a revenue to the State, a serviceable one I mean; or can the good wishes or confidence of a people be increased by the operation of a law, whose penalty they prefer to its obligation? I am convinced that under another name these impositions would not be tolerated, and that an insurrection would follow the exercise of them.

If the annual expence of Pennsylvania for training her Militia be 386,666 dollars, and if we consider her as an eighth part of the United States, the aggregate expence of the United States in times of perfect peace, for the instruction of men to whom she cannot risque her fate in war, will be annually 3,113,328 dollars; what it would be in war is beyond all calculation, but it may not be amiss to take a view of the obviously additional sources which must then take place. It is I believe an acknowledged fact, that the expence of any corps will depend upon its discipline. An old soldier will live upon half the allowance of a new levy—not because he has less appetite, but because he has more care and more management. The one will regard his arms and accoutrements with all the solicitude of friendship; the other with all the indifference of contempt. The veteran, taught by the diseases he has felt or the observations he has made, is attentive to his health, and though attentive to his duty avoids everything which would most probably expose it; the militiaman, or new levy, fatigued and disheartened perhaps by the march of a single day, and measuring the tedious hours of his enlistment, throws himself down without any regard to the place or situation; rises in the morning reluctant and languid, and perhaps for want of attention to himself incapable of performing his duty. These are facts which cannot be contradicted, and which hold up to your view some articles of expence, which should be considered, though they cannot be ascertained.

There are many other of the same description; such for instance is the loss sustained by the inefficiency of convoys and the inattention of guards, and such the loss in calling forth a Farmer, a Mechanic, or a Merchant at a shilling a day; the Farmer it is true loses less than either, but still there is no proportion between the profits of his farm and the wages of his sword. Under these considerations trade and agriculture cannot remain unhurt, they must feel some unkind influence foreign to their habits, and unfriendly to their genius. But there is still another more pressing and calamitous: I mean the Rotation Service. For example: A State whose Militia consists of 100,000 men is invaded, the whole cannot be called forth—10,000 may be equal to the contest—but unless the war be almost instantly closed, and that is not to be expected, the principle of rotation must be adopted, and the first detachment is relieved by a second, the second by a third, and the third by a fourth, so that in reality the State must a very large proportion of the time pay and feed 20,000 men, to have 10,000 in the field. How then are these defects to be supplied? I answer by changing their constitution, and lessening their numbers. The Militia of the United States may be calculated at 400,000 men; on what occasion, or for what purpose, shall we ever want this number? The difficulty of bringing a twentieth part of them together has been sufficiently evinced; the impossibility of instructing, and what is still more of feeding them if collected, wants no proof. Giving up therefore the chimerical idea of having 400,000 Militia, and that every Citizen is a Soldier, let us look for a number that will be less expensive, sooner collected, and more easily taught, those lessons necessary for a Soldier to know.

At one period of the late war, Great-Britain attacked us with an army of more than 40,000 effectives; where is the European Power that can do more? We cannot therefore want 400,000 men, nor do we want 50,000; for as we cannot be surprised, an army of 25,000 will be equal to any foreign attack, or internal convulsion, that may happen to exist. I would therefore repeat my proposal, that in addition to the established Continental Legion, that Seven Legions be formed from the whole militia force of the United States; call them the Established Militia, and let their composition and construction be exactly the same with your Continental Legion.

To determine what proportion of the corps will fall to each State, an exact register of the numbers in each should be previously obtained; but not to stop at what is very immaterial in mere proportion, I would hazard the following: North Department, to New Hampshire, Massachusetts, Rhode Island, and Connecticut, Two Legions. Middle Department, to New York, Jersey, Pennsylvania, and Maryland, Three Legions. Southern Department, to Virginia, North Carolina, South Carolina, and Georgia, Two Legions.

It is to simplify the system, and to render its operations easy, that I make this division into departments; the proportion of the States composing each may be easily determined—the smaller will give companies, the larger Battalions, until the several Legions are compleat. In the appointment of Officers for the established Militia, I think the following method should be pursued. Each State appoints the Officers necessary for its own contingent of troops. If either send a Company only, they send no Officer higher than a Captain; if a Battalion, a Lieutenant-Colonel and Major; if a Regiment, a Colonel; if two Regiments, a Brigadier; and if two Brigades, a Major-General. In instances where neither State sends a sufficient number to give these higher ranks, the superior Officers are called from the district which has furnished the largest contingent.

These Officers remain absolutely subject to the State which has sent them, and are dismissed with the same formality with which they have been appointed. For instance: If a Court-Martial should sentence to disgrace a Major, who belongs to a state which only furnishes a Company, the approbation or disapprobation belongs to the Supreme of that State which furnishes the largest part of the Regiment. If a Colonel or Brigadier belonging to a State which has furnished only a Battalion or Regiment, should be tried by a Court-Martial, the sentence is invalid without the approbation of the Grand Convention of the Empire.

Officers or whatever rank will receive pay only for those days which they actually spend in the service of the Public; they will have a right to resign their places after each yearly review, but while they hold their commissions, they will be subject to whatever ordinance may be issued by Government. This ordinance will regulate the pay and emoluments of each grade; determine the uniformity of the discipline, arms, and accoutrements, and the duties of the service in general. With regard to the men the following regulations should take place.

I. That the first class be engaged for three different periods; one third for two years, one third for three, and one third for four; that is, in a company of seventy-two men, twenty-four will be engaged for two years, twenty-four for three years, and twenty-four for four years.

II. That after the expiration of the time of the two years men, their places shall be supplied by another enlistment of the same number of men for three years, and that all subsequent engagements shall be for no less time than this. By this arrangement when the times of one third of a corps expire, a like number will be enlisted; this will prevent a total expiration, and there will be always two-thirds disciplined troops to one-third recruits.

III. That none but Citizens be received.

IV. That their age be not less than eighteen, nor more than twenty-four.

V. That each man be well formed and at least five feet six inches high.

VI. That both Negroes and Mulattoes be excluded.

The best method of engaging men in service is by bounty; the expence will not be great, and the inconveniency and ill humour which attends draughting be avoided. The bounty need not exceed ten dollars per man; to this must be added for the whole term of service, a hat, coat, vest, pair of overalls, pair of shoes, and a stock; and at the expiration of his service, provided he has not been capitally censured, his arms and accoutrements should be given to him. In the operation of this system, at the expiration of every third year 7000 well disciplined men, with their arms and accoutrements, will be added to the effective force of the United States, and the best possible magazine for a Republic firmly established, (*viz.*) arms and accoutrements in the course of a few years be put into the hands of every member of the community, and a perfect knowledge of the duties of a soldier engraved on the mind of every citizen. This will secure you a respectable station amongst the Powers of Europe; and if not ensure you a perfect peace, at least furnish you with the ability of checking the ardour of any Power that may be hardy enough to attack you.

The whole annual expence of this establishment will not exceed fifteen dollars per man per annum, and for this he subjects himself to military discipline thirty-one days in a year, twelve of which he will be employed in exercise, in detail, and twelve in learning the evolutions and maneuvres, and seven in reviews.

The time for these exercises must depend upon the season of year and the place, upon the population of the State, etc., etc., but it were to be wished that at each rendezvous of inspection, one Legion compleat might be assembled, and that on every third year all the troops of the department would encamp together.

The Soldier and the State must come under this farther obligation to each other, that each months service (exclusive of the time taken up in repairing to the rendezvous for which he will receive a certain stipulated allowance) shall count for a year; but should an invasion or any other cause make it necessary for Government to call him out, he shall be obliged to repair to the place appointed on the shortest notice, and to serve any length of time not exceeding one year, which Government may deem expedient. For this time he shall receive that pay and emoluments annexed to a war establishment. By such an arrangement, I dare assure to the United States, an army as useful and as respectable as that of any Republic in Europe; and as to its expence, I will venture again to advance, that it will not cost more than one third of the sum which is now expended; and this may be levied upon every man who falls under the present system, and will not demand from him but twelve shillings and sixpence per annum, in lieu of forty, which simply considered is evidently more eligible; but when viewed as a discharge from the irksome routine of militia duty, I cannot but suppose but it must be embraced with ardour by every individual at present enrolled in the Militia.

As I have in a former instance made the Militia establishment of Pennsylvania a subject of calculation, it may not be improper to say what would be the expence of that Commonwealth, under the operation of the system proposed. For the support of her share of a board of war and inspection, the Continental Legion, Corps of Artillerists and others, her share of the expence will be 65,000 dollars, and for her proportion of the seven Militia Legions 35,000 dollars, the whole annual expence then will amount to 10,000 dollars, and consequently she must have yearly 286,666 dollars—how striking is this difference.

Should it be objected that the scale upon which I have gone is too small, the proportion of each State may be increased without breaking in upon the principles of formation, or should the finances of any State permit, or her politics require another corps, it may be raised upon the same plan.

Much of what has been said on the uses of the federal Legion may be applied to the Militia Corps, like that in peace they will be a most excellent school for the instruction of the young, and in war present an immediate guard or barrier, behind which Government may take its further measures of defence with confidence and ease; and if necessary in war, the rank and file of your army may be doubled, and the list of your officers remain the same; for being perfectly trained in the military schools, which the operation of this plan will establish, I should without hesitation pledge myself for their abilities in their professions. Having now filled up the limits which I had prescribed for myself upon this occasion, I cannot but hope a plan so clearly efficient, as well as economical will not fail to secure the attention of the United States. I foresee, however, it will be subject to one very popular objection, "It is in fact a Standing Army." Yes Fellow Citizens I admit it—it is a Standing Army, but composed of your brothers and your sons. Can you require or conceive a better security— are they not your natural guardians? And shall it be supposed a cockade and feather, the *Vox et preteria nihil* of the military character, can alienate either their affections or their interests: Be assured you reflect upon yourselves by nourishing the suspicion, and wound the feelings of men who at least are entitled to your gratitude and esteem.

Letter, George Washington to Frederick Steuben, March 15, 1784

George Washington's response to Baron von Steuben revealed an emerging national sense of the role for a militia versus the standing army.

My Dear Baron: I have perused with attention the plan which you have formed for establishing a Continental Legion, and for training a certain part of the Arms bearing men of the Union as a Militia in times of peace; and with the small alterations which have been suggested and made, I very much approve of it.

... Yours of maturer thought and better digestion, I, at the same time that I hinted the *propriety* of a Continental Militia; glided almost insensibly into what I thought *would*, rather than what I conceived *ought* to be a proper peace Establishment for this Country.

A peace establishment ought always to have two objects in view. The one present security of Posts, of Stores and the public tranquillity. The other, to be prepared, if the latter is impracticable, to resist with efficacy, the sudden attempts of a foreign or domestic enemy. If we have no occasion of Troops for the first purposes, and were certain of not wanting any for the second; then all expence of every nature and kind whatsoever on this score, would be equally nugatory and unjustifiable; but while men have a disposition to wrangle, and to disturb the peace of Society, either from ambitious, political or interested motives, common prudence and foresight requires such an establishment as is likely to ensure to us the blessings of Peace, altho' the undertaking should be attended with difficulty and expence; and I can think of no plan more likely to answer the purpose, than the one you have suggested; which (the principle being established) may be enlarged, or diminished at pleasure, according to circumstances; it therefore meets my approbation and has my best wishes for its success. I have the honor etc.

Resolution of the Continental Congress Creating the Peace Establishment, June 3, 1784

The Continental Congress's response to the suggestions of founding a standing army is contained in this resolution.

Whereas a body of troops, to consist of seven hundred noncommissioned officers and privates, properly officered, are immediately and indispensably necessary for taking possession of the western posts, as soon as evacuated by the troops of his britannic Majesty, for the protection of the northwestern frontiers, and for guarding the public stores;

Resolved, That it be, and it is hereby recommended to the states hereafter named, as most conveniently situated, to furnish forthwith from their militia, seven hundred men, to serve for twelve months, unless sooner discharged, in the following proportions, viz.

Connecticut, 165
New Jersey, 110
New York, 165
Pensylvania, 260
—700

Resolved, That the Secretary in the War Office take order for forming the said troops when assembled, into one regiment, to consist of eight companies of infantry, and two of artillery, arming and equipping them in a soldier-like manner; and that he be authorised to direct their destination and operations, subject to the order of Congress, and of the Committee of the states in the recess of Congress.

Resolved, That the pay, subsistance and rations of the officers and men shall be the same as has been heretofore allowed to the troops of the United States; and that each officer and soldier shall receive one month's pay after they are embodied, before their march.

Resolved, That the staff and commissioned officers of the said troops, consist of the following, and be furnished by the several states hereinafter mentioned; that is to say, one lieutenant colonel commandant from Pensylvania; two majors, one from Connecticut, and one from New York, each major to command a company; eight captains from the several states furnishing the troops in the nearest proportion to the number of the men furnished; ten lieutenants, one to act as adjutant; ten ensigns; one regimental chaplain; one surgeon; four mates.

Resolved, That the secretary in the War office give the necessary order for the inferior arrangements and organization of the said troops, and make the apportionment of the officers to be furnished by the several states, not herein particularly directed.

Resolved, That the said troops when embodied, on their march, on duty, and in garrison, shall be liable to all the rules and regulations formed for the government of the late army of the United States, or such rules and regulations as Congress or a committee of the states may form.

Resolved, That the Superintendant of the finances of the United States, take order for furnishing, on the warrant of the secretary in the war office, the sums requisite for carrying the foregoing resolutions into effect.

Resolution of the Continental Congress Ascertaining the Powers and Duties of the Secretary at War, January 27, 1785

One aspect of establishing a standing military is the rights and responsibilities of the official charged with administering it.

The ordinance for ascertaining the powers and duties of the Secretary at War, was taken up and being read a third time, was passed as follows:

An Ordinance for ascertaining the powers and duties of the Secretary at War.

Be it ordained by the United States in Congress Assembled, that the powers and duty of the Secretary at War shall be as follows, to wit: To examine into the present state of the war department, the returns and present state of the troops, ordnance, arms, ammunition, cloathing and supplies of the Troops of these states, and report the same to Congress: To keep exact and regular returns of all the forces of these states, and of all the military stores, equipments and supplies in the Magazines of the United States, or in other places for their use; and to receive into his care, from the officers in whose possession they may be, all such as are not in actual service; to form estimates of all such stores, equipments and supplies as may be requisite for the military service, and for keeping up competent magazines, and to report the same to the Commissioners of the treasury of the United States, that measures may be taken in due time, for procuring the same; to prepare estimates for paying and recruiting the troops of these United States; to carry into effect all ordinances and resolves of Congress for raising and equipping troops for the service of the United States, and for inspecting the said troops; and to direct the arrangement, destination and operation of such troops as are or may be in service, subject to the Orders of Congress or of the Committee of the States in the recess of Congress; to make out, seal and countersign the commissions of all such military officers as shall be employed in the service of the United States; to take order for the transportation, safe keeping and distributing the necessary supplies for such troops and garrisons as may be kept up by the United States. He shall appoint and remove at pleasure all persons employed under him, and shall be responsible for their conduct in office; all which appointments shall be immediately certified to Congress, and such certificate, or the substance thereof, registered in a book to be kept for that purpose in the office of the Secretary of Congress. He shall keep a public and convenient Office in the place where Congress shall reside. He shall, at least once a year, visit all the magazines and deposits of public stores, and report the state of them with proper arrangements to Congress; and shall twice a year, or oftner if thereto required, settle the accounts of his department. That as well the Secretary at war, as his assistants or clerks, before they shall enter on the duties of their Office, shall respectively take and subscribe an Oath or affirmation of fidelity to the United States, and for the faithful execution of the trust reposed in them; and which oaths or affirmations shall be administered by the Secretary of Congress, and a certificate thereof filed in his Office. The Oath of fidelity shall be in the words following: "I A. B. appointed to the office of _____ do acknowledge that I do owe faith and true allegiance to the United States of America, and I do swear (or affirm) that I will, to the utmost of my power, support, maintain and defend the said United States in their freedom, sovereignty and independence, against all opposition whatsoever." And the Oath of Office shall be in the words following: "I, A. B. appointed to the office of _____ do swear (or affirm) that I will faithfully, truly, and impartially execute the office of _____ to which I am so appointed, according to the best of my skill and judgment; and that I will not disclose or reveal any thing, that shall come to my knowledge in the execution of the said office, or from the confidence I may thereby acquire, which, in my own judgment, or by the injunction of my superiors, ought to be kept secret." That the form of the oath of fidelity heretofore prescribed by Congress, and all former resolutions of Congress, relative to the department of war, be, and they are hereby repealed..

Resolutions of the Continental Congress Renewing the Peace Establishment, April 1, 7, and 12, 1785

The aspects of establishing this institution have been revisited often in U.S. history.

Congress took into consideration the report of a committee, to whom were referred sundry motions relative to the western frontiers, and a paragraph thereof relative to the raising of troops being under debate, a motion was made by Mr. [David] Howell, seconded by Mr. [John] Beatty, that the same be postponed, in order to take up the following: "That it is necessary, that a body of troops, consisting of non-commissioned officers and privates, be raised to serve for the term of three years, unless sooner discharged, for the protection of the north western frontiers, and for guarding public stores; to be raised by the States in the following proportions, viz. N. H. &c.

It is the opinion of the Committee that the United States in Congress assembled should proceed . . . to make requisitions on the states for men and money in order to establish such garrisons.

. . . *Resolved,* That it is necessary that a body of troops consisting of 700 noncommissioned officers and privates, be raised to serve for the term of three years, unless sooner discharged, for the protection of the northwestern frontiers, to defend the settlers on the land belonging to the United States, from the depredations of the Indians, and to prevent unwarrantable intrusions thereon, and for guarding the public stores..

Ordered, That the further consideration thereof be postponed.

That the 700 non commissioned officers and privates determined to be necessary, by the act of 1 April, be raised by the following states, in the following proportions:.

That it be recommended to the states hereafter named, as most conveniently situated, to furnish forthwith, from their militia, the seven hundred non commissioned officers and men, agreed to be raised by the resolution of 1 April, in the following proportions, viz.

Thursday, April 7, 1785. That the 700 non commissioned officers and privates determined to be necessary, by the act of 1 April, be raised by the following states, in the following proportions: . . .

That it be recommended to the states hereafter named, as most conveniently situated, to furnish forthwith, from their militia, the seven hundred non commissioned officers and men, agreed to be raised by the resolution of 1 April, in the following proportions, viz..

Resolved, That it be recommended to the states hereafter named, as most conveniently situated, to furnish forthwith, the seven hundred non commissioned officers and men, agreed to be raised by the resolution of 1 April, in the following proportions:

Ordered, That the remainder of the report be committed, and that the committee be instructed to report the states to be called upon, and the proportions to be furnished by them respectively.

Tuesday, April 12, 1785. *Resolved,* That the non commissioned Officers and privates to be raised by the resolution of the seventh day of the present month April, be furnished by the states hereinafter mentioned, in the following proportions:

Connecticut, 165
New Jersey, 110
New York, 165
Pennsylvania, 260
—700

. . . One lieutenant colonel from Pennsylvania. Two majors, one from Connecticut, and one from New York, each to command a company.

Eight captains, ten lieutenants, one to act as adjutant, one as quarter master, and one as pay master. Ten ensigns, one surgeon and four mates, to be furnished by the said States in proportion to the number of privates which they respectively furnish.

That the pay of the lieutenant colonel be 50 dollars per month; that of the Major, 45; Captain, 35; lieutenant, 26; Ensign, 20; Serjeant, 6; Corporal, 5; Drum, 5; Fife, 5; private, 4; Surgeon, 45; Mate, 30.

That the lieutenants acting as adjutant, quarter master and pay master, shall receive, in consideration of the said extra duty, each 10 dollars per month.

That each Officer and soldier shall receive one month's pay after they are embodied, before their march.

That the Secretary at War be directed to form the said troops when raised into one regiment, consisting of eight companies of infantry, and two of artillery, to appoint their places of rendezvous, direct their subsequent operations, and make all other inferior necessary arrangements not herein particularly mentioned, subject to the Order of Congress, and of the Committee of the States in the recess of Congress; and That the Commissioners of the treasury be instructed to furnish on his warrant, the sums necessary for carrying the same into effect.

That the said troops when embodied, on their march, on duty, or in garrison, shall be subject to all the rules and regulations formed for the government of the late army, or such other rules as Congress or a Committee of the States may form.

That the Secretary at War ascertain the necessary clothing and rations proper for the troops, and report the same to Congress.

That the Commissioners of the treasury contract for the supply of rations at such places and in such quantities as the Secretary at War shall judge necessary.

Resolution of the Continental Congress Expanding the Peace Establishment, October 20, 1786

Because of the strongly held, diverse opinions about a standing Army (meaning military in general), the need to put this issue before the Continental Congress for general approval was crucial to the evolving debate on what we now call public policy in the United States.

The committee was referred the letter from the war Office, with the papers enclosed, containing intelligence of the hostile intentions of the Indians in the Western country, having reported,

That the uniform tenor of the intelligence from the western country plainly indicates the hostile disposition of a number of Indian Nations, particularly the Shawanese, Puteotamies, Chippawas, Tawas and Twightwees: That these nations are now assembling in the Shawanese towns, and are joined by a banditti of desperadoes, under the name of Mingoes and Cherokees, who are outcasts from other nations, and who have associated and settled in that country for the purpose of war and plunder: That they are labouring to draw in other nations to unite with them in a war with the Americans: That it is expected one thousand warriors will soon be collected in the Shawanese towns, from whence they have already despatched parties to commence hostilities: That from the motions of the Indians to the southward as well as the northward, and the exertions made in different quarters to stimulate the various nations against the Americans, there is the strongest reason to believe that, unless the speediest measures are taken effectually to counteract and defeat their plan, the war will become general, and will be attended with the most dangerous and lasting Consequences: That the committee, therefore, deem it highly necessary that the troops in the service of the United States be immediately augmented, not only for the protection and support of the frontiers of the states, bordering on the western territory and the valuable settlements on and near the margin of the Mississippi, but to establish the possession and facilitate the surveying and selling of those intermediate lands which have been so much relied on for the reduction of the debts of the United States: Whereupon,

Resolved unanimously, That the number of one thousand three hundred and forty noncommissioned Officers and privates be raised for the term of three years, unless sooner discharged, and that they, together with the troops now in service, be formed into a legionary corps, to consist of 2040 noncommissioned Officers and privates:.

That the Secretary at War inform the executive authorities of the respective states, in which the troops are to be raised, the number and rank of commissioned Officers to be furnished by each State, in proportion to the men.

That the pay and allowances to the troops, to be raised by this resolve, be the same as established by the Act of Congress of the 12 of April, 1785.

That the said troops shall be subject to the existing articles of war, or such as may hereafter be formed by Congress or a committee of the States.

That the board of treasury contract for a supply of Cloathing and rations, at such places and in such quantities as the Secretary at war shall judge necessary.

Resolved unanimously, That the states above-mentioned be, and they are hereby requested to use their utmost exertions, to raise the quotas of troops respectively assigned them, with all possible expedition, and that the executive of the said states be, and hereby are requested, in case any of their legislatures should not be in session, immediately to convene them for this purpose, as a delay may be attended with the most fatal Consequences.

Ordered, That the board of treasury, without delay, devise ways and means for the pay and support of the troops of the United States upon the present establishment, and report the same to Congress.

A Plan for the General Arrangement of the Militia of the United States (1786)

Secretary of War Henry Knox's decision to support the creation of the militia was crucial to the decision to keep it in the society. This plan went to Congress in January 1790.

That a well constituted Republic is more favorable to the liberties of society, and that its principles give an higher elevation to the human mind than any other form of Government, has generally been acknowledged by the unprejudiced and enlightened part of mankind.

But it is at the same time acknowledged, that unless a Republic prepares itself by proper arrangements to meet those exigencies to which all States are in a degree liable, that its peace and existence are more precarious than the forms of Government in which the will of one directs the conduct of the whole for the defence of the nation.

A Government whose measures must be the result of multiplied deliberations, is seldom in a situation to produce instantly those exertions which the occasion may demand; therefore it ought to possess such energetic establishments as should enable it by the vigor of its own citizens, to controul events as they arise instead of being convulsed or subverted by them . . .

May the United States avoid the errors and crimes of other Governments, and possess the wisdom to embrace the present invaluable opportunity of establishing such institutions as shall invigorate, exalt, and perpetuate, the great principles of freedom— an opportunity pregnant with the fate of millions, but rapidly borne on the wings of time, and may never again return.

The public mind unbiased by superstition or prejudice seems happily prepared to receive the impressions of wisdom—The latent springs of human action ascertained by the standard of experience, may be regulated and made subservient to the noble purpose of forming a dignified national character.

The causes by which nations, have ascended and declined through the various ages of the world, may be calmly and accurately determined; and the United States may be placed in the singularly fortunate condition of commencing their career of Empire with the accumulated knowledge of all the known societies and Governments of the Globe.

The strength of the Government like the strength of any other vast and complicated machine will depend on a due adjustment of its several parts—Its agriculture, its commerce, its laws, its finance, its system of defence, and its manners and habits all require consideration, and the highest exercise of political wisdom.

It is the intention of the present attempt to suggest the most efficient system of defence which may be compatible with the interests of a free people; a system which shall not only produce the expected effect, but in its operations shall also produce those habits and manners which will impart strength and durability to the whole Government.

The modern practice of Europe with respect to the employment of standing Armies has created such a mass of opinion in their favor that even Philosophers, and the advocates for liberty have frequently confessed their use and necessity in certain cases.

But whoever seriously and candidly estimates the power of discipline and the tendency of military habits will be constrained to confess, that whatever may be the efficacy of a standing Army in War, it cannot in peace be considered as friendly to the rights of human nature—The recent instance in France cannot with propriety be brought to overturn the general principle built upon the uniform experience of mankind—It may be found on examining the causes that appear to have influenced the Military of France, that while the springs of power were wound up in the nation to the highest pitch, that the discipline of the army was proportionably relaxed—But any argument on this head may be considered as unnecessary to the enlightened citizens of the United States.

A small Corps of well disciplined and well informed Artillerists and Engineers—and a Legion for the protection of the frontiers, and the Magazines and Arsenals are all the Military establishment which may be required for the present use of the United States—The privates of the Corps to be enlisted for a certain period and after the expiration of which to return to the mass of the Citizens.

An energetic National Militia is to be regarded as the *capital security* of a free republic, and not a standing Army forming a distinct class in the community.

It is the introduction and diffusion of vice and corruption of manners into the mass of the people that render a standing army necessary—It is when public spirit is despised, and avarice, indolence, and effeminacy of manners, predominate and prevent the establishment of institutions, which would elevate the minds of the youth in the paths of virtue and honor, that a standing Army is formed and rivetted forever.

Without this vital principle, the Government would be invaded or overturned and trampled upon by the bold and ambitious—no community can be long held together unless its arrangements are adequate to its probable exigencies.

If it should be decided to reject a standing Army for the military branch of the Government of the United States as possessing too feirce an aspect, and being hostile to the principles of liberty it will follow that a well constituted Militia ought to be established. A consideration of the subject will show the impracticability of disciplining at once the mass of the people. All discussions on the subject of a powerful Militia will result in one or the other of the following principles.

First: Either efficient institutions must be established for the military education of the youth, and that the knowledge acquired therein shall be diffused throughout the community by the mean of rotation.

Or Secondly: That the Militia must be formed of substitutes.

If the United States possess the vigor of mind to establish the first institution, it may reasonably be expected to produce the most unequivocal advantages—A glorious national spirit will be introduced with its extensive train of political consequences—the youth will imbibe a love of their country—reverence and obedience to its laws—courage and elevation of mind—openness and liberality of character—accompanied by a just spirit of honor. In addition to which their bodies will acquire a robustness—greatly conducive to their personal happiness as well as the defence of their country—While habit with its silent but efficacious operations will durably cement the system.

Habit that powerful and universal law, incessantly acting on the human race, well deserves the attention of legislatures . . .

The well informed members of the community, actuated by the highest motives of self love, would form the real defence of the country—Rebellions would be prevented or suppressed with ease. Invasions of such a Government would be undertaken only by madmen and the virtues and knowledge of the people would effectually oppose the introduction of Tyranny.

But the second principle—a Militia of substitutes—is pregnant in a degree with the mischeifs of a standing Army. Wealthy families proud of distinctions which riches may confer will prevent their sons from serving in the Militia of substitutes—the plan will degenerate into habitual contempt—a standing Army will be introduced, and the liberties of the people subjected to all the contingencies of events.

The expence attending an energetic establishment of militia may be strongly urged as an objection to the institution, but it is to be remembered that this objection is levelled at both systems, whether by, rotation, or by substitutes—For if the numbers are equal the expence will also be equal—The estimate of the expence will show its unimportance when compared with the magnitude, and beneficial effects of the institution.

But the people of the United States will cheerfully consent to the expences of a measure calculated to serve as a perpetual barrier to their liberties—especially as they well know that the disbursements will be made among the members of the same community, and therefore cannot be injurious.

Every intelligent mind would rejoice in the establishment of an institution, under whose auspices, the youth and vigor of the Constitution, would be renewed with each successive generation, and which would appear to secure the great principles of freedom and happiness, against the injuries of time and events.

The following plan is formed on these general principles.

1st. That it is the indispensible duty of every nation to establish all necessary institutions for its own perfection and defence.

2'ndly, That it is a capital security to a free State for the great body of the people to possess a competent knowledge of the military art.

3'dly, That this knowledge cannot be attained in the present state of society but by establishing adequate institutions for the military education of youth—And that the knowledge acquired therein should be diffused throughout the community by the principles of rotation.

4'thly That every man of the proper age, and ability of body is firmly bound by the social compact to perform personally his proportion of military duty for the defence of the State.

5'thly; That all men of the legal military age should be armed, enrolled and held responsible for different degrees of military service.

And 6thly, That agreeably to the Constitution the United States are to provide for organizing, arming and disciplining the Militia, and for governing such part of them as may be employed in the service of the United States, reserving to the States respectively the appointment of the officers, and the authority of training the Militia according to the discipline prescribed by Congress . . .

Constitution of the United States (1787)

The Constitution of the United States is the governing document on national military service. The United States drew its jurisprudence from a number of political philosophies, and these different strains melded into a unique view of the role of the military in society and as a mechanism for defending the nation.

Article 1, Section 8. The Congress shall have Power To lay and collect Taxes, Duties, Imposts and Excises, to pay the Debts and provide for the common Defence and general Welfare of the United States.

We the People of the United States, in Order to form a more perfect Union, establish Justice, insure domestic Tranquility, provide for the common defense, promote the general Welfare, and secure the Blessings of Liberty to ourselves and our Posterity, do ordain and establish this Constitution for the United States of America.

Article I, Section 8. To raise and support Armies, but no Appropriation of Money to that Use shall be for a longer Term than two Years

To provide and maintain a Navy

To make Rules for the Government and Regulation of the land and naval Forces;

To provide for calling forth the Militia to execute the Laws of the Union, suppress Insurrections and repel Invasions

To provide for organizing, arming, and disciplining, the Militia, and for governing such Part of them as may be employed in the Service of the United States, reserving to the States respectively, the Appointment of the Officers, and the Authority of training the Militia according to the discipline prescribed by Congress;

Article 1, Section 10. No State shall, without the Consent of Congress, lay any Duty of Tonnage, keep Troops, or Ships of War in time of Peace, enter into any Agreement or Compact with another State, or with a foreign Power, or engage in War, unless actually invaded, or in such imminent Danger as will not admit of delay.

Article 2, Section 2. The President shall be Commander in Chief of the Army and Navy of the United States, and of the Militia of the several States, when called into the actual Service of the United States; he may require the Opinion, in writing, of the principal Officer in each of the executive Departments, upon any Subject relating to the Duties of their respective Offices, and he shall have Power to grant Reprieves and Pardons for Offences against the United States, except in Cases of Impeachment.

Militia Act of 1792

Because of the historic tensions of the colonial period, the United States has an explicit document providing for the authority of the president to call out the militia. In most nations around the world, governments or individuals in position of governance would (and regularly do) view this as an inherent power. Not so for the United States.

Second Congress, Session I. Chapter XXVIII, Passed May 2, 1792 providing for the authority of the president to call out the Militia.

Section 1. . . . it shall be lawful for the President of the United States, to call forth such number of the militia of the state or states most convenient to the place of danger or scene of action as he may judge necessary to repel such invasion, and to issue his orders for that purpose, to such officer or officers of the militia as he shall think proper; and in case of an insurrection in any state, against the government thereof, it shall be lawful for the President of the United States, on application of the legislature of such state, or of the executive (when the legislature cannot be convened) to call forth such number of the militia of any other state or states, as may be applied for, or as he may judge sufficient to suppress such insurrection.

Section 2. *And be it further enacted,* That whenever the laws of the United States shall be *opposed or the execution thereof obstructed,* in any state, by combinations too powerful to be suppressed by the ordinary course of judicial proceedings, or by the powers vested in the marshals by this act, the same being notified to the President of the United States, by an associate justice or the district judge, it shall be lawful for the President of the United States to call forth the militia of such state to *suppress* such combinations, and to cause the laws to be duly executed. And if the militia of a state, where such combinations may happen, *shall refuse,* or be insufficient to suppress the same, it shall be lawful for the President, if the legislature of the United States be not in session, to call forth and employ such numbers of the militia of any other state or states most convenient thereto, as may be necessary, and the use of militia, so to be called forth, may be continued, if necessary, until the expiration of thirty days after the commencement of the ensuing session.

Section 3. *Provided always, and be it further enacted,* That whenever it may be necessary, in the judgment of the President, to use the military force hereby directed to be called forth, the President shall forthwith, . . . by proclamation, command such insurgents to disperse, and retire peaceably to their respective abodes, within a limited time.

Section 4. *And be it further enacted,* That the militia employed in the service of the United States, shall receive the same pay and allowances, as the troops of the United States, who may be in service at the same time, or who were last in service, and shall be subject to the same rules and articles of war: And that no officer, non-commissioned officer or private of the militia shall be compelled to serve more than three months in any one year, nor more than in due rotation with every other able-bodied man of the same rank in the battalion to which be belongs.

Section 5. *And be it further enacted,* That every officer, non-commissioned officer or private of the militia, who shall fail to obey the orders of the President of the United States in any of the cases before recited, shall forfeit a sum not exceeding one year's pay, and not less than one month's pay, to be determined and adjudged by a court martial; and such officers shall, moreover, be liable to be cashiered by sentence of a court martial: and such non-commissioned officers and privates shall be liable to be imprisoned by the like sentence, or failure of payment of the fines adjudged against them, for the space of one calendar month for every five dollars of such fine.

Section 6. *And be it further enacted,* That court martial for the trial of militia be composed of militia officers only.

Section 7. *And be it further enacted,* That all fines to be assessed, as aforesaid, shall be certified by the presiding officer of the court martial before whom the same shall be assessed, to the marshal of the district, in which the delinquent shall reside, or to one of his deputies; and also the supervisor of the revenue of the same district, who shall record the said certificate in a book to be kept for that purpose. The said marshal or his deputy shall forthwith proceed to levy the said fines with costs, by distress and sale of the goods and chattels of the delinquent, which costs and manner of proceeding, with respect to the sale of the goods distrained, shall be agreeable to the laws of the state, in which the same shall be, in other cases of distress; and where any non-commissioned officer or private shall be adjudged to suffer imprisonment, there being no goods or chattels to be found, whereof to levy the said fines, the marshal of the district or his deputy may commit such delinquent to gaol, during the term, for which he shall be so adjudged to imprisonment, or until the fine shall be paid, in the same manner as other persons condemned to fine and imprisonment at the suit of the United States, may be committed.

Section 8. *And be it further enacted,* That the marshals and their deputies shall pay all such fines by them levied to the supervisor of the revenue, in the district in which they are collected, within two months after they shall have received the same, deducting therefrom five per centum, as a compensation for their trouble; and in case of failure, the same shall be recoverable by action of debt or information in any court of the United States, of the district, in which such fines shall be levied, having cognizance therefor, to be sued for, prosecuted and recovered, in the name of the supervisor of the district, with interest and costs.

Section 9. *And be it further enacted,* That the marshals of the several districts and deputies, shall have the same powers in executing the laws of the United States, as sheriffs, and their deputies in the several states have by law, in executing the laws of their respective states.

Section 10. *And be it further enacted,* That this act shall continue and be in force, for and during the term of two years, and from thence to the end of the next session of Congress thereafter, and no longer.

James Madison's State of the Union Address, December 5, 1815 (excerpt)

President Madison's views after the troubling War of 1812 about the need to solidify a "military peace establishment" were viewed with a new lens after the first conflict of the young nation's history.

The execution of the act for fixing the military peace establishment has been attended with difficulties which even now can only be overcome by legislative aid. The selection of officers, the payment and discharge of the troops enlisted for the war, the payment of the retained troops and their reunion from detached and distant stations, the collection and security of the public property in the Quartermaster, Commissary, and Ordnance departments, and the constant medical assistance required in hospitals and garrisons rendered a complete execution of the act impracticable on the 1st of May, the period more immediately contemplated. As soon, however, as circumstances would permit, and as far as it has been practicable consistently with the public interests, the reduction of the Army has been accomplished; but the appropriations for its pay and for other branches of the military service having proved inadequate, the earliest attention to that subject will be necessary; and the expediency of continuing upon the peace establishment the staff officers who have hitherto been provisionally retained is also recommended to the consideration of Congress.

Militia Act of 1862 (July 17, 1862)

The nation's fabric was stretched thin during the war between the states, as were the military forces used to fight the conflict. Early in the Civil War the Militia Act tried to regularize the forces used in the conflict.

Chapter CCI. An Act to amend the Act calling forth the Militia to execute the Laws of the Union, suppress Insurrections, and repel Invasions, approved February twenty-eight, seventeen hundred and ninety-five, and the Acts amendatory thereof, and for other Purposes.

Section 12. *And be it further enacted,* That the President be, and he is hereby, authorized to receive into the service of the United States, for the purpose of constructing intrenchments, or performing camp service or any other labor, or any military or naval service for which they may be found competent, persons of African descent, and such persons shall be enrolled and organized under such regulations, not inconsistent with the Constitution and laws, as the President may prescribe.

Section 13. *And be it further enacted,* That when any man or boy of African descent, who by the laws of any State shall owe service or labor to any person who, during the present rebellion, has levied war or has borne arms against the United States, or adhered to their enemies by giving them aid and comfort, shall render any such service as is provided for in this act, he, his mother and his wife and children, shall forever thereafter be free, any law, usage, or custom whatsoever to the contrary notwithstanding: Provided, That the mother, wife and children of such man or boy of African descent shall not be made free by the operation of this act except where such mother, wife or children owe service or labor to some person who, during the present rebellion, has borne arms against the United States or adhered to their enemies by giving them aid and comfort

Section 14. *And be it further enacted,* That the expenses incurred to carry this act into effect shall be paid out of the general appropriation for the army and volunteers.

Section 15. *And be it further enacted,* That all persons who have been or shall be hereafter enrolled in the service of the United States under this act shall receive the pay and rations now allowed by law to soldiers, according to their respective grades: *Provided,* That persons of African descent, who under this law shall be employed, shall receive ten dollars per month and one ration, three dollars of which monthly pay may be in clothing.

APPROVED, July 17, 1862.

Posse Comitatus (1878)

One of the more often cited laws about U.S. military service, the 1878 act prohibited the U.S. armed forces from being used in domestic situations, responding to those who still feared that an unreasonable government or individual could use the standing military to oppress American citizens.

Chapter 263. An act making appropriations for the support of the Army for the fiscal year ending June thirtieth, eighteen hundred and seventy-nine, and for other purposes.

Section 15. From and after the passage of this act it shall not be lawful to employ any part of the Army of the United States, as a posse comitatus, or otherwise, for the purpose of executing the laws, except in such cases and under such circumstances as such employment of said force may be expressly authorized by the Constitution or by act of Congress; and no money appropriated by this act shall be used to pay any of the expenses incurred in the employment of any troops in violation of this section And any person willfully violating the provisions of this section shall be deemed guilty of a misdemeanor and on conviction thereof shall be punished by fine not exceeding ten thousand dollars or imprisonment not exceeding two years or by both such fine and imprisonment.

10 U.S.C. (United States Code) 375. Section 375. Restriction on direct participation by military personnel. The Secretary of Defense shall prescribe such regulations as may be necessary to ensure that any activity (including the provision of any equipment or facility or the assignment or detail of any personnel) under this chapter does not include or permit direct participation by a member of the Army, Navy, Air Force, or Marine Corps in a search, seizure, arrest, or other similar activity unless participation in such activity by such member is otherwise authorized by law.

18 U.S.C. 1385. Section 1385. Use of Army and Air Force as posse comitatus. Whoever, except in cases and under circumstances expressly authorized by the Constitution or Act of Congress, willfully uses any part of the Army or the Air Force as a posse comitatus or otherwise to execute the laws shall be fined under this title or imprisoned not more than two years, or both.

The Dick Act (1903)

Between 1903 and the 1920s, new legislation strengthened the Army National Guard as a component of the national defense force. The Dick

Act of 1903 replaced the 1792 Militia Act and affirmed the National Guard as the Army's primary organized reserve. The Dick Act of 1903 regularized the militia forces from each state into the National Guard, which now operates in each state and under the governor's dictates in the states. This standardization was crucial to the nation's sense of national service.

57th Congress, 2nd Session. Report No. 2129.
Efficiency of the Militia. December 4, 1902—Ordered to be printed.

Mr. Proctor, from the Committee on Military Affairs, submitted the following report to accompany H. R. 15345..

The Committee on Military Affairs, to whom was referred the bill (H. R. 15345) to promote the efficiency of the militia, and for other purposes, have considered the same and submit the following report:

The President in his message to Congress recommends the passage of the bill: The measure providing for the reorganization of the militia system and for securing the highest efficiency in the National Guard, which has already passed the House, should receive prompt attention and action. It is of great importance that the relation of the National Guard to the militia and volunteer forces of the United States should be defined, and that in place of our present obsolete laws a practical and efficient system should be adopted.

The Secretary of War, in his very able annual report, explains the measure so clearly and concisely in the following language that in the opinion of your committee little further need be said:

I earnestly urge that this measure be made a law. It is really absurd that the nation which maintains but a small Regular Army and depends upon unprofessional citizen soldiery for its defense should run along as we have done for one hundred and ten years under a militia law which never worked satisfactorily in the beginning, and which was perfectly obsolete before any man now fit for military duty was born. The result is that we have practically no militia system, notwithstanding the fact that the Constitution makes it the duty of the Federal Congress "to provide for organizing, arming, and disciplining the militia," and "for calling forth the militia to execute the laws of the Union, suppress insurrections, and repel invasions."

The National Guard organizations of the several States have grown up in default of any national system, and to meet local requirements. Their relations to the Federal Government have never been defined or settled. The confusion, controversy, and bad feeling arising from this uncertain status were painfully apparent at the beginning of the war with Spain; and it must always be the same until Congress shall exercise its constitutional power over the subject. Repeated efforts have been made to accomplish this result. Two years after the passage of the present law of 1792, President Washington addressed Congress on the subject in these words: "The devising and establishing of a well-regulated militia would be a genuine source of legislative honour and a perfect title to public gratitude. I therefore entertain a hope that the present session will not pass without carrying to its full energy the power of organizing, arming, and disciplining the militia, and thus providing, in the language of the Constitution, for calling them forth to execute the laws of the Union, suppress insurrection, and repel invasions."

President Jefferson, eleven years later, in 1805, said: "I can not, then, but earnestly recommend to your early consideration the expediency of so modifying out militia system as, by a separation of the more active part from that which is less so, we may draw from it, when necessary, an efficient corps for real and active service, etc."

And in 1808 he said: "For a people who are free, and who mean to remain so, a well-organized and armed militia is their best security. It is therefore incumbent on us at every meeting to revise the condition of the militia and to ask ourselves if it is prepared to repel a powerful enemy at every point of our territories exposed to invasion. Some of the States have paid a laudable attention to this subject; but every degree of neglect is to be found among others. Congress alone has power to produce a uniform state of preparation in this great organ of defense. The interest which they so deeply feel; in their own and their country's security will present this as among the most important objects of their deliberation."

President Madison said in 1816: "An efficient militia is authorized and contemplated by the Constitution and required by the spirit and safety of free government. The present organization of our militia is universally regarded as less efficient than it ought be made, and no organization can be better calculated to give to it its due force than a classification which will assign the foremost place in the defense of the country to that portion of its citizens whose activity and animation best enable them to rally to its standard, etc."

President Monroe said in 1817: "An improvement in the organization and discipline of the militia is one of the great objects which claims the unremitted attention of Congress."

Almost every President, from Washington down, has urged the importance of this subject upon the attention of Congress. The chief reason why nothing has been done has been that nobody could agree upon any one system. Everybody was agreed upon the general principle, but a majority of all the people interested were opposed to every particular concrete method suggested to give it effect.

The bill which has now passed the House is the result of extensive and painstaking conference among representatives of all the classes of citizens especially interested in the subject and especially qualified to express opinions upon it. It does not represent fully anyone's view, but it contains many important provisions upon which a general agreement has been reached; and it will, I am sure, if enacted, be a great step in advance toward effective preparation for war otherwise than by the maintenance of a standing army.

The fundamental idea of the bill is to recognize the value to the National Government of the National Guard, which is capable of being utilized, first, as active militia when called out by the President for the specific purposes enumerated in the Constitution; second, as an already organized volunteer force when its organizations respond as such to calls for volunteers. The bill undertakes to regulate and provide for these various relations of the National Guard and its members to the general system; to conform the organization, armament, and disciple of the guard to that of the Regular and Volunteer armies of the United States; to establish closer relations and better cooperation between the National Guard and the Regular Army; to promote the efficiency and dignity of the guard as a apart of the military system of the United States.

To aid in accomplishing these objects, and in recognition of the benefits to the General Government that come from the Guard altogether outside of its service to the individual States. the bill provides that the General Government shall furnish to the Guard the same arms which it furnishes to the Regular Army, and for the voluntary participation by the Guard with Regular Army in maneuvers and field exercises for brief periods in each year. The bill also contains provisions making National Guard organizations which choose voluntarily to go beyond the limitations of militia service in effect a First Volunteer Reserve, and further provisions for the enrollment of a Second Volunteer reserve not exceeding 100,000 to be composed of trained men who have served in the National Guard or in the Regular Army or the volunteer armies of the United States. These would constitute the first volunteer regiments after the National Guard Volunteers under any call by Congress. It also provides for ascertaining by practical tests, in advance of a call for volunteers, the fitness of members of the National Guard, graduates of the military schools and colleges, and other citizens with military training, to hold volunteer commissions, thus constituting an eligible list from which in case of a call for volunteers the officers of the Second Reserve must be taken, and officers of the general body of volunteers may be taken. With the system provided for by the bill carried into effect we should be able while maintaining a standing army of but 60,000 men to put a force of at least 250,000 well-trained men into the field instantly upon a declaration of war, and the cost would be less than to maintain but a few additional regiments of regular troops.

The military force of the United States would then be as follows:

First. The Regular Army, capable of enlargement by the President, when he sees war coming, to 100,000.

Second. Such of the organized militia (already trained as a national guard, and just as valuable, when used in the manner hereinafter indicated, as any other troops) as the President shall see fit to call into the service of the United States for not exceeding nine months, to repel invasion.

Third. A First Volunteer Reserve, composed of such companies, troops, and regiments of the organized militia already trained as a national guard as volunteers by organizations with all their officers and men.

Fourth. A Second Volunteer Reserve, composed of men previously enrolled and having previous military training in the National Guard, the Regular Amy, or the Volunteer Army, and commanded by officers whose fitness has been previously ascertained by practical tests under the provisions of the militia act.

Fifth. Such further volunteers as it may be necessary to call forth from the States, according to their respective quotas, and commanded by regimental officers appointed by the governors of the States.

A conservative estimate of the number which would be included in the first four classes of troops, who have already had military service and will be available for immediate action, is from 250,000 to 300,000.

The number of the fifth class—volunteers who may or may not have had previous service—has no limit, except the possibilities of transportation and supply.

The capacity of the National Guard organization in general to serve effectively as organizations, either militia or volunteer, in the National Army in case of war depends very largely upon the aid which they receive from the National Government. The guard is now armed with a variety of weapons of different kinds and calibers, including two different calibers of the obsolete Springfield rifle, the Lee, the Remington-Lee, the Winchester, and the Krag-Jörgenson. In several instances different National Guard organizations of the same State are armed with different weapons of different calibers. Among all the 115,000 National Guardsmen of the different States and Territories only about 4,000 have the modern service rifle of the United States Army. With the exception of these 4,000 rifles the arms of the guard would be practically worthless in time of war, not merely because they are inferior, but because the guard would have to look to the United States Government for their ammunition, and the Government will have no ammunition for the kind of rifles they carry; they would have to look to the Government to replace the arms lost or broken in service, and the Government will be unable to supply the same kind. The militia and the volunteer National Guard organizations in general would therefore be obliged to throw away their present arms at the beginning or a war and get reequipped with weapons the use of which they had never learned.

The Committee on Militia in the House of Representatives make a very elaborate and full report, and unanimously recommend the passage of the bill.

Your committee, after full consideration, also recommend the passage of the bill.

National Defense Act, 1916

The National Defense Act of 1916, which immediately preceded U.S. entry to World War I, was probably the most important U.S. law of the twentieth century because it organized forces into the National Guard beyond what the Dick Act had stated. These forces had regular pay, training, and a title.

Chapter 134, 39 Stat. 166—An Act for making further and more effectual provision for the national defense, and for other purposes.

Be it enacted by the Senate and House of Representatives of the United States in Congress assembled, That the Army of the United States shall consist of the Regular Army, the Volunteer Army, the Officers' Reserve Corps, the Enlisted Reserve Corps, the National Guard while in the service of the United States, and such other land forces as are now or may thereafter be authorized by law.

Section 2. Composition of the Regular Army

The Regular Army of the United States, including the existing organizations, shall consist of regiments of Infantry, regiments of Cavalry, regiments of Field Artillery, a Coast Artillery Corps, . . .the Regular Army Reserve, all organized as hereinafter provided, and the following as now authorized by law: The officers and enlisted men on the retired list; the additional officers; the professors, the Corps of Cadets, the general Army service detachment, and detachments of Cavalry, Field Artillery, and

Engineers, and the band of the United States Military Academy; the post noncommissioned staff officers; the recruiting parties, the recruit depot detachments, and unassigned recruits; the disciplinary organizations; the Indian Scouts, and such other officers and enlisted men as are now or may be hereafter provided for: Provided, That hereafter the enlisted personnel of all organizations of the Regular Army shall at times be maintained at a strength not below the minimum strength fixed by law: Provided further, That the total enlisted force of the line of the Regular Army . . . shall not at any time, except in the event of actual or threatened war or similar emergency in which the public safety demands it, exceed one hundred seventy-five thousand men: Provided further, That the unassigned recruits at depots or elsewhere shall at no time, except in time of war, exceed by more than seven per centum the total authorized enlisted strength . . .

   Section 23. Original Appointments to Be Provisional. Hereafter all military appointments of persons other than graduates of the United States Military Academy to the grade of second lieutenant in the Regular Army shall be provisional for a period for two years, at the close of which period such appointments shall be made permanent if the appointees shall have demonstrated, under such regulations as the President may prescribe, their suitability and moral, professional, and physical fitness for such permanent appointment, but should any appointee fail so to demonstrate his suitability and fitness, his appointment shall terminate; and should any officer become eligible for promotion to a vacancy in a higher grade and quality therefor before the expiration of two years from the date of his original appointment, he shall receive a provisional appointment in such higher grade, which appointment shall be made permanent when he shall have qualified for permanent appointment upon the expiration of two years from the date of his original appointment, or shall terminate if he shall fail so to qualify . . .

   Vacancies in the grade of second lieutenant, created or caused by the increases due to this Act, in any fiscal year shall be filled by the appointment in the following order:

   1.   Of cadets graduated from the United States Military Academy during the preceding fiscal year for whom vacancies did not become available during the fiscal year in which they were graduated;

   2.   Under the provisions of existing law, of enlisted men, including officers of the Philippine Scouts, whose fitness for promotion shall have been determined by competitive examination;

   3.   Of members of the Officers' Reserve Corps between the ages of twenty-one and twenty-seven years;

4. Of commissioned officers of the National Guard between the ages of twenty-one and twenty-seven years;

5. Of such honor graduates, between the ages of twenty-one and twenty-seven years, of distinguished colleges as are now or may hereafter be entitled to preference by general orders of the War Department; and

6. Of candidates from civil life between the ages of twenty-one and twenty-seven years; and the President is authorized to make the necessary rules and regulations to carry these provisions into effect; *Provided,* That any such original vacancies not so filled, and remaining at the time of graduation of any class at the United States Military Academy, may be filled by the appointment of members of that class; and all vacancies in the grade of second lieutenant not created or caused by the increases due to this Act shall be filled as provided in the Act . . .

Section 30. Composition of the Regular Army Reserve. The Regular Army Reserve shall consist of, first, all enlisted men now in the Army Reserve or who shall hereafter become members of the Army Reserve under the provisions of existing law; second, all enlisted men furloughed to or enlisted in the Regular Army Reserve under the provisions of this Act; and, third, any person holding an honorable discharge from the Regular Army with character reported at least good who is physically qualified for the duties of a soldier and not over forty-five years of age who enlists in the Regular Army Reserve for a period of four years.

Section 31. The President is authorized to assign members of the Regular Army Reserve as reserves to particular organizations of the Regular Army, or to organize the Regular Army Reserve, or any part in such manner as he may prescribe, and to assign to such units and detachment officers of the Regular Army or of the Officers' Reserve Corps herein provided for; and he may summon the Regular Army during such periods of training; and in the event of actual or threatened hostilities he may mobilize the Regular Army Reserve in such manner as he may determine, and thereafter retain it, or any part thereof, in active service for such period as he may determine the conditions demand: *Provided,* That all enlistments in the Regular Army, including those in the Regular Army Reserve, which are in force on the date of the outbreak of war shall continue in force for one year, unless sooner terminated by order of the Secretary of War, but noting herein shall be construed to shorten the time of enlistment prescribed: *Provided further,* That subject to such regulars as the President may prescribe for their proper identification, and location, and physical condition, the members of the Regular Army Reserve shall be paid semiannually at the rate of $24 a year while in the reserve.

Section 32. Regular Army Reserve in Time of War. When mobilized by order of the President, the members of the Regular Army Reserve shall, so long as they may remain in active service, receive the pay and allowances of enlisted men of the Regular Army of like grades: *Provided,* That any enlisted man who shall have reenlisted in the Regular Army Reserve shall receive during such active service the additional pay now provided by law for enlisted men in his arm of the service in the second enlistment period: *Provided further,* That upon returning for duty, and being found physically fit for service, members of the Regular Army shall receive a sum equal to $3 per month for each month during which they shall have belonged to the reserve, as well as the actual necessary cost of transportation and subsistence from their homes to the places at which they may be ordered to report for duty under such summons: *And provided further,* That service in the Regular Army Reserve shall confer no right to retirement or retired pay, and members of the Regular Army Reserve shall become entitled to pension only through disability incurred while on active duty in the service of the United States.

Section 37. the Officers' Reserve Corps. For the purpose of securing a reserve of officers available for service as temporary officers in the Regular Army, as provided for in this Act and in section eight of the Act approved April twenty-fifth, nineteen hundred and fourteen, as officers of the Quartermaster Corps and other staff corps and departments, as officers for recruit rendezvous and depots, and as officers of volunteers, there shall be organized, under such rules and regulations of this Act, an Officers' Reserve Corps of the Regular Army. Said corps shall consist of sections corresponding to the various arms, staff corps, and departments of the Regular Army. Except as otherwise herein provided, a member of the Officers' Reserve Corps shall not be subject to call for service in time of peace, and whenever called upon for service shall not, without his consent, be so called in a lower grade than tat held by him in said reserve corps.

The President alone shall be authorized to appoint and commission as reserve officers in the various sections of the Officers' Reserve Corps, in all grades up to and including that of major, such citizens as, upon examination prescribed by the President, shall be found physically, mentally, and morally qualified to hold such commissions: *Provided,* That the proportion of officers in any section of the Officers' Reserve Corps shall not exceed the proportion for the same grade in the corresponding arm, corps, or department of the Regular Army, except that the number of commissioned in the lowest authorized grade in any section of the Officers' Reserve Corps shall not be limited . . .

Section 38. the Officers' Reserve Corps in War. In time of actual or threatened hostilities the President may order officers of the Officers' Reserve Corps, subject to such subsequent physical examinations as he may prescribe, to temporary duty with the Regular Army in grades thereof which can not, for the time being, be filled by promotion, or as officers in volunteer or other organizations that may be authorized by law, or as officers at recruit rendezvous and depots, or on such other duty as the President may prescribe. While such reserve officers are on such service they shall, by virtue of their commission as reserve officers, exercise command appropriate to their grades in the Regular Army with increase of pay for length of active service, as allowed by law for officers of the Regular Army, from the date upon which they shall be required by the terms of their orders to obey the same: *Provided,* That officers so ordered to active service shall take temporary rank among themselves, and in their grades in the organization to which assigned, according to the dates of orders placing them on active service, to vacancies in volunteer organizations or to temporary vacancies in the Regular Army thereafter occurring in the organizations in which they shall be serving: *Provided further,* That officers of the Officers' Reserve Corps shall not be entitled to retirement incurred in the line of duty and while in active service.

Any officer who, while holding a commission in the Officers' Reserve Corps, shall be ordered to active service by the Secretary of War shall, from time he shall be required by the terms of his order to obey the same, be subject to the laws and regulations for the government of the Army for the United States, in so far as they are applicable to officers whose permanent retention in the military service is not contemplated.

Section 39. Instruction of Officers of the Officers' Reserve Corps. To the extent provided for from time to time by appropriations for this specific purpose, the Secretary of War is authorized to order reserve officers to duty with troops or at field exercises, or for instruction, for periods not to exceed fifteen days in any one calendar year, and while so servicing such officers shall receive the pay and allowances of their respective grades in the Regular Army . . .

Section 40. The Reserve Officers' Training Corps. The President is hereby authorized to establish and maintain in civil educational institutions a Reserve Officers' Training Corps, which shall consist of a senior division organized at universities and colleges requiring four years of collegiate study for a degree, including State universities and those State institutions that are required to provide instruction in military tactics under the provisions of the Act of Congress of July second, eighteen hundred and sixty-two, donating lands for the establishment of colleges where the leading object shall be practical instruction in agriculture and the mechanical arts, including military tactics, and a junior division organized at all other public or private educational institutions, except that units of the senior division may be organized at those essentially military schools which do not confer an academic degree but which as a result of the annual inspection of such institutions by the War Department, are specially designated by the Secretary of War as qualified for units of the senior division, and each division shall consist of units of the several arms or corps in such number and of such strength as the President may prescribe.

Section 41. The President may, upon the application of any State institution described in section forty of this Act, establish and maintain at such institution one or more units of the Reserve Officers' Training Corps: *Provided,* That no such unit shall be established or maintained at any such institution until an officer of the Army shall have been detailed as professor of military science and tactics, nor until such institution shall maintain under military instruction at least one hundred physically fit male students . . .

Section 43. The Secretary of War is hereby authorized to prescribe standard courses of theoretical and practical military training for units of the Reserve Officers' Training Corps, and no unit of the senior division shall be organized or maintained at any educational institution the authorities of which fail or neglect to adopt into their curriculum the prescribed courses of military training for the senior division or to devote at least an average of three hours per week per academic year to such military training; and no unit of the junior division shall be organized or maintained at any educational institution the authorities of which fail or neglect to adopt into their curriculum the prescribed courses or military training for the junior division, or to devote at least an average of three hours per week per academic year to such military training.

Section 44. Eligibility to membership in the Reserve Officers' Training Corps shall be limited to students of institutions in which units of such corps may be established who are citizens of the United States, who are not less than fourteen years of age, and whose bodily condition indicates that they are physically fit to perform military duty, or will be so upon arrival at military age . . .

Section 48. The Secretary of War is hereby authorized to maintain camps for the further practical instruction of the members of the Reserve Officers' Training Corps, no such camps to be maintained for a period longer than six weeks in any one year, except in time of the actual or threatened hostilities; to transport members of such corps to and from such camps at the expense of the United States so far as appropriations will permit; to subsist them at the expense of the united States while traveling to and from such camps and while remaining therein so far as appropriations will permit; to use the Regular Army, such other military forces as Congress from time to time authorizes, and such Government property as he may deem in attendance at such camps; to prescribe regulations for the government of such corps; and to authorize, in his discretion, the formation of company units thereof into battalion and regimental units . . .

Section 54. Training Camps. The Secretary of War is hereby authorized to maintain, upon military reservations or elsewhere, camps for the military instruction and training of such citizens as may be selected for such instruction and training . . . to use, for the purpose of maintaining said camps and imparting military instruction and training threat, such arms, ammunition, accouterments, equipments, tentage, field equipage, and transportation belonging to the United States as he may deem necessary; to furnish, at the expense of the United States, uniforms, subsistence, transportation by the most usual and direct route within such limits as to territory as the Secretary of War may prescribe, and medical supplies to persons receiving instruction at said camps during the period of their attendance thereat, to authorize such expenditures from proper Army appropriations, as he may deem necessary for water, fuel, light, temporary structures, not including quarters for officers nor barracks for men, screening, and damages resulting from field exercises, and other expenses incidental to the maintenance of said camps, and the theoretical winter instruction in connection therewith; and to sell to persons receiving instruction at said camps, for cash and at cost price plus ten per centum, quartermaster and ordnance property, the amount of such property sold to any one person to be limited to that which is required for is proper equipment. All moneys arising from such sales shall remain available throughout the fiscal year in which the sales are made, for the purpose of that appropriation from which the property sold was authorized to be supplied at the time for the sale. The Secretary of War is authorized further to prescribe the courses of theoretical and practical instruction to be pursued by persons attending the camps authorized by this section . . .

Section 55. The Enlisted Reserve Corps. For the purpose of security an additional reserve of enlisted men for military service . . . an Enlisted Reserve Corps, to consist of such number of enlisted men of such grade or grades as may be designated by the President from time to time, is hereby authorized . . .

There may be enlisted in the grade or grades herein before specified, for a period of four years, under such rules as may be prescribed by the President, citizens of the United States, or persons who have declared their intentions to become citizens of the United States, subject to such physical, educational, and practical examination as may be prescribed in said rules. For men enlisting in said grade or grades certificates of enlistment in the Enlisted Reserve Corps shall be issued by the Adjutant General of the Army, but no such man shall be enlisted in said corps unless he shall be found physically, mentally, and morally qualified to hold such certificate and unless man shall be between the ages of eighteen and forty-five years. The certificates so given shall confer upon the holders when called into the active service or for purposes of instruction and training, and during the period of such active service, instruction, or training, all the authority, rights, and privileges of like grades of the Regular Army. Enlisted men of the Enlisted Reserve Corps shall take precedence in said corps according to the dates of their certificates of enlistment therein and when called into active service or when called out for purposes of instruction or training shall take precedence next below all other enlisted men of like grades in the Regular Army . . .

Section 57. Composition of the Militia. The militia of the United States shall consist of all able-bodied male citizens of the United States and all other able-bodied males who have or shall have declared their intention to become citizens of the United States, who shall have declared their intention to become citizens of the United States, who shall be more than eighteen years of age and, except as hereinafter provided, not more than forty-five years of age, and said militia shall be divided into three classes, the National Guard, the Naval Militia, and the Unorganized Militia.

Section 58. Composition of the National Guard. The National Guard shall consist of the regularly enlisted militia between the ages of eighteen and forty-five years organized, armed, and equipped as hereinafter provided, and of commissioned officers between the ages of twenty-one and sixty-four years . . .

Section 60. Organization of National Guard Units. Except as otherwise specifically provided herein, the organization of the National Guard, including the composition of all units thereof, shall be the same as that which is or may hereafter be prescribed for the Regular Army, subject in time of peace to such general exceptions as may be authorized by the Secretary of War . . .

Section 61. Maintenance of Other Troops by the States. No State shall maintain troops in time of peace other than as authorized in accordance with the organization prescribed under this Act: *Provided,* That nothing contained in this Act shall be construed as limiting the rights of the States and Territories in the use of the National Guard within their respective borders in time of peace: *Provided further,* That nothing contained in this Act shall prevent the organization and maintenance of State police or constabulary . . .

Section 67. Appropriation, Apportionment, and Disbursement of Funds for the National Guard. A sum of money shall hereafter be appropriated annually, to be paid out of any money in the Treasury not otherwise appropriated, for the support of the National Guard, including the expense of providing arms, ordnance stores, quartermaster stores, and camp equipage, and all other military supplies for issue to the National Guard, and such other expenses pertaining to said guard as are now or may hereafter be authorized by law . . .

The governor of each State and Territory and commanding general of the National Guard of the District of Columbia shall appoint, designate, or detail subject to the approval of the Secretary of War, an officer of the National Guard of the State, Territory, or District of Columbia who shall be regarded as property and disbursing officer for the United States . . .

Section 78. The National Guard Reserve. Subject to such rules and regulations as the President may prescribe, a National Guard Reserve shall be organized in each State, Territory, and the District of Columbia, and shall consist of such organizations, officers, and enlisted men as the President may prescribe, or members thereof may be assigned as reserves to an active organization of the National Guard: *Provided,* That members of said reserve, when engaged in field or coast-defense training with the active National Guard, shall receive the same Federal pay and allowances as enlisted men of like grade on the active list of said guard when likewise engaged: *Provided further,* That, except as otherwise specifically provided in this Act, no commissioned or enlisted reservist shall receive any pay or allowances out of any appropriation made by Congress for National Guard purposes . . .

Section 91. Discipline to Conform to That of Regular Army. The discipline (which includes training) of the National Guard shall conform to the system which is now or may hereafter be prescribed for the Regular Army, and the training shall be carried out by the several States, Territories, and the District of Columbia so as to conform to the provisions of this Act . . .

Section 94. Encampments and Maneuvers. Under such regulations as the President may prescribe the Secretary of War is authorized to provide for the participation of the whole or any part of the National Guard in encampments, maneuvers, or other exercises, including outdoor target practice, for field or coast-defense instruction, either independently or in conjunction with any part of the Regular Army, and there may be set aside from the funds appropriated for that purpose and allotted to any State, Territory, or the District of Columbia, such portion of said funds as may be necessary for the payment, subsistence, transportation, and other proper expenses of such portion of the National Guard of such State, Territory, or the District of Columbia as shall participate in such encampments, maneuvers, or other exercises, including outdoor target practice, for field and coast-defense instruction; and the officers and enlisted men of such National Guard while so engaged shall be entitled to the same pay, subsistence, and transportation of officers and enlisted men of corresponding grades of the Regular Army are or hereafter may be entitled by law . . .

Section 99. National Guard Officers and Men at Service Schools, and So Forth. Under such regulations as the President may prescribe, the Secretary of War may, upon the recommendation of the governor of any State or Territory or the commanding general of the National Guard of the District of Columbia, authorize a limited number of selected officers or enlisted men of the National Guard to attend and pursue a regular course of study at any military service school of the United States, except the United States Military Academy; or to be attached to an organization of the same arm, corps, or department to which such officer or enlisted man shall belong, for routine practical instruction at or near an Army post during a period of field training or other outdoor exercises; and such officer or enlisted man shall receive, out of any National Guard allotment of funds available for the purpose, the same travel allowances and quarters, or commutation of quarters, and the same pay, allowances, and subsistence to which an officer or enlisted man of the Regular Army would be entitled for attending such school, college, or practical course of instruction under orders from proper military authority, while in actual attendance at such school, college, or practical course of instruction: *Provided*, That in no case shall the pay and allowances authorized by this section exceed those of a captain . . .

Section 101. National Guard, When Subject to Laws Governing Regular Army. The National Guard when called as such into the service of the United States shall, from the time they are required by the terms of the call to respond thereto, be subject to the laws and regulations governing the Regular Army, so far as such laws and regulations are applicable to the officers and enlisted men whose permanent retention in the military service, either on the active list or on the retired list, is not contemplated by existing law . . .

Section 111. National Guard When Drafted into Federal Service. When Congress shall have authorized the use of the armed land forces of the United States, for any purpose requiring the use of troops in excess of those of the Regular Army, the President may, under such regulations, including such physical examination, as he may prescribe, draft into the military service of the United States, to serve therein for the period of the war unless sooner discharged, any or all members of the National Guard and of the National Guard Reserve . . .

Subsequent Amendments to This Law Since Enactment.
U.S. Code, amendments. 65 Stat. 710, Ch. 655, Oct. 31, 1951; Amendment in sec. 53 at 65 Stat. 728

Armed Forces Reserve Act of 1952. 66 Stat. 481, Ch. 608, July 9, 1952; Amendment in sec. 806 at 66 Stat. 506

National Defense Act, amendment. 67 Stat. 35, Ch. 69, May 27, 1953; Amendment at 67 Stat. 35

National Defense Act, amendment. 68 Stat. 451, Ch. 462, July 6, 1954; Amendment at 68 Stat. 451

National Defense Act, amendment. 68 Stat. 896, Ch. 1039, Aug. 28, 1954; Amendment at 68 Stat. 896

Reserve Officer Personnel Act of 1954. 68 Stat. 1147, Ch. 1257, Sept. 3, 1954; Amendment in sec. 702(b) at 68 Stat. 1188

State Defense Forces. 69 Stat. 686, Ch. 802, Aug. 11, 1955; Amendment at 69 Stat. 686

U.S. Code, titles 10 and 32. 70 Stat. 1126, Ch. 1041, Aug. 10, 1956; Amendment in sec. 53(b) at 70A Stat. 641

Selective Training and Service Act of 1940

The 1940 law, written not long before the United States entered World War II, began to establish a size of the national force (and its components) to protect national security. This was crucial to the concept of national service. The 1940 act remained a basic law for selective service throughout the period from World War II to 1973. Subsequently, training remained important, but it appealed to a different type of military.

Public Law No. 783, Compilation of the Military Selective Service Act (MSSA); 50 U.S.C. App. 451 et seq.

To provide for the common defense by increasing the personnel of the armed forces of the United States and providing for its training.

Be it enacted by the Senate and House of Representatives of the United States of America in Congress assembled, That

(a) the Congress hereby declares that it is imperative to increase and train the personnel of the armed forces of the United States.

(b) The Congress further declares that in a free society the obligations and privileges of military training and service should be shared generally in accordance with a fair and just system of selective compulsory military training and service.

(c) The Congress further declares, in accordance with our traditional military policy as expressed in the National Defense Act of 1916, as amended, that it is essential that the strength and organization of the National Guard, as an integral part of the first-line defenses of this Nation, be at all times maintained and assured. To this end, it is the intent of the Congress that whenever the Congress shall determine that troops are needed for the national security in excess of those in the Regular Army and those in active training and service under section 3 (b), the National Guard of the United States, or such part thereof as may be necessary, shall be ordered to active Federal service and continued therein so long as such necessity exists.

Section 2. Except as otherwise provided in this Act, it shall be the duty of every male citizen of the United States, and of every male alien residing in the United States, who, on this day or days fixed for the first or any subsequent registration, is between the ages of twenty-one and thirty-six, to present himself for and submit to registration at such time or times and place or places, and in such manner and in such age group or groups, as shall be determined by rules and regulations prescribed hereunder.

Section 3. (a) Except as otherwise provided in this Act, every male citizen of the United States, and every male alien residing in the United States who has declared his intention to become such a citizen, between the ages of twenty-one and thirty-six at the time fixed for his registration, shall be liable for training and service in the land or naval forces of the United States. The President is authorized from time to time, whether or not a state of war exists, to select and induct into the land and naval forces of the United States for training and service, in the manner provided in this Act, such number of men as in his judgment is required for such forces in the national interest: Provided, That within the limits of the quota determined under section 4 for the subdivision in which he resides, any person, regardless of race or color, between the ages of eighteen and thirty-six, shall be afforded an opportunity to volunteer for induction in the land or naval forces of the United States for the training and service prescribed in subsection (b), but no person who so volunteers shall be inducted for such training and service so long as he is deferred after classification: Provided further, That no man shall be inducted for training and service under this Act unless and until he is acceptable to the land or naval forces for such training and service and his physical and mental fitness for such training and service has been satisfactorily determined: Provided further, That no men shall be inducted for such training and service until adequate provision shall have been made for such shelter, sanitary facilities, water supplies, eating and lighting arrangements, medical care, and hospital accommodations, for such men, as may have been determined by the Secretary of War or the Secretary of the Navy, as the case may be, to be essential to public and personal health: Provided further, That except in time of war there shall not be in activities training or service the land forces of the United States at any one time under subsection (b) more than nine hundred thousand men inducted under the provisions of the Act. The men inducted into the land or naval forces for training and service under this Act shall be assigned to camps or units of such forces.

(b) Each man inducted under the provisions of subsection (a) shall serve for a training and service period of twelve consecutive months, unless sooner discharged, except that whenever the Congress had declared that the national interest is imperiled, such twelve-month period may be extended by the President to such time as may be necessary in the interests of national defense.

(c) Each such man, after the completion of his period of training and service under subsection (b), shall be transferred to a reserve component of the land or naval forces of the United States; and until he attains the age of forty-five, or until the expiration of a period of ten years after such transfer, or until he is discharged from such reserve component, whichever occurs first, he shall be deemed to be a member of such reserve component and shall be subject to such additional training and service as may now or thereafter be prescribed by law: Provided, That any man who completes at least twelve months' training and service in the land forces under subsection (b), and who thereafter serves in the land forces under subsection (b), and who thereafter serves satisfactorily in the Regular Army or in the active National Guard for a period of at least two years, shall, in time of peace, be relieved from any liability to service in any such man, while in a reserve component of such forces, from being ordered or called to active duty in such forces.

(d) With respect to the men inducted for training and service under this Act there shall be paid, allowed, and extended the same pay, allowances, pensions, disability and death compensation, and other benefits as are provided by law in the case of other enlisted men of like grades and length of service of that component of the land or naval forces to which they are assigned, and after transfer to a reserve component of the land or naval forces as provided in subsection (c) there shall be paid, allowed, and extended with respect to them the same benefits as are provided by law in like cases with respect to other members of such reserve component. Men in such training and service and men who have been so transferred to reserve components shall have an opportunity to qualify for promotion.

(e) Persons inducted into the land forces of the United States under this Act shall not be employed beyond the limits of the Western Hemisphere except in the Territories and possessions of the United States, including the Philippine Islands.

(f) Nothing contained in this or any other Act shall be construed as forbidding the payment of compensation by any person, firm, or corporation to persons inducted into the land or naval forces of the United States for training and service under this Act, or to members of the reserve components of such forces now or hereafter on any type of active duty, who, prior to their induction or commencement of active duty, were receiving compensation from such person, firm, or corporation.

Section 4. (a) The selection of men for training and service under section 3 (other than those who are voluntarily inducted pursuant to this Act) shall be made in an impartial manner, under such rules and regulations as the President may prescribe, from the men who are liable for such training and service and who at the time of selection are registered and classified but not deterred or exempted: Provided, That in the selection and training of men under this Act, and in the interpretation and execution of the provisions of this Act, there shall be no discrimination against any person on account of race or color . . .

Section 5. (a) Commissioned officers, warrant officers, pay clerks, and enlisted men of the Regular Army, the Navy, the Marine Corps, the Coast Guard, the Coast and Geodetic Survey, the Public Health Service, the federally recognized active National Guard, the Officers' Reserve Corps, the Regular Army Reserve, the Enlisted Reserve Corps, the Naval Reserve, the Marine Corps Reserve; cadets, United States Military Academy; midshipmen, the United States Naval Academy; cadets, United States Coast Guard Academy; men who have been accepted for admittance (commencing with the academic year net succeeding such acceptance) to the United States Military Academy as cadets, to the United States Naval Academy as midshipmen, or to the United States Coast Guard Academy as cadets, but only during the continuance of such acceptance; cadets of the advanced course, senior division, Reserve Officers' Training Corps or Naval Reserve Officers' Training Corps; diplomatic representatives, technical attachés of foreign embassies and legations, consuls general, consuls, vice consuls, and consular agents of foreign countries, residing in the United States, who are not citizens of the United States, and who have not declared their intention to become citizens of the United States, shall not be required to be registered under section 2 and shall be relieved from liability for training and service under section 3 (b).

(b) Any man who shall have satisfactorily served for at least three consecutive years in the Regular Army before or after and partially after the time fixed for registration under section 2.

Any man who as a member of the active National Guard shall have satisfactorily served for at least one year in active Federal service in the Army of the United States, and subsequent thereto for at least two consecutive years in the Regular Army or in the active National Guard, before or after or partially before and partially after the time fixed for registration under section 2.

Any man who is in the active National Guard at the time fixed for registration under section 2, and who shall have satisfactorily served therein on the eligible list for at least six consecutive years, before or after or partially before and partially after the time fixed for such registration.

Any man who is in the Officers' Reserve Corps on the eligible list at the time fixed for registration under section 2, and who shall have satisfactorily served therein on the eligible list for at least six consecutive years, before or after or partially before and partially after the time fixed for such registration: Provided, That nothing in this subsection shall be construed to prevent the persons enumerated in this subsection, while in reserve components of the land or naval forces of the United States, from being ordered or called to active duty in such forces.

(c) (1) The Vice President of the United States, the Governors of the several States and Territories, members of the legislative bodies of the United States and of the several States and Territories, judges of the courts of record of the United States and of the several States and Territories and the District of Columbia, shall, while holding such offices, be deferred from training and service under this Act in the land and naval forces of the United States.

(2) The President is authorized . . . to provide for the deferment from training and service under this Act . . . any person holding an office . . . under the United States or any State, Territory, or District of Columbia, whose continued service in such office is found in accordance with . . . maintenance of public health, safety, or interest.

(d) Regular or duly ordained ministers of religion, and students who are preparing for the ministry in theological or divinity schools recognized as such . . . under this Act.

(e) The President is authorized . . . to provide for the deferment from training and service under this Act in the forces of the United States of those men whose employment in industry, agriculture, or other occupations or employment, or whose employment in industry, agriculture, or other occupations or employment, or whose activity in other endeavors, is found . . . necessary to the maintenance of national health, safety or interest.

(f) Any person who, during the year 1940, entered upon attendance for the academic year 1940–1941—

(1) At any college or university which grants a degree in arts or science, to pursue a course of instruction satisfactory completion of which is prescribed by such a college or university as a prerequisite to either of such degrees; or

(2) at any university described in paragraph (1), to pursue a course of instruction . . . and who, while pursuing such course of instruction at such college, is selected for training and service under this Act prior to the end of such academic year, or prior to July 1, 1941, whichever occurs first, shall, upon his return, be deferred from induction in the land or naval forces for such training and service until the end of such academic year, but in no event later than July 1, 1941.

(g) Nothing contained in this Act shall be construed to require any person to be subject to combatant training and service in the land or naval forces of the United States, who by reason of religious training and belief, is conscientiously opposed to participation in war in any form. Any such person claiming such exemption from combatant training and service because of such conscientious objection whose claim is sustained by the local board shall, if he is inducted into the land or naval forces under this Act, be assigned to noncombatant service as defined by the president . . .

(h) No exception from registration, or exemption or deferment from training and service, under this Act, shall continue after the cause therefore ceases to exist.

Section 6. The President shall have authority to induct into the land and naval forces of the United States under this Act no greater number of men than the Congress shall hereafter make specific appropriation for from time to time.

Section 7. No bounty shall be paid to induce any person to enlist in or be inducted into the land or naval forces of the United States . . .

Section 10 (a). The President is authorized to prescribe the necessary rules and regulations to carry out the provisions of this Act; to create and establish a Selective Service System, and shall provide for the classification of registrants and of persons who volunteer for induction under this Act . . .

Section 18. This Act may be cited as the "Selective Training and Service Act of 1940."

Approved September 16, 1940, 3:08 p.m., E.S.T.

National Security Act of 1947 (As Amended July 26, 1947)

The 1947 National Security Act and its subsequent 1949 revision established the Department of Defense and a number of other components of the national security community, including the creation of an Air Force and replacement of the War Department and Service Departments, with the Defense Department overseeing all branches of the services.

Be it enacted by the Senate and House of Representatives of the United States of America in Congress assembled, that [50 U.S.C. 401 note] this Act may be cited as the "National Security Act of 1947."

Title II – The Department of Defense. Section 201 [Subsections (a) and (b) were repealed by section 30 of Public Law 87–651. Act of September 7, 1962, 76 Stat. 526 Subsection (c) consisted of an amendment to another Act] (d) [50 U.S.C. 408] Except to the extent inconsistent with the provisions of this Act, the provisions of title IV of the Revised Statutes. Title IV of the Revised Statutes consisted of sections 158–198 of the Revised Statutes. Sections 176 and 193 are codified as sections 492–1 and 492–2 of title 31, United States Code. The remainder of those sections have been repealed or replaced by provisions of title 5, United States Code as enacted. See the "Tables" volume of the United States Code for the distribution of specific sections] as now of hereafter amended shall be pplicable to the Department of Defense [Sections 202–204 were repealed by section 307 of Public Law 87–651 (Act of September 7, 1962, 76 Stat. 526).]

Department of the Army. Section 205 [Subsections (a), (d), and (e) were repealed by the law enacting titles 10 and 32, United States Code (Act of August 10, 1956, 70A Stat. 676)].

(b) All laws, orders, regulations, and other actions relating to the Department of War or to any officer or activity whose title is changed under this section shall, insofar as they are not inconsistent with the provisions of this Act, be deemed to relate to the Department of the Army within the Department of Defense or to such officer or activity designated by his or its new title.

(c) [50 U.S.C. 409(a)] the term "Department of the Army" as used in this Act shall be construed to mean the Department of the Army at the seat of government and all field headquarters, forces, reserve components, installations, activities, and functions under the control or supervision of the Department of the Army.

Department of the Navy. Section 206 (a) [50 U.S.C. 409(b)] The term "Department of the Navy" as used in this Act shall be construed to mean the Department of the Navy at the seat of government; the headquarters, United States Marine Corps; the entire operating forces of the United States Navy, including naval aviation, and of the United States Marine Corps, including the reserve components of such forces, all field activities, headquarters, forces, bases, installations, activities and functions under the control or supervision of the Department of the Navy; and the United States Coast Guard when operating as a part of the Navy pursuant to law. [Subsections (b) and (c) were repealed by the law enacting titles 10 and 32, United States Code (Act of August 10, 1956, 70A Stat. 676).]

Department of the Air Force. Section 2075 [Subsections (a), (b), (d), (e), and (f) were repealed by the law enacting titles 10 and 32, United States Code (Act of August 10, 1956, 70A Stat. 676)].

(c) [(50 U.S.C. 409(c)] The term "Department of the Air Force" as used in this Act shall be construed to mean the Department of the Air Force at the seat of government and all field headquarters, forces, reserve components, installations, activities, and functions under the control or supervision of the Department of the Air Force.

[Section 208 (less subsection (c)) was repealed by the law enacting titles 10 and 32, United States Code (Act of August 10, 1956, 70A Stat. 676). Section 208 (c) was repealed by the law enacting title 5, United States Code (Public Law 89–544, September 6, 1966, 80 Stat. 654).]

[Sections 209–214 were repealed by the law enacting titles 10 and 32, United States Code (Act of August 10, 1956, 70A Stat. 676).]

Harry S Truman's Presidential Directive to Desegregate the Military, June 1948

The desegregation efforts of the U.S. military are not among the nation's proudest moments. President Harry Truman, after feeling stonewalled, particularly by his own Army, issued the following Presidential Proclamation to desegregate U.S. forces.

EXECUTIVE ORDER 9981
Establishing the President's Committee on Equality of Treatment and Opportunity in the Armed Forces.

WHEREAS it is essential that there be maintained in the armed services of the United States the highest standards of democracy, with equality of treatment and opportunity for all those who serve in our country's defense:

NOW THEREFORE, by virtue of the authority vested in me as President of the United States, by the Constitution and the statutes of the United States, and as Commander in Chief of the armed services, it is hereby ordered as follows:

1. It is hereby declared to be the policy of the President that there shall be equality of treatment and opportunity for all persons in the armed services without regard to race, color, religion or national origin. This policy shall be put into effect as rapidly as possible, having due regard to the time required to effectuate any necessary changes without impairing efficiency or morale.

2. There shall be created in the National Military Establishment an advisory committee to be known as the President's Committee on Equality of Treatment and Opportunity in the Armed Services, which shall be composed of seven members to be designated by the President.

3. The Committee is authorized on behalf of the President to examine the rules, procedures and practices of the Armed Services in order to determine in what respect such rules, procedures and practices may be altered or improved with a view to carrying out the policy of this order. The Committee shall confer and advise the Secretary of Defense, the Secretary of the Army, the Secretary of the Navy, and the Secretary of the Air Force, and shall make such recommendations to the President and to said Secretaries as in the judgment of the Committee will effectuate the policy hereof.

4. All executive departments and agencies of the Federal Government are authorized and directed to cooperate with the Committee in its work, and to furnish the Committee such information or the services of such persons as the Committee may require in the performance of its duties.

5. When requested by the Committee to do so, persons in the armed services or in any of the executive departments and agencies of the Federal Government shall testify before the Committee and shall make available for use of the Committee such documents and other information as the Committee may require.

6. The Committee shall continue to exist until such time as the President shall terminate its existence by Executive order.

Harry Truman. The White House. July 26, 1948.

Universal Military and Training Act of 1951; *see* Military Selective Service Act

The War Powers Act of 1973 (Public Law 93–148, November 7, 1973)

Congressional frustration with the Johnson and Nixon administrations' handling of the Vietnam War, coupled with the reaction to Nixon's foibles as revealed by the Watergate scandal, led to the War Powers Act. It has never been tested before the courts because neither the Executive (which completely rejects it) nor the Legislature (which supports it depending on whether the party in the White House is the same as that ruling the Legislature) is certain of its value in any particular instance.

Joint Resolution. Section 1. This joint resolution may be cited as the "War Powers Resolution."

Purpose and Policy. Section 2. (a) It is the purpose of this joint resolution to fulfill the intent of the framers of the Constitution of the United States and insure that the collective judgement of both the Congress and the President will apply to the introduction of United States Armed Forces into hostilities, or into situations where imminent involvement in hostilities is clearly indicated by the circumstances, and to the continued use of such forces in hostilities or in such situations.

(b) Under article I, section 8, of the Constitution, it is specifically provided that the Congress shall have the power to make all laws necessary and proper for carrying into execution, not only its own powers but also all other powers vested by the Constitution in the Government of the United States, or in any department or officer thereof.

(c) The constitutional powers of the President as Commander-in-Chief to introduce United States Armed Forces into hostilities, or into situations where imminent involvement in hostilities is clearly indicated by the circumstances, are exercised only pursuant to (1) a declaration of war, (2) specific statutory authorization, or (3) a national emergency created by attack upon the United States, its territories or possessions, or its armed forces.

Consultation. Section 3. The President in every possible instance shall consult with Congress before introducing United States Armed Forces into hostilities or into situations where imminent involvement in hostilities is clearly indicated by the circumstances, and after every such introduction shall consult regularly with the Congress until United States Armed Forces are no longer engaged in hostilities or have been removed from such situations.

Reporting. Section 4. (a) In the absence of a declaration of war, in any case in which United States Armed Forces are introduced—

(1) into hostilities or into situations where imminent involvement in hostilities is clearly indicated by the circumstances;

(2) into the territory, airspace or waters of a foreign nation, while equipped for combat, except for deployments which relate solely to supply, replacement, repair, or training of such forces; or

(3) (A) the circumstances necessitating the introduction of United States Armed Forces; (B) the constitutional and legislative

authority under which such introduction took place; and (C) the estimated scope and duration of the hostilities or involvement.

(b) The President shall provide such other information as the Congress may request in the fulfillment of its constitutional responsibilities with respect to committing the Nation to war and to the use of United States Armed Forces abroad.

(c) Whenever United States Armed Forces are introduced into hostilities or into any situation described in subsection (a) of this section, the President shall, so long as such armed forces continue to be engaged in such hostilities or situation, report to the Congress periodically on the status of such hostilities or situation as well as on the scope and duration of such hostilities or situation, but in no event shall he report to the Congress less often than once every six months.

Goldwater-Nichols Department of Defense Reorganization Act of 1986 (Public Law 99–433, October 1, 1986)

The Goldwater-Nichols Reforms of 1986 were the last major revisions to the national service, enhancing the role of "jointness," "joint education," and other moves to make a more cohesive, coherent national military.

Be it enacted by the Senate and House of Representatives of the United States of America in Congress assembled,

Title I: Department of Defense Generally.

Section 102. Powers and Duties of the Secretary of Defense

Post, pp. 1022, Section 113 (as transferred and redesignated by section 101(a)(2)) is 1075, amended by adding at the end the following new subsections:

(f) When a vacancy occurs in an office within the Department of Defense and the office is to be filled by a person appointed from civilian life by the President, by and with the advice and consent of the Senate, the Secretary of Defense shall inform the President of the qualifications needed by a person serving in that office to carry out effectively the duties and responsibilities of that office.

(g) (1) The Secretary of Defense, with the advice and assistance of the Chairman of the Joint Chiefs of Staff, shall provide annually to the heads of Department of Defense components written policy guidance for the preparation and review of the program recommendations and budget proposals of their respective components.

Such guidance shall include guidance on

(A) national security objectives and policies;

(B) the priorities of military missions; and

(C) the resource levels projected to be available for the period of time for which such recommendations and proposals are to be effective.

(2) The Secretary of Defense, with the approval of the President and after consultation with the Chairman of the Joint Chiefs of Staff, shall provide annually to the Chairman written policy guidance for the preparation and review of contingency plans. Guidance shall include guidance on the specific force levels and specific supporting resource levels projected to be available for the period of time for which such plans are to be effective.

(h) The Secretary of Defense shall keep the Secretaries of the military departments informed with respect to military operations and activities of the Department of Defense that directly affect their respective responsibilities . . .

Section 103. Modification of Authority of Secretary of Defense to Reorganize the Department of Defense. *Post,* pp. 1022, Section 125 is amended–1055.

(1) by striking out "unless the Secretary" in the second sentence of subsection (a) and all that follows in that subsection and inserting in lieu thereof a period; and

(2) by inserting "vested by law in the Department of Defense, or an officer, official, or agency thereof" in subsection (b) after "function, power, or duty."

Section 104. Office of the Secretary of Defense. Chapter 4 (as amended by section 101(a)) is further amended by inserting after the table of sections the following new section:

Title II—Military Advice and Command Functions.
Part A—Joint Chiefs of Staff

Section 201. Revised Functions of Chairman; Establishment of Vice Chairman. Chapter 5 is amended to read as follows:

151. Joint Chiefs of Staff: composition; functions.

152. Chairman: appointment; rank.

153. Chairman: functions.

154. Vice Chairman.

155. Joint Staff.

§ 151. Joint Chiefs of Staff: composition; functions 10 USC 151.

(a) COMPOSITION. There are in the Department of Defense the Joint Chiefs of Staff, headed by the Chairman of the Joint Chiefs of Staff. The Joint Chiefs of Staff consist of the following:

(1) The Chairman.

(2) The Chief of Staff of the Army.

(3) The Chief of Naval Operations.

(4) The Chief of Staff of the Air Force.

(5) The Commandant of the Marine Corps.

(b) FUNCTION AS MILITARY ADVISERS.

(1) The Chairman of the Joint Chiefs of Staff is the principal military adviser to the President, the National Security Council, and the Secretary of Defense.

(2) The other members of the Joint Chiefs of Staff are military advisers to the President, the National Security Council, and the Secretary of Defense as specified in subsections (d) and (e).

(c) CONSULTATION BY CHAIRMAN.

(1) In carrying out his functions, duties, and responsibilities, the Chairman shall, as he considers appropriate, consult with and seek the advice of

(A) the other members of the Joint Chiefs of Staff; and

(B) the commanders of the unified and specified combatant commands.

(2) Subject to subsection (d), in presenting advice with respect to any matter to the President, the National Security Council, or the Secretary of Defense, the Chairman shall, as he considers appropriate, inform the President, the National Security Council, or the Secretary of Defense, as the case may be, of the range of military advice and opinion with respect to that matter.

(d) ADVICE AND OPINIONS OF MEMBERS OTHER THAN CHAIRMAN.

(1) A member of the Joint Chiefs of Staff (other than the Chairman) may submit to the Chairman advice or an opinion in disagreement with, or advice or an opinion in addition to, the advice presented by the Chairman to the President, the National Security Council, or the Secretary of Defense. If a member submits such advice or opinion, the Chairman shall present the advice or opinion of such member at the same time he presents his own advice to the President, the National Security Council, or the Secretary of Defense, as the case may be.

(2) The Chairman shall establish procedures to ensure that the presentation of his own advice to the President, the National Security Council, or the Secretary of Defense is not unduly delayed by reason of the submission of the individual advice or opinion of another member of the Joint Chiefs of Staff.

(e) ADVICE ON REQUEST. The members of the Joint Chiefs of Staff, individually or collectively, in their capacity as military advisers, shall provide advice to the President, the National Security Council, or the Secretary of Defense on a particular matter when the President, the National Security Council, or the Secretary requests such advice.

(f) RECOMMENDATIONS TO CONGRESS. After first informing the Secretary of Defense, a member of the Joint Chiefs of Staff may make such recommendations to Congress relating to the Department of Defense as he considers appropriate.

(g) MEETINGS OF JCS.

(1) The Chairman shall convene regular meetings of the Joint Chiefs of Staff.

(2) Subject to the authority, direction, and control of the President and the Secretary of Defense, the Chairman shall

(A) preside over the Joint Chiefs of Staff;

(B) provide agenda for the meetings of the Joint Chiefs of Staff (including, as the Chairman considers appropriate, any subject for the agenda recommended by any other member of the Joint Chiefs of Staff);

(C) assist the Joint Chiefs of Staff in carrying on their business as promptly as practicable; and

(D) determine when issues under consideration by the Joint Chiefs of Staff shall be decided.

Section 152, Chairman: appointment; rank.

(a) APPOINTMENT TERM OF OFFICE

(1) There is a Chairman of the Joint Chiefs of Staff, appointed by the President, by and with the advice and consent of the Senate from the officers of the regular components of the armed forces. The Chairman serves at the pleasure of the President for a term of two years, beginning on October 1 of odd-numbered years. Subject to paragraph (3), an officer serving as Chairman may be reappointed in the same manner for two additional terms. However, in time of war there is no limit on the number of reappointments.

(2) In the event of the death, retirement, resignation, or reassignment of the officer serving as Chairman before the end of the term for which the officer was appointed, an officer appointed to fill the vacancy shall serve as Chairman only for the remainder of the original term, but may be reappointed as provided in paragraph (1).

(3) An officer may not serve as Chairman or Vice Chairman of the Joint Chiefs of Staff if the combined period of service of such officer in such positions exceeds six years. However, the President may extend to eight years the combined period of service an officer may serve in such positions if he determines such action is in the national interest. The limitations of this paragraph do not apply in time of war.

(b) REQUIREMENT FOR APPOINTMENT.

(1) The President may appoint an officer as Chairman of the Joint Chiefs of Staff only if the officer has served as

(A) the Vice Chairman of the Joint Chiefs of Staff;

(B) the Chief of Staff of the Army, the Chief of Naval Operations, the Chief of Staff of the Air Force, or the Commandant of the Marine Corps; or

(C) the commander of a unified or specified combatant command.

(2) The President may waive paragraph (1) in the case of an officer if the President determines such action is necessary in the national interest.

(c) GRADE AND RANK. The Chairman, while so serving, holds the grade of general or, in the case of an officer of the Navy, admiral and outranks all other officers of the armed forces. However, he may not exercise military command over the Joint Chiefs of Staff or any of the armed forces.

Section 153. Chairman: functions 10 USC 153.

(a) PLANNING ADVICE; POLICY FORMULATION. Subject to the authority, direction, and control of the President and the Secretary of Defense, the Chairman of the Joint Chiefs of Staff shall be responsible for the following:

(1) STRATEGIC DIRECTION. Assisting the President and the Secretary of Defense in providing for the strategic direction of the armed forces.

(2) STRATEGIC PLANNING.

(A) Preparing strategic plans, including plans which conform with resource levels projected by the Secretary of Defense to be available for the period of time for which the plans are to be effective.

(B) Preparing joint logistic and mobility plans to support those strategic plans and recommending the assignment of logistic and mobility responsibilities to the armed forces in accordance with those logistic and mobility plans.

(C) Performing net assessments to determine the capabilities of the armed forces of the United States and its allies as compared with those of their potential adversaries.

(3) CONTINGENCY PLANNING PREPAREDNESS.

(A) Providing for the preparation and review of contingency plans which conform to policy guidance from the President and the Secretary of Defense.

(B) Preparing joint logistic and mobility plans to support those contingency plans and recommending the assignment of logistic and mobility responsibilities to the armed forces in accordance with those logistic and mobility plans.

(C) Advising the Secretary on critical deficiencies and strengths in force capabilities (including manpower, logistic, and mobility support) identified during the preparation and review of contingency plans and assessing the effect of such deficiencies and strengths on meeting national security objectives and policy and on strategic plans.

(D) Establishing and maintaining, after consultation with the commanders of the unified and specified combatant commands, a uniform system of evaluating the preparedness of each such command to carry out missions assigned to the command.

(4) ADVICE ON REQUIREMENTS, PROGRAMS, AND BUDGET.

(A) Advising the Secretary, under section 163(b)(2) of this title, on the priorities of the requirements identified by the commanders of the unified and specified combatant commands.

(B) Advising the Secretary on the extent to which the program recommendations and budget proposals of the military departments and other components of the Department of Defense for a fiscal year conform with the priorities established in strategic plans and with the priorities established for the requirements of the unified and specified combatant commands.

(C) Submitting to the Secretary alternative program recommendations and budget proposals, within projected resource levels and guidance provided by the Secretary, in order to achieve greater conformance with the priorities referred to in clause (B).

(D) Recommending to the Secretary, in accordance with section 166 of this title, a budget proposal for activities of each unified and specified combatant command.

(E) Advising the Secretary on the extent to which the major programs and policies of the armed forces in the area of manpower conform with strategic plans.

(F) Assessing military requirements for defense acquisition programs.

(5) DOCTRINE, TRAINING, AND EDUCATION.

(A) Developing doctrine for the joint employment of the armed forces.

(B) Formulating policies for the joint training of the armed forces.

(C) Formulating policies for coordinating the military education and training of members of the armed forces.

(6) OTHER MATTERS.

(A) Providing for representation of the United States on the Military Staff Committee of the United Nations in accordance with the Charter of the United Nations.

(B) Performing such other duties as may be prescribed by law or by the President or the Secretary of Defense.

(b) REPORT ON ASSIGNMENT OF ROLES AND MISSIONS.

(1) Not less than once every three years, or upon the request of the President or the Secretary of Defense, the

Chairman shall submit to the Secretary of Defense a report containing such recommendations for changes in the assignment of functions (or roles and missions) to the armed forces as the Chairman considers necessary to achieve maximum effectiveness of the armed forces. In preparing each such report, the Chairman shall consider (among other matters) the following:

(A) Changes in the nature of the threats faced by the United States.

(B) Unnecessary duplication of effort among the armed forces.

(C) Changes in technology that can be applied effectively to warfare.

(2) The Chairman shall include in each such report recommendations for such changes in policies, directives, regulations, and legislation as may be necessary to achieve the changes in the assignment of functions recommended by the Chairman.

Section 154. Vice Chairman.

(a) APPOINTMENT.

(1) There is a Vice Chairman of the Joint Chiefs of Staff, appointed by the President, by and with the advice and consent of the Senate, from the officers of the regular components of the armed forces.

(2) The Chairman and Vice Chairman may not be members of the same armed force. However, the President may waive the restriction in the preceding sentence for a limited period of time in order to provide for the orderly transition of officers appointed to serve in the positions of Chairman and Vice Chairman.

(3) The Vice Chairman serves at the pleasure of the President for a term of two years and may be reappointed in the same manner for two additional terms. However, in time of war there is no limit on the number of reappointments.

(b) REQUIREMENT FOR APPOINTMENT.

(1) The President may appoint an officer as Vice Chairman of the Joint Chiefs of Staff only if the officer

(A) Has the joint specialty under section 661 of this title; and

(B) Has served in at least one joint duty assignment (as defined under section 668(b) of this title) as a general or flag officer.

(2) The President may waive paragraph (1) in the case of an officer if the President determines such action is necessary in the national interest.

(c) DUTIES. The Vice Chairman performs such duties as may be prescribed by the Chairman with the approval of the Secretary of Defense.

(d) FUNCTION AS ACTING CHAIRMAN. When there is a vacancy in the office of Chairman or in the absence or disability of the Chairman, the Vice Chairman acts as Chairman and performs the duties of the Chairman until a successor is appointed or the absence or disability ceases.

(e) SUCCESSION AFTER CHAIRMAN AND VICE CHAIRMAN. When there is a vacancy in the offices of both Chairman and Vice Chairman or in the absence or disability of both the Chairman and the Vice Chairman, or when there is a vacancy in one such office and in the absence or disability of the officer holding the other, the President shall designate a member of the Joint Chiefs of Staff to act as and perform the duties of the Chairman until a successor to the Chairman or Vice Chairman is appointed or the absence or disability of the Chairman or Vice Chairman ceases.

(f) PARTICIPATION IN JCS MEETINGS. The Vice Chairman may participate in all meetings of the Joint Chiefs of Staff, but may not vote on a matter before the Joint Chiefs of Staff except when acting as Chairman.

(g) GRADE AND RANK. The Vice Chairman, while so serving, holds the grade of general or, in the case of an officer of the Navy, admiral and outranks all other officers of the armed forces except the Chairman. The Vice Chairman may not exercise military command over the Joint Chiefs of Staff or any of the armed forces.

Section 155. Joint Staff.

(a) APPOINTMENT OF OFFICERS TO JOINT STAFF.

(1) There is a Joint Staff under the Chairman of the Joint Chiefs of Staff. The Joint Staff assists the Chairman and, subject to the authority, direction, and control of the Chairman, the other members of the Joint Chiefs of Staff and the Vice Chairman in carrying out their responsibilities.

(2) Officers of the armed forces (other than the Coast Guard) assigned to serve on the Joint Staff shall be selected by the Chairman in approximately equal numbers from

(A) the Army;

(B) the Navy and the Marine Corps; and

(C) the Air Force.

(3) Selection of officers of an armed force to serve on the Joint Staff shall be made by the Chairman from a list of officers submitted by the Secretary of the military department having jurisdiction over that armed force. Each officer whose name is submitted shall be among those officers considered to be the most

outstanding officers of that armed force. The Chairman may specify the number of officers to be included on any such list.

(b) DIRECTOR. The Chairman of the Joint Chiefs of Staff, after consultation with the other members of the Joint Chiefs of Staff and with the approval of the Secretary of Defense, may select an officer to serve as Director of the Joint Staff.

(c) MANAGEMENT OF JOINT STAFF. The Chairman of the Joint Chiefs of Staff manages the Joint Staff and the Director of the Joint Staff. The Joint Staff shall perform such duties as the Chairman prescribes and shall perform such duties under such procedures as the Chairman prescribes.

(d) OPERATION OF JOINT STAFF. The Secretary of Defense shall ensure that the Joint Staff is independently organized and operated so that the Joint Staff supports the Chairman of the Joint Chiefs of Staff in meeting the congressional purpose set forth in the last clause of section 2 of the National Security Act of 1947 (50 U.S.C. 401) to provide:

(1) for the unified strategic direction of the combatant forces;

(2) for their operation under unified command; and

(3) for their integration into an efficient team of land, naval, and air forces.

(e) Prohibition of Function as Armed Forces General Staff. The Joint Staff shall not operate or be organized as an overall Armed Forces General Staff and shall have no executive authority. The Joint Staff may be organized and may operate along conventional staff lines.

(f) Tour of Duty of Joint Staff Officers.

(1) An officer who is assigned or detailed to permanent duty on the Joint Staff may not serve for a tour of duty of more than four years. However, such a tour of duty may be extended with the approval of the Secretary of Defense.

(2) In accordance with procedures established by the Secretary of Defense, the Chairman of the Joint Chiefs of Staff may suspend from duty and recommend the reassignment of any officer assigned to the Joint Staff. Upon receipt of such a recommendation, the Secretary concerned shall promptly reassign the officer.

(3) An officer completing a tour of duty with the Joint Staff may not be assigned or detailed to permanent duty on the Joint Staff within two years after relief from that duty except with the approval of the Secretary.

(4) Paragraphs (1) and (3) do not apply

(A) in time of war; or

(B) during a national emergency declared by the President or Congress.

(g) Composition of Joint Staff.

(1) The Joint Staff is composed of all members of the armed forces and civilian employees assigned or detailed to permanent duty in the executive part of the Department of Defense to perform the functions and duties prescribed under subsections (a) and (c).

(2) The Joint Staff does not include members of the armed forces or civilian employees assigned or detailed to permanent duty in a military department.

Chapter 6—Combatant Commands

Section 161: Establishment of Combatant Commands and Authority of Commanders

(a) UNIFIED AND SPECIFIED COMBATANT COMMANDS. With the advice and assistance of the Chairman of the Joint Chiefs of Staff, the President, through the Secretary of Defense, shall—

(1) establish unified combatant commands and specified combatant commands to perform military missions; and

(2) prescribe the force structure of those commands.

(b) PERIODIC REVIEW.

(1) The Chairman periodically (and not less than every two years)

(A) review the missions, responsibilities (including geographic boundaries), and force structure of each combatant command; and

(B) recommend to the President, through the Secretary of Defense, any changes to such missions, responsibilities, and force structures as may be necessary.

(2) Except during time of hostilities or imminent threat of hostilities, the President shall notify Congress not more than 60 days after

(A) establishing a new combatant command; or

(B) significantly revising the missions, responsibilities, or force structure of an existing combatant command.

(c) DEFINITIONS. In this chapter:

(1) The term "unified combatant command" means a military command which has broad, continuing missions and which is composed of forces from two or more military departments.

(2) The term "specified combatant" command means a military command which has broad, continuing missions and which is normally composed of forces from a single military department.

(3) The term "combatant command" means a unified combat approved by the President.

Section 162. Combatant commands: assigned forces; chain of command

(a) ASSIGNMENT OF FORCES.

(1) Except as provided in paragraph (2), the Secretaries of the military departments shall assign all forces under their jurisdiction to unified and specified combatant commands or to the United States element of the North American Aerospace Defense Command to perform missions assigned to those commands. Such assignments shall be made as directed by the Secretary of Defense, including direction as to the command to which forces are to be assigned. The Secretary of Defense shall ensure that such assignments are consistent with the force structure prescribed by the President for each combatant command.

(2) Except as otherwise directed by the Secretary of Defense, forces to be assigned by the Secretaries of the military departments to the combatant commands or to the United States element of the North American Aerospace Defense Command under paragraph (1) do not include forces assigned to carry out functions of the Secretary of a military department listed in sections of this title or forces assigned to multinational peacekeeping organizations.

(3) A force assigned to a combatant command or to the United States element of the North American Aerospace Defense Command under this section may be transferred from the command to which it is assigned only—

(A) by authority of the Secretary of Defense; and

(B) under procedures prescribed by the Secretary and approved by the President.

(4) Except as otherwise directed by the Secretary of Defense, all forces operating within the geographic area assigned to a unified combatant command shall be assigned to, and under the command of, the commander of that command. The preceding sentence applies to forces assigned to a specified combatant command only as prescribed by the Secretary of Defense.

(b) CHAIN OF COMMAND. Unless otherwise directed by the President, the chain of command to a unified or specified combatant command runs—

(1) from the President to the Secretary of Defense; and

(2) from the Secretary of Defense to the commander of the combatant command.

§ 163. Role of Chairman of Joint Chiefs of Staff

(a) COMMUNICATIONS THROUGH CHAIRMAN OF JCS; ASSIGNMENT OF DUTIES. Subject to the limitations in section 152(c) of this title, the President may

(1) direct that communications between the President or the Secretary of Defense and the commanders of the unified and

specified combatant commands be transmitted through the Chairman of the Joint Chiefs of Staff; and

(2) assign duties to the Chairman to assist the President and the Secretary of Defense in performing their command function.

(b) OVERSIGHT BY CHAIRMAN OF JOINT CHIEFS OF STAFF.

(1) The Secretary of Defense may assign to the Chairman of the Joint Chiefs of Staff responsibility for overseeing the activities of the combatant commands. Such assignment by the Secretary to the Chairman does not confer any command authority on the Chairman and does not alter the responsibility of the commanders of the combatant commands prescribed in section 164(b)(2) of this title.

(2) Subject to the authority, direction, and control of the Secretary of Defense, the Chairman of the Joint Chiefs of Staff serves as the spokesman for the commanders of the combatant commands, especially on the operational requirements of their commands. In performing such function, the Chairman shall—

(A) confer with and obtain information from the commanders of the combatant commands with respect to the requirements of their commands;

(B) evaluate and integrate such information;

(C) advise and make recommendations to the Secretary of Defense with respect to the requirements of the combatant commands, individually and collectively; and

(D) communicate, as appropriate, the requirements of the combatant commands to other elements of the Department of Defense.

President William J. Clinton's Remarks at the National Defense University, Announcing the New Policy on Gays and Lesbians in the Military (July 19, 1993)

President Clinton announced immediately after his inauguration his intention to normalize gay/lesbian participation in the military but did not announce his modified policy for six months, during which time opponents mobilized to provoke this more restrained policy.

THE PRESIDENT: Thank you very much. Secretary Aspin, General Powell, members of the Joint Chiefs, Admiral Kime; to our host, Admiral Smith, ladies and gentlemen.

I have come here today to discuss a difficult challenge and one which has received an enormous amount of publicity and public and private debate over the last several months—our nation's policy toward homosexuals in the military.

I believe the policy I am announcing today represents a real step forward. But I know it will raise concerns in some of your minds. So I wanted you to hear my thinking and my decision directly and in person, because I respect you and because you are among the elite who will lead our Armed Forces into the next century, and because you will have to put this policy into effect and I expect your help in doing it.

The policy I am announcing today is, in my judgment, the right thing to do and the best way to do it. It is right because it provides greater protection to those who happen to be homosexual and want to serve their country honorably in uniform, obeying all the military's rules against sexual misconduct.

It is the best way to proceed because it provides a sensible balance between the rights of the individual and the needs of our military to remain the world's number one fighting force. As President of all the American people, I am pledged to protect and to promote individual rights. As Commander in Chief, I am pledged to protect and advance our security. In this policy, I believe we have come close to meeting both objectives.

Let me start with this clear fact: Our military is one of our greatest accomplishments and our most valuable assets. It is the world's most effective and powerful fighting force, bar none. I have seen proof of this fact almost every day since I became President. I saw it last week when I visited Camp Casey along the DMZ in Korea. I witnessed it at our military academies at Annapolis and West Point when I visited there. And I certainly relied on it three weeks ago when I ordered an attack on Iraq after that country's leadership attempted to assassinate President Bush.

We owe a great deal to the men and women who protect us through their service, their sacrifice and their dedication. And we owe it to our own security to listen hard to them and act carefully as we consider any changes in the military. A force ready to fight must maintain the highest priority under all circumstances.

Let me review the events which bring us here today. Before I ran for President, this issue was already upon us. Some of the members of the military returning from the Gulf War announced their homosexuality in order to protest the ban. The military's policy has been questioned in college ROTC programs. Legal challenges have been filed in court, including one that has since succeeded. In 1991, the Secretary of Defense Dick Cheney was asked about reports that the Defense Department spent an alleged $500 million to separate and replace about 17,000 homosexuals from the military service during the 1980s, in spite of the findings of a government report saying there was no reason to believe that they could not serve effectively and with distinction.

Shortly thereafter, while giving a speech at the Kennedy School of Government at Harvard, I was asked by one of the students what I thought of this report and what I thought of lifting the ban. This question had never before been presented to me, and I had never had the opportunity to discuss it with anyone. I stated then what I still believe: that I thought there ought to be a presumption that people who wish to do so should be able to serve their country if they are willing to conform to the high standards of the military, and that the emphasis should be always on people's conduct, not their status.

For me, and this is very important, this issue has never been one of group rights, but rather of individual ones—of the individual opportunity to serve and the individual responsibility to conform to the highest standards of military conduct. For people who are willing to play by the rules, able to serve, and make a contribution, I believe then and I believe now we should give them the chance to do so.

The central facts of this issue are not much in dispute. First, notwithstanding the ban, there have been and are homosexuals in the military service who serve with distinction. I have had the privilege of meeting some of these men and women, and I have been deeply impressed by their devotion to duty and to country.

Second, there is no study showing them to be less capable or more prone to misconduct than heterosexual soldiers. Indeed, all the information we have indicates that they are not less capable or more prone to misbehavior.

Third, misconduct is already covered by the laws and rules which also cover activities that are improper by heterosexual members of the military.

Fourth, the ban has been lifted in other nations and in police and fire departments in our country with no discernible negative impact on unit cohesion or capacity to do the job, though there is, admittedly, no absolute analogy to the situation we face and no study bearing on this specific issue.

Fifth, even if the ban were lifted entirely, the experience of other nations and police and fire departments in the United States indicates that most homosexuals would probably not declare their sexual orientation openly, thereby, making an already hard life even more difficult in some circumstances.

But as the sociologist, Charles Moskos, noted after spending many years studying the American military, the issue may be tougher to resolve here in the United States than in Canada, Australia, and in some other nations because of the presence in our country of both vocal gay rights groups and equally vocal antigay rights groups, including some religious groups who believe that lifting the ban amounts to endorsing a lifestyle they strongly disapprove of.

Clearly, the American people are deeply divided on this issue, with most military people opposed to lifting the ban because of the feared impact on unit cohesion, rooted in disapproval of homosexual lifestyles, and the fear of invasion of privacy of heterosexual soldiers who must live and work in close quarters with homosexual military people.

However, those who have studied this issue extensively have discovered an interesting fact. People in this country who are aware of having known homosexuals are far more likely to support lifting the ban. In other words, they are likely to see this issue in terms of individual conduct and individual capacity instead of the claims of a group with which they do not agree; and also to be able to imagine how this ban could be lifted without a destructive impact on group cohesion and morale.

Shortly after I took office and reaffirmed my position, the foes of lifting the ban in the Congress moved to enshrine the ban in law. I asked that congressional action be delayed for six months while the Secretary of Defense worked with the Joint Chiefs to come up with a proposal for changing our current policy. I then met with the Joint Chiefs to hear their concerns and asked them to try to work through the issue with Secretary Aspin. I wanted to handle the matter in this way on grounds of both principle and practicality.

As a matter of principle, it is my duty as Commander in Chief to uphold the high standards of combat readiness and unit cohesion of the world's finest fighting force, while doing my duty as President to protect the rights of individual Americans and to put to use the abilities of all the American people. And I was determined to serve this principle as fully as possible through practical action, knowing this fact about our system of government: While the Commander in Chief and the Secretary of Defense can change military personnel policies, Congress can reverse those changes by law in ways that are difficult, if not impossible, to veto.

For months now, the Secretary of Defense and the service chiefs have worked through this issue in a highly charged, deeply emotional environment, struggling to come to terms with the competing consideration and pressures and, frankly, to work through their own ideas and deep feelings.

During this time many dedicated Americans have come forward to state their own views on this issues. Most, but not all, of the military testimony has been against lifting the ban. But support for changing the policy has come from distinguished combat veterans including Senators Bob Kerrey, Chuck Robb, and John

Kerry in the United States Congress. It has come from Lawrence Korb, who enforced the gay ban during the Reagan administration; and from former Senator Barry Goldwater, a distinguished veteran, former Chairman of the Senate Arms Services Committee, founder of the Arizona National Guard, and patron saint of the conservative wing of the Republican Party.

Senator Goldwater's statement, published in *The Washington Post* recently, made it crystal clear that when this matter is viewed as an issue of individual opportunity and responsibility rather than one of alleged group rights, this is not a call for cultural license, but rather a reaffirmation of the American value of extending opportunity to responsible individuals and of limiting the role of government over citizens' private lives.

On the other hand, those who oppose lifting the ban are clearly focused not on the conduct of individual gay service members, but on how nongay service members feel about gays in general and, in particular, those in the military service.

These past few days I have been in contact with the Secretary of Defense as he has worked through the final stages of this policy with the Joint Chiefs. We now have a policy that is a substantial advance over the one in place when I took office. I have ordered Secretary Aspin to issue a directive consisting of these essential elements: One, servicemen and women will be judged based on their conduct, not their sexual orientation. Two, therefore, the practice, now six months old, of not asking about sexual orientation in the enlistment procedure will continue. Three, an open statement by a service member that he or she is a homosexual will create a rebuttable presumption that he or she intends to engage in prohibited conduct, but the service member will be given an opportunity to refute that presumption; in other words, to demonstrate that he or she intends to live by the rules of conduct that apply in the military service. And four, all provisions of the Uniform Military Justice will be enforced in an even-handed manner as regards both heterosexuals and homosexuals. And, thanks to the policy provisions agreed by the Joint Chiefs, there will be a decent regard to the legitimate privacy and associational rights of all service members.

Just as is the case under current policy, unacceptable conduct, either heterosexual or homosexual, will be unacceptable twenty-four hours a day, seven days a week, from the time a recruit joins the service until the day he or she is discharged. Now, as in the past, every member of our military will be required to comply with the Uniform Code of Military Justice, which is federal law and military regulations, at all times and in all places.

Let me say a few words now about this policy. It is not a perfect solution. It is not identical with some of my own goals. And it certainly will not please everyone, perhaps not anyone, and clearly not those who hold the most adamant opinions on either side of this issue.

But those who wish to ignore the issue must understand that it is already tearing at the cohesion of the military, and it is today being considered by the federal courts in ways that may not be to the liking of those who oppose any change. And those who want the ban to be lifted completely on both status and conduct must understand that such action would have faced certain and decisive reversal by the Congress and the cause for which many have fought for years would be delayed probably for years.

Thus, on grounds of both principle and practicality, this is a major step forward. It is, in my judgment, consistent with my responsibilities as President and Commander in Chief to meet the need to change current policy. It is an honorable compromise that advances the cause of people who are called to serve our country by their patriotism, the cause of our national security and our national interest in resolving an issue that has divided our military and our nation and diverted our attention from other matters for too long.

The time has come for us to move forward. As your Commander in Chief, I charge all of you to carry out this policy with fairness, with balance and with due regard for the privacy of individuals. We must and will protect unit cohesion and troop morale. We must and will continue to have the best fighting force in the world. But this is an end to witch hunts that spend millions of taxpayer dollars to ferret out individuals who have served their country well. Improper conduct, on or off base, should remain grounds for discharge. But we will proceed with an even hand against everyone regardless of sexual orientation.

Such controversies as this have divided us before. But our nation and our military have always risen to the challenge before. That was true of racial integration of the military and changes in the role of women in the military. Each of these was an issue because it was an issue for society as well as for the military. And in each case our military was a leader in figuring out how to respond most effectively.

In the early 1970s, when President Nixon decided to transform our military into an all-volunteer force, many argued that it could not work. They said it would ruin our forces. But the leaders of our military not only made it work, they used the concept of an all-volunteer force to build the very finest fighting force our nation and the world have ever known.

Ultimately, the success of this policy will depend in large measure on the commitment it receives from the leaders of the military services.

I very much respect and commend the Joint Chiefs for the good-faith effort they have made through this whole endeavor. And I thank General Powell, the Joint Chiefs, and the Commandant of the Coast Guard for joining me here today and for their support of this policy.

I would also like to thank those who lobbied aggressively in behalf of changing the policy, including Congressman Barney Frank, Congressman Gary Studds, and the Campaign for Military Service, who worked with us and who clearly will not agree with every aspect of the policy announced today, but who should take some solace in knowing that their efforts have helped to produce a strong advance for the cause they seek to serve.

I must now look to General Powell, to the Joint Chiefs, to all the other leaders in our military to carry out this policy through effective training and leadership. Every officer will be expected to exert the necessary effort to make this policy work. That has been the key every time the military has successfully addressed a new challenge, and it will be key in this effort, too.

Our military is a conservative institution, and I say that in the very best sense, for its purpose is to conserve the fighting spirit of our troops; to conserve the resources and the capacity of our troops; to conserve the military lessons acquired during our nation's existence; to conserve our very security; and yes, to conserve the liberties of the American people. Because it is a conservative institution, it is right for the military to be wary of sudden changes. Because it is an institution that embodies the best of America and must reflect the society in which it operates, it is also right for the military to make changes when the time for change is at hand.

I strongly believe that our military, like our society, needs the talents of every person who wants to make a contribution and who is ready to live by the rules. That is the heart of the policy that I have announced today. I hope in your heart you will find the will and the desire to support it and to lead our military in incorporating it into our nation's great asset and the world's best fighting force.

Thank you very much. (Applause.)

NOTE: The President spoke at 2:36 p.m.

Secretary Rumsfeld's Interview with Juan Williams of NPR (July 16, 2004)

The George W. Bush administration had problems with retention of forces after the extent of the Iraqi insurgency became clear. This interview illustrates how hard it was for the administration to acknowledge this difficulty.

Q: Mr. Secretary, I've been given the cut-off sign, but I have two quick questions, if I could. One is when we were talking about recruitment, retention, have you ruled out the idea of reinstituting a draft?

SEC. RUMSFELD: Of course, Juan, as you know, I'm not the government of the United States. I am just one person. But if you ask me personally would I rule it out, the answer is absolutely. Back in the 1960s, when I was a congressman, I was one of the first members to introduce legislation to create an all-volunteer force.

I testified before the House and Senate committees back in those days. It has worked brilliantly for our country. We do not need a draft. The recruiting and retention process is going forward. It's working very well to the extent we end up with some areas of concern, all we have to do is to turn the dials up and increase the incentives and reduce the disincentives. We can do that. We're perfectly capable of doing it. There were a lot of inequities in a draft—in any draft. There certainly were inequities in the ones that existed back in the '60s and '70s. And I would argue vigorously against reinstituting a draft.

7

Directory of Organizations

One of the most important tools for anyone interested in national military service is an understanding of the organizations concerned with this topic, even indirectly. This chapter identifies international organizations (meaning they have a significant participation in the U.S. national service dialogue while having links abroad), as well as not-for-profit, for-profit, and governmental organizations. The not-for-profit category is found in the U.S. Tax Code, generally that of a 501 (c)(3), which means the organization cannot spend more than 10 percent of its time on partisan or political activity and must attempt a nonpartisan assessment of topics.

This list is not exhaustive because organizations come and go; instead it attempts to offer a genuinely broad discussion of groups in the nation's capital and outside the Beltway. The chapter does not, however, include two obvious, prominent groups: Mormon missions and Jesuit missionaries. Both of these organizations operate as religious missionaries, and their work is very similar to the national military service or represents an alternative to military service. They are excluded because both groups possess a decidedly proselytizing goal.

International Organizations

Amnesty International
International Secretariat
1 Easton Street
London WC1 XOD
United Kingdom

Voice: 44.20.74135500
Facsimile: 44.20.79561157
Web page: www.amnesty.org
Local offices around the world, including
Amnesty International USA
5 Penn Plaza, 14th floor
New York, New York 10001
Voice: 212.807.8400
Facsimile: 212.463. 9193 or 212.627.1451
Electronic mail: admin-us@aiusa.org
Web page: www.amnestyusa.org

Amnesty International (AI) began in the 1960s in Britain in hopes of guaranteeing that all individuals around the world would receive the protections espoused in the Universal Declaration of Human Rights (1947). Seen by many as excessively critical of most governments around the world because of the organization's fears that human rights cannot be compromised without gradual erosion of the protections they guarantee, AI prides itself on being fair and impartial in protecting the rights of individual men and women around the world. One of the AI's auxiliary interests is monitoring national service obligations, particularly for children, in effect under national service policies around the world. Amnesty International organizes much of its work around international campaigns, such as against child soldiers, against the death penalty, monitoring refugees, and a host of other concerns. AI also issues reports on human rights conditions and concerns in individual countries and regions of the world.

Much of the work conducted by AI is facilitated through grassroots support around the world. While AI receives grants, it also has support from millions of individuals who make personal contributions to its work. Much AI work concentrates on educating the citizenry of the world about conditions created by government actions and armed opposition groups seeking to change the international climate. The Web page maintained by the international secretariat contains a vast array of electronic links to other human rights organizations and studies.

Human Rights Watch
350 Fifth Avenue, 34th Floor
New York, New York. 10018–3299

Voice: 212.290.4700
Facsimile: 202.736.1300
Electronic mail: hrwnyc@hrw.org
Web page: www.hrw.org

Human Rights watch originally had the name "Helsinki Watch" when it was associated with human rights violations exclusively behind the Iron Curtain. With the greater international awareness that globalization increasingly allowed, the organization absorbed human rights monitoring groups in various regions and, after its first decade, took on its current look. Human Rights Watch, despite its title, has a major advocacy role in precluding people who do not want to engage in national service from doing so. Headquartered in New York, it also has offices in London, Toronto, Brussels, Moscow, Tashkent, San Francisco, Los Angeles, Washington, and Hong Kong. Human Rights Watch also includes a component of individuals engaged in or trying to avoid national service around the world, especially in repressive regimes.

International Coalition to Stop the Use of Child Soldiers
International Secretariat
2–12 Pentonville Road
2nd floor
London N1 9HF
United Kingdom
Voice: 44.20.7713.2761
Facsimile: 44.20.771.2794
Electronic mail: info@child-soldiers.org
Web page: www.child-soldiers.org/coalition

Formed in 1998 with several international organizations as its basis, the coalition aims to "end the recruitment and use of boys and girls as soldiers, to secure their demobilization and to promote their reintegration into their communities." The concentration of research, education, and coordinated advocacy is seen as the key to ending any obligatory national service or forced participation by children under 18 who are too young to protect themselves, often abandoned or orphaned in highly violent, contested areas of the world. The coalition has worked across the world, as explained in the organization's reports, studies, and press releases.

The coalition's Web site contains an impressive array of resources, and their electronic links tie the reader to various groups around the world in this field.

Quaker United Nations Office–Geneva
13 Avenue de Mervelet
1209 Geneva
Switzerland
Voice: 41.22.748.4800
Facsimile: 41.22.748.4819
Electronic mail: quno@quno.ch
Web page: www.quaker.org/quno

Begun as a movement in the 1650s to foster the kind of life preached by Jesus Christ, the Religious Society of Friends is better known as the Quakers. Though begun in England, Quakers are now most commonly found in the Western Hemisphere or Africa. Quakers emphasize the peaceful prevention of conflict. In the United States they are often referred to as pacifists and have issued a number of statements that govern the movement's attempts to prevent war around the world (see the Web site for these statements). The Quakers have an active organization in the United States (the American Friends Service Committee) but function with United Nations' offices in Geneva and New York to highlight the movement's belief that dialogue can prevent conflict but must be worked at in a deliberate, sustained manner. The Quaker offices associated with the United Nations engage in and promote this dialogue. Two relevant publications of the Quaker United Nations Office (QUNO) include reports on child soldiers around the world, *Child Soldiers: Deprived of Parental Care* (July 2005), and a variety of specific studies on child and particularly girl soldiers in major conflicts around the world (e.g., Colombia, the Philippines, Sri Lanka). These are available on the Web site. Similarly, the Quakers have an extensive series of publications on conscientious objection status in conflicts and in general around the globe. These studies and statements are also available through the Web site.

The Religious Society of Friends (Quakers)
Quaker United Nations Office–New York
777 United Nations Plaza

New York, New York 10017
Voice: 212.682.2745
Facsimile: 212.983.0034
Electronic mail: qunony@afsc.org

The Society of Jesus (Jesuits)
U.S. Jesuit Conference
1616 P Street, N.W., Suite 300
Washington, D.C. 20036–1420
Voice: 202.462.0400
Electronic mail: webmaster@jesuit.org
Web page: www.jesuit.org

Dating to the death of St. Ignatius of Loyola, a fifteenth-century Spanish priest who inspired an international movement within the Catholic Church, the Jesuits are one of the largest orders of the Church with a presence in more than 100 countries around the world. Jesuits are often called the educators of the Catholic Church and have frequently been a thorn in the side of the hierarchy in Rome. Their role in national service is that of an order working in countries where many young men are forced into national service (or forced into service by groups fighting any government). Often labeled caretakers of social justice concerns within the Catholic faith, Jesuits have been involved in preventing forced participation for many years. The Web site maintained by the Jesuit Conference of the United States discusses pastoral work on issues relating to national service in as many as forty countries around the world.

Not-for-Profits in the United States

Air Force Association
1501 Lee Highway
Arlington, Virginia 22209–1198
Voice: 800.727.3337
Electronic mail: service@afa.org
Web page: www.afa.org

The Air Force Association is an educational, not-for-profit organization aimed at advancing public understanding of air power and the role of the Air Force in the U.S. national services. The association proudly reminds its members of ties dating back to a founder of the Air Force, General Billy Mitchell, during World War I when the United States did not possess a first-class air force. Use of airpower during World War I under General "Hap" Arnold brought greater understanding of the importance of this form of warfare. Ultimately, the Defense Reorganization Act of 1947 led to the creation of the Department of the Air Force as a force separate from the Army. The Air Force Association, formally begun in 1946, has long prided itself on providing the most comprehensive understanding and education of air power available to the public. In addition, the AFA pushes its members' needs by working to educate the Congress along with the public on what the commitment to join the Air Force means. The association is led by volunteers across the United States in one international and thirteen regional components. The AFA's daily activities are carried out by the national headquarters in Arlington, Virginia, with access not only to the Congress but also to the Air Force hierarchy in the Pentagon. For calendar year 2006, for example, the association lists eleven major policy concerns, including Concern for Airmen, Total Force Concerns, Civilian Workforce Concerns, and Veteran and Retiree Concerns. These are handled through education as well as through its various programs and charities. AFA publishes a monthly, *Air Force Magazine*, that reaches more than 135,000 subscribers, along with *Newsline* (about the association's regular activities) and *Visions Newsletter*, which covers current educational work. Along with individual members, AFA has a significant corporate membership that is crucial to its work.

Association for the U.S. Army
2425 Wilson Boulevard
Arlington, Virginia 22201
Voice: 800.336.4570
Web page: www.ausa.org

With 126 chapters around the globe, the Association of the United States Army (AUSA) offers three types of membership: individual, corporate, or sustaining. Along with receiving the monthly publications about the Army and AUSA, the association is heavily involved in overall debate and education on the Army's role in the United States and its national security. Dating to 1950, the association concerns itself with active-duty, Reserve, National

Guard, retired, and civilian Department of the Army employees. Its interests in educating about and enhancing the Army's role in national security are extensive. AUSA holds numerous meetings around the nation, many of which are orchestrated through the individual chapters. The AUSA Institute of Land Warfare is a research facility designed to enhance one's grasp of security concerns, with a land-conflict emphasis. Finally, AUSA also has a Directorate of Government Affairs that coordinates its policy lobbying activities and overall monitoring of legislation affecting the Army. AUSA has a significant program of activities for NCO and enlisted personnel as well as for Army families. The *ARMY Magazine* is a monthly on activities of interest to members.

The Brookings Institution
1776 Massachusetts Avenue, N.W.
Washington, D.C. 20036
Voice: 202.797.6000 (general inquiries)
Voice: 202.797.6404 (Web content inquiries)
Voice: 202.797.6252 (Brookings Press inquiries)
Web page: www.brookings.edu

The Brookings Institution began in 1916 when a group of reformers from the Institute for Government Research began to push for better public policy discussion in the United States through a formal study organization. Six years later, Robert Somers Brookings, a St. Louis businessman, established two parallel organizations for similar purposes. The three organizations seeking to study policy questions merged into the Brookings Institution in 1927. The institution, often tagged as liberal, considers itself a research body without political advocacy but with an emphasis on encouraging greater debate. With a generous endowment and various other contributions, the institution hosts more than 140 scholars who work on an entire range of foreign and domestic policy issues, including a substantial number relating to national military service. Specifically, Brookings works on defense modernization, personnel, readiness, restructuring, transformation, civil-military relations, and other aspects of national service. Brookings' work appears in conferences, conference reports, studies, newsletters, and other publications. It also concentrates on post–Cold War conflicts around the world and overall use of military force. Brookings offers Executive Brookings, which includes a two-day seminar that is run annually for those who want a broad understanding of the challenges facing the United States, including national service issues. Speakers for this highly popular series have included former Secretary of Defense Robert McNamara and former Central Command Combatant Commander Anthony Zinni, USMC.

Carnegie Endowment for International Peace
1779 Massachusetts Avenue, N.W.
Washington, D.C. 20036–2013
Voice: 202.483.7600
Facsimile: 202.483.1840
Electronic mail: info@ceip.org
Web page: www.ceip.org

Located along the Massachusetts Avenue research band (adjacent to the Brookings Institution, the Johns Hopkins University School of Advanced International Studies, and the International Institute for Economics), the Carnegie Endowment took its name from Scottish steel magnate Andrew Carnegie's 1910 bequest for a nonpartisan research facility to study how to prevent conflict around the world. Carnegie holds an abundance of conferences on a range of issues as well as operating an office in Moscow to promote similar studies in the Russian capital. With a plethora of researchers, Carnegie is one of the most prominent research institutions around the world. Its work in national service is illustrated by its projects on America in the world, America and the war in Iraq, and religion and U.S. foreign policy to study whether religion plays a peculiar role in U.S. activities around the globe. Carnegie researchers regularly publish opinion pieces. Many leave the organization to take positions in presidential administrations. Carnegie staff members include some of the most often cited public policy voices in the United States, such as Robert Kagan.

Catholic Peace Fellowship
P.O. Box 4232
South Bend, Indiana 46634
Voice: 574.232.2295
Electronic mail: staff@catholicpeacefellowship.org
Web page: www.catholicpeacefellowship.org

The Catholic Peace Fellowship openly and deliberately supports Catholic conscientious objectors who prefer not to engage in national service, proudly citing the call by Dorothy Day to "urge a mighty league of conscientious objectors." The group uses a three-pronged approach: educating members of the Catholic Church about peace and war; working with those who have been engaged in national service but now see the need to invoke conscientious objector status; and publishing the monthly journal, *The Sign of Peace*. The organization's Web page cites chapters around the nation and operates a GI Rights Hotline to answer questions from those already engaged in national service but now facing doubts.

Cato Institute

1000 Massachusetts Avenue, N.W.
Washington, D.C. 20001–5403
Voice: 202.842.0200
Facsimile: 202.842.3490
Web page: www.cato.org

Begun through the efforts of Edward Crane in 1977, the Cato Institute holds an avowedly libertarian approach to public policy discussion, hoping to extract the United States from many foreign adventures and to keep government out of many aspects of individuals' lives. While Cato offers analysis on a wide range of public policy questions within the defense field, it studies several specific concerns relating to national service: military readiness, military personnel, conscription, and defense spending. It takes a minimalist view of the reasons the United States should commit its men and women to fight abroad, establishing only a direct threat to national interests of the territorial United States as a major threshold. The Institute publishes not only opinion pieces but also studies, such as Doug Bandow's "Feeling a Draft?" *Cato Policy Report*, 21, no. 2 (1999) or his "Fighting the War against Iraq: Elite Forces, Yes; Conscripts, No," *Cato Foreign Policy Analysis* 430 (2002).

Center for American Progress

1333 H Street, N.W., Tenth Floor
Washington, D.C. 20005
Voice: 202.682.1611
Electronic mail: progress@americanprogress.org
Web page: www.americanprogress.org

Bursting on the public policy scene at the turn of the millennium, the Center for American Progress has become one of the most prolific organizations sponsoring public policy events to debate a range of national priorities. Proclaiming a progressive agenda, the center maintains that its work is nonpartisan and not-for-profit under the 501(c)(3) status of the U.S. tax code. Advocating a strong, sharp military, the center acknowledges many threats to the United States around the world but has evaluated some existing public policy decisions differently from other significant think tanks, such as the American Enterprise Institute or the Heritage Foundation. A number of the fellows at the center have strong liberal credentials, several having served in the Clinton administration, but this is not uniformly true. A prominent and often-cited fellow at the Center for America Progress is Reagan administration Department of Defense official Lawrence J. Korb. The center has three core topics for research and debate, one of them including defense. Within that vast topic, there have been several studies, press announcements, and conferences on national service issues. The center has a large number of reports that focus on its belief in the need to revise the current national service system, such as the December 2004 "For Soldier and Country: Saving the All Volunteer Force," "Base Closings Meant to Bypass Politics" in May 2005, and "Transforming the Reserve Component" in September 2004. Each of these studies presents an executive summary online along with the PDF link to the entire study. They are easily accessible to anyone reaching this site and illustrate one of the most modern uses in the think tank community today of the new technology that has revolutionized communications by aggressively making the center's products available in any medium. Similarly, the center issued an evaluation of the current applications of the 1986 Goldwater-Nichols Military Reform Act of 1986, and hence the use of national military service, to the threats against the United States, through a widely covered press conference in June 2005.

The center is also expanding its work from the Washington base to campus activities around the country.

Center for Defense Information
1779 Massachusetts Avenue, N.W.
Washington, D.C. 20036–2109
Voice: 202.332.0600
Facsimile: 202.462.4559

Electronic mail: info@cdi.org
Web page: www.cdi.org

The Center for Defense Information (CDI) has a long history of providing analysis on national security concerns, including national service. It bucks the trend in Washington because it does not take any governmental funding, and it advocates strengthening national security through greater cooperation around the world instead of greater defense against conflict. It was long run by two retired U.S. rear admirals, and the president is now former Air Force missile officer and scholar Bruce Blair. CDI's work is often cited by the press. Blair took CDI from its private status to its participation as a subsection of the World Security Institute, which also oversees the International Media and Azimuth Media and International Programs that operate in Washington, Beijing, Moscow, and Brussels. Two projects highlighting CDI's work on national service issues are Children and Armed Conflict and the Straus Military Reform Project. In the latter case, it is intended to generate public policy debate about how the United States deploys and accesses national service personnel.

Center for Security Policy
Suite 210
1920 L Street, N.W.
Washington, D.C. 20036
Voice: 202.835.9077
Facsimile: 202.835.9066
Web page: www.centerforsecuritypolicy.org

The Center for Security Policy, established in 1988 by former Reagan Defense Department official Frank Gaffney, focuses on national service issues through the broader lens of what is threatening the United States, at home and abroad. The center covers a range of traditional security concerns such as military readiness, transformation, the threats posed by China and Russia, terrorists, Operation Iraqi Freedom, and energy overdependence. It goes beyond these issues to raise red flags about the "peace movement" (these are the organization's quotation marks) and the threats posed by the Islamic world. The Center for Security Policy is often viewed as conservative because of Gaffney's role in its founding, but it has a nonpartisan, educational goal as its stated mission. The center aggressively promotes putting out its analyses through facsimiles and media reports. It hosts conferences and issues studies on security questions. The center has a Web page that is particularly useful for electronic links to other organizations and materials.

Center for Strategic and Budgetary Assessments
1730 Rhode Island Avenue, N.W., Suite 912
Washington, D.C. 20036
Voice: 202.331.7990
Facsimile: 202.331.8019
Web page: www.csba.org

The Center for Strategic and Budgetary Assessments (CSBA) is a not-for-profit analysis organization that focuses on defense assessments in the broadest sense of the term, including the challenges of national military service. Started to provide timely, impartial, visionary analysis of the various angles of defense, the center is acknowledged as one of the most respected groups in the country because it does not lean toward any particular position but instead offers solid answers to some of the greatest challenges facing the nation. Much of its credibility lies in its employment of retired military officers who provide nuts-and-bolts studies that are impeccably sourced and researched. The work of CSBA falls into two broad categories: defense studies and strategic studies, with the defense studies founding the most relevant portion of the center's work on national military service questions. CSBA issues regular and as-needed reports, press releases, and other information pieces. Defense budget studies consider readiness, military operations, weapons systems, and the budgetary process, among other topics. The center provides a wide array of publications, some of which are targeted at Congress and others at the public. It also holds a range of public events, such as the December 2005 discussion on U.S. policy in Iraq, which attracted much participation and was repeatedly rebroadcast on C-Span in subsequent months.

Center for Strategic and International Studies
1800 K Street, N.W.
Washington, D.C. 20036
Voice: 202.887.0200

Facsimile: 202.775.3199
Web page: www.csis.org

The Center for Strategic and International Studies (CSIS) is probably the single most prominent think tank in the United States today in international affairs, with a major involvement in analysis of defense issues. A subsection of that work relates to national military service. An outgrowth of the American Enterprise Institute research activities located at Georgetown University in the early 1960s, CSIS became independent in 1966 when it moved from the Jesuit campus to the K Street area of Washington, D.C. In the years after achieving autonomy, CSIS aggressively built an impressive stable of experts who were available to the press. CSIS has three research foci: defense and security issues, regional concerns, and global trends. In the area of defense, six distinct programs allow the range of study in this field: defense policy, homeland security, postconflict reconstruction, international security, proliferation prevention, and terrorism and transnational threats. In defense policy, CSIS targets half a dozen distinct but interrelated aspects of the conditions at work. These include a three-phased initiative on Goldwater-Nichols in the twenty-first century, to include Phase I on military reform, Phase II on interagency reconsiderations, and Phase III on National Guard and Reserve functions in the United States. Other work examines the defense industrial base, European defense integration, the military balance around the world, the Project on Nuclear Issues, and the Seven Revolutions, which examine the range of changes that can be considered in making defense-related decisions. CSIS, with its large budget and tremendous range of outreach, engages in media and publishing ventures. CSIS has a wide number of publications but concentrates on studies accessible online and/or through its Web page as well as for purchase. CSIS also holds a large number of events, most of which are open to the public, to encourage public policy debate on many of these issues.

Center for the Study of Sexual Minorities in the Military
University of California–Santa Barbara
Department of Political Science
Santa Barbara, California 93106–9420

Web page: http://www.gaymilitary.ucsb.edu/Publications/
evans3.htm

The Center for the Study of Sexual Minorities in the Military
(CSSMM), a 501 (c)(3) located at the University of California in
Santa Barbara, offers studies and education on the role of gays
and lesbians in the U.S. armed forces. The center has published a
number of studies challenging the assumptions behind the current "don't ask, don't tell" policy, which de jure precludes active
national service by gays and lesbians. Studies are presented for
public and congressional debate. The CSSMM Web page offers a
long list of studies the center has produced as well as a listing of
research and teaching resources for scholars and interested
citizens.

Center on Conscience and War
1830 Connecticut Avenue, N.W.
Washington, D.C. 20009
Voice: 202.483.2200 or 1.800.379.2679
Facsimile: 202.483.1246
Web page: www.centeronsonscience.org

Formerly the National Interreligious Service Board for Conscientious Objectors which began in 1940, the Center on Conscience
and the War works to help conscientious objectors exercise their
right to preclude military service. The organization's Web site
notes clearly that it opposes all forms of military conscription. Its
services apply to anyone who is a natural-born U.S. citizen, a nat-
uralized citizen, a permanent resident, a citizen of another country, or an undocumented alien in the United States. This not-for-
profit operates across the country through objector counseling, a
hotline for GIs, and lobbying of Congress under the auspices of a
parallel organization. The center holds meetings across the country to counsel potential objectors while also working to shut
down the School of the Americas in Georgia, which trains Latin
American military officers.

Central Committee for Conscientious Objectors
405 14th Street, Suite 205
Oakland, California 94612
Voice: 510.45.1617

Facsimile: 510.465.2459
1515 Cherry Street
Philadelphia, Pennsylvania 19102
Voice: 215.563.8787
Facsimile: 215.563.8890
Electronic mail: info@objector.org
Web page: www.objector.org

The Central Committee for Conscientious Objectors aggressively argues against national military service. Its Web site portrays a variety of options available to young people tempted to enlist in the military while warning that the current policies of the United States are positioning the nation to require a return to the draft. Many of its sponsors are longtime activists dating back to the Vietnam-era antiwar movement, such as singer Joan Baez or academic Noam Chomsky. It is a not-for-profit organization but acknowledges that it rarely receives funding from mainline foundations or the government. The committee publishes a magazine, *The Objector,* which merged two prior publications, *CCCO News Notes* and *The Objector: A Journal of Draft and Military Counseling,* in 1995. The committee also has aggressive programs to advocate withdrawing military recruitment personnel from schools and promotes talks by prominent resisters or individuals who rejected the military after their service was completed. The student body within the Central Committee is the Student Coalition Resisting Enlistment and Militarism, subsumed by the CCCO Web site.

Friends Committee on National Legislation
245 Second Street, N.E.
Washington, D.C. 20002
Voice: 202.547.6000
Toll-free Voice: 800.630.1330
Web page: www.fcnl.org

The Friends Committee for National Legislation (FCNL) is a legally registered lobby organization under the federal tax code, meaning it does not have tax-exempt status, nor is the committee obligated to present a nonpartisan, balanced view of its concerns. The organization's not-for-profit parallel group is the Friends Committee on National Legislation Education Fund, which is a 501 (c)(3) requiring nonpartisan education. FCNL prides itself on being "the biggest peace lobby" as well as "the oldest registered ecumenical lobby" in the nation's capital, with a history beginning in 1943 with its founding by the Society of Friends (Quakers). With its history of pacifism, the FCNL has a mission statement noting its desire for a world "free of war and the threat of war," among four goals. The committee has public policy priorities conforming to its mission statement, including significant annual work on the defense budget, nuclear disarmament, and prevention of war. Lobby activities are targeted on the nation's capital, but the committee also has work in local communities where it attempts to raise public awareness about war. The FCNL issues many press statements and reports to influence public policy debate. It also encourages grassroots lobbying and citizen action, especially at lower ages. The committee receives much of its funding from public contributions.

G.I. Rights Hotline
405 Fourteenth Street, Suite 205
Oakland, California 94612
Voice: 215.563.4620
Toll-free Voice: 800.394.9544
Facsimile: 510.465.2459
Electronic mail: girights@objector.org
Web page: www.girights.objector.org

The hotline is a coalition of activists that aims to provide a range of advice and assistance to those serving in the U.S. military. Topics it covers include the "don't ask, don't tell" policy against homosexuality in the service, termination of service through discharge or absence without leave (AWOL) status, and issues relating to being stationed overseas. One unique feature of the organization is its Web page, which makes a conscious effort to include materials in both English and Spanish. The G.I. Rights project also provides a wealth of information to anyone using its Web page on absence without leave (AWOL) or unauthorized absence (UA) status, discharge procedures, and other procedures for separating from national service. The project receives the bulk of its funding from public donations. G.I. Rights is part of a coalition of organizations under the umbrella organization, Central Commission for Conscientious Objectors.

Global Volunteers
375 East Little Canada Road
St. Paul, Minnesota 55117–1628
Voice: 800.487.1074
Facsimile: 651.482.0915
Web page: www.globalvolunteers.org

Begun in 1984, Global Volunteers promotes community service around the world, with specific targets in several portions of the United States. Global Volunteers is somewhat unique in that its work has a specified short-term aspect, attempting to assist those in need through service. Within the United States, Global Volunteers has service projects in West Virginia, Hawaii, South Dakota, Minnesota, Montana, Florida, and Mississippi. These activities are heavily related to poor or underprivileged portions of the United States.

Heritage Foundation
214 Massachusetts Avenue, N.W.
Washington, D.C. 20002–4999
Voice: 202.546.4400
Facsimile: 202.546.8328
Electronic mail: info@heritage.org
Web page: www.heritage.org

The Heritage Foundation may well be the most influential think tank in Washington, D.C. It was begun in 1973 to give conservatives a more visible presence in the public policy debate through funding by Coors Beer magnate Peter Coors and other important corporate donors. From that beginning, Heritage has gradually increased its presence from its Capitol Hill location to a remarkable degree in all discussions, including that about national service. With substantial resources behind its work, Heritage actually publishes principles on its various and extensive research fields. In defense, the principles include taking steps for the Defense Department to use its resources responsibly while alleviating any stresses on the armed forces and deploying them where the United States alone can accomplish global missions. The Foundation also provides suggested readings, suggested national priorities, and various other positions supporting its perspective on how to best defend the United States. Much of the Heritage material is published simultaneously online and in hard copy. In addition, Heritage holds a vast number of public conferences, making many of them available through simultaneous Webcasts on the Internet.

Inter-University Seminar on Armed Forces and Society
Department of Political Science
Loyola University–Chicago
6525 North Sheridan Road
Chicago, Illinois 60626
Voice: 773.508.3047
Electronic mail: asigart@luc.edu
Web page: www.iusafs.org

The Inter-University Seminar on Armed Forces and Society (IUS) is an internationally respected research organization made up of fellows, the term for Inter-University Seminar on Armed Forces and Society (IUS) members, from across the globe. Founded under the guiding hand of University of Chicago military sociologist Morris Janowitz, the IUS has been perhaps the most influential academic research organization since its inception in 1960. Janowitz's successors at the helm of the group—Sam C. Sarkesian of Loyola University–Chicago, Charles Moskos of Northwestern University, David Segal at the University of Maryland–College Park, and John Allen Williams of Loyola–Chicago—have helped the organization retain its unique position in the field. IUS holds biennial conferences in the United States and around the world, with a unique format of a single presenter offering all the papers on a panel, followed by a discussant's analyses of the papers prior to the papers' authors actually answering audience queries on the material. The IUS journal, *Armed Forces & Society*, is the most influential multidisciplinary publication on issues relating to national service because of the quality of the peer-reviewed articles and the global nature of the authors. Many of the *Armed Forces & Society* articles focus on induction, retention, lifestyle issues, family concerns, and other themes at the heart of the national military service debate around the world.

Lexington Institute
1600 Wilson Boulevard
Suite 900
Arlington, Virginia 22209

Voice: 703.522.5828
Facsimile: 703.522.5837
Web page: www.lexingtoninstitute.org

The Lexington Institute has a strong history of examining public policy issues in the United States. One of its specialties is national service questions. An organization founded in the 1980s to focus on the national security, immigration, government reform, education, and economics topics that characterize a strong national state, the institute has a major focus, shown on its Web site, on defense, much of it hitting hard on national service. In 2005 alone, national service appeared in four issues briefs and a white paper with such topics as "No to a Larger Army!" and "Paying Homage to a Great Old Warrior"; Loren Thompson's "Air Guard Attacks BRAC Process with Dumb Bombs" (June) and "Fighter Plan Is Latest Evidence of Military Decay (July); and Dan Gouré and Ivan Susak's white paper "Logistics Transformation: Still Fighting the Last War?" (June). The institute also holds meetings and cosponsors them with others to get the public discussion going.

Mennonite Central Committee
21 South 12th Street, Box 500
Akron, Pennsylvania 17501–0500
Voice: 717.859.1151
Toll-free Voice: 888.563.4676
Web page: www.mcc.org

The Mennonite Central Committee (MCC) was organized in the wake of the Russian civil war of 1918–1920 to find a way to engage in the religion's biblical vision of the responsibility people have to help others. Some forty years later, in 1963, Canadian Mennonites joined their U.S. brethren to work toward relief where it is necessary around the world. A significant portion of the MCC's activities revolve around conscientious objectors and attempts to preclude people from being drawn into conflict. The MCC Web page has part of the site called "Ask a Vet," including stories on conscientious objectors. Two prominent projects of the MCC in the United States are Peace Education, to keep people from becoming enmeshed in conflict around the world or at home, and Peacebuilding, which is aimed at what the MCC views as meaningful conflict resolution activities. The MCC is part of the G.I. Rights project.

Military Officers Association of America
201 North Washington Street
Alexandria, Virginia 22314
Voice: 800.234.6622
Web page: www.moaa.org

The Military Officers Association of America (MOAA, formerly known as the Retired Officers' Association or TROA) is a diverse organization that focuses on the needs of retired, active-duty, and National Guard officers of the United States. MOAA has a range of activities, some educational and others involving lobbying, designed to enhance the lives of its members as they have given so much to their nation. Organized around local chapters and regional councils, the activities of MOAA allow for networking, promoting discussion on relevant topics, ensuring high-quality health care, providing financial services and advice, guaranteeing educational benefits, and generally monitoring the quality of life available to its members. In the late 1990s, when Congress eliminated the "double-dipping" prohibition against retired military collecting their full retirement if they were subsequently hired as federal employees, MOAA was a major force behind that change in the law. MOAA has a Legislative Action Center that provides updates on bills in progress, indicates what hearings are being held, recommends resources on relevant topics, and indicates how to contact the appropriate representatives to lobby for a position. MOAA holds an annual meeting for its membership and appropriate local meetings for each chapter or council. In addition, MOAA dedicates a portion of its extensive Web page to those "fully retired" as well as family and spouses.

National Association for Uniformed Services
5525 Hempstead Way
Springfield, Virginia 22151
Voice: 703.750.1342
Web page: www.naus.org

The National Association for Uniformed Services (NAUS) began in 1968, priding itself on being the only organization in the nation to represent all services in the officer and enlisted corps as a whole family group. As a veterans' organization of 501 (c) (19) status under the tax code, NAUS engages with the Congress, the

Pentagon, and the White House on behalf of the seven uniform branches of service (Air Force, Navy, Marine Corps, Army, National Oceanographic and Atmospheric Administration, Public Health Service, and Coast Guard). The NAUS mission includes helping military widows, active-duty families left stateside, and an array of other issues that are at the core of asking someone to serve his or her nation. The Web site is quite user-friendly and offers a great deal of information, especially on relevant current legislative developments on Capitol Hill.

National Defense Industrial Association

Voice: 703.247.2558 (customer support)
Electronic mail: tfletcher@ndia.org
Web page: www.ndia.org

The National Defense Industrial Organization (NDIA) dates back to 1997 when the American Defense Preparedness Association merged with the National Security Industrial Association. It currently consists of twenty-nine divisions and five industrial groups to link its vast network of individual and corporate members who come together to form "strength through industry and technology." NDIA has chapters in many places across the country where defense and industry coincide, such as the Aberdeen Training Ground in Maryland; San Diego, California; or the Virginia area called Greater Hampton Roads. The NDIA Web page indicates an extensive list of meetings of varying sizes for chapters of the national organization. NDIA also has an advocacy arm whereby it works to bring public and congressional attention to the need to retain the defense industrial base as well as the defense conditions for those engaged in national service. Major foci of that advocacy include privatization of military activities and outsourcing. Along with producing reports and media updates, NDIA publishes *National Defense Magazine* to highlight issues relating to national service.

National Guard Association of the United States

One Massachusetts Avenue, N.W.
Washington, D.C. 20001
Voice: 202.789.0031
Toll-free Voice: 1.888.22NGAUS
Facsimile: 202.682.9358

Electronic mail: ngaus@ngaus.org
Web page: www.ngaus.org

The National Guard Association (NGAUS), dating to 1878, has local chapters through which potential members must join and through which members of the association are able to pursue united goals to promote the Guard's concerns in the Congress, making certain the Guard takes its appropriate and well-re-sourced role within the national military service of the nation. Its targeted individual participants, organized into regional chapters across the country, are the commissioned and warrant officers of the Army and Air National Guard. Corporate membership through cognate industry groups is also welcome. The association's annual meetings bring industry together with the individual members. In promoting its membership's needs, the assocation also provides many services, such as discounted auto insurance and improved health-care benefits, which are available through a larger group activity. The NGAUS tracks legislation of interest to members and makes that available by phone (888.22NGAUS) or through the Internet (bphelps@ngaus.org). One of its primary interests over the years has been the Base Realignment and Closing (BRAC) process whereby the nation's military basing structure is altered through a supposedly nonpartisan committee process that the Guard Association often opposes. The association itself is not a not-for-profit organization, but its parallel National Guard Educational Fund is a tax-deductible 501 (c)(3) group. The association also maintains the National Guard Association Memorial Museum in Washington, D.C., along with a library on pertinent Guard materials. Contained within the association are also the Adjutants' General Association and the Enlisted Association of the National Guard for relevant members.

National Institute for Military Justice
Washington, D.C.
Web page: www.nimj.org

This is a peculiar organization in that the contact information listed above is an extensive Web page with impressive links but no further details. The institute and its primary public voice, Eugene Fidell, are prominently involved in virtually all of the military justice cases that appear in the contemporary scene, ranging from gays and lesbians in the military service opposing the "Don't

Ask, Don't Tell" policy to the role of women in national service to the staggeringly complex arguments at work in the legal cases forming the post-9/11 world of military justice. Fidell himself frequently appears in the media to discuss the legal questions, and the institute has taken on some of the most controversial legal cases of the era, including filing amicus briefings in the *Hamdan v. Rumsfeld* and other legal cases relating to the war in Iraq. The institute's mission is to improve public understanding of military justice while making an effort to see the "fair administration" of military justice. Lawyers affiliated with the institute have been some of the most frequent commentators in the media on the dilemmas and legal questions relating to both the prison scandal at Abu Ghraib and the questions relating to whether the military is subject to the Geneva Conventions as it wages the "war on terrorism." While the Web site does not give any further contact information, it does provide a postmaster function by which the public can send electronic mail to individual lawyers with ties to the institute. In 2005, the institute established an affiliation with the Washington College of Law at American University.

National Priorities Project
17 New South Street
Northampton, Massachusetts 01060
Voice: 413.584.9556
Facsimile: 413.586.9647
Web site: www.nationalpriorities.org

The National Priorities Project is a not-for-profit organization seeking to clarify the federal budget's impact on local, state, and city spending priorities. The institutions that provide roughly 75 percent of its operating budget include the Carnegie Corporation and the Rockefeller Brothers Fund. A component of its work gauges the impact of military recruiting on any population across the country with an eye toward encouraging the national dialogue on a range of public policy issues. The project's roots were in the coping mechanisms that citizens used in western Massachusetts in the face of budget cuts in 1983. The data include a section, begun in 2005, on how national security spending affects individual communities around the world. Embedded in this is specific spending for 400 communities in the United States where comparative assessments of the impact of national security can be made. The national security component is broken down into military spending, preventative measures, general data on security, and homeland security. Information appears in a variety of formats. This organization provides significant information on military recruiting, separated into individual zip codes across the country and available by service and Reserve versus active duty. Much of the project's work is available online.

The Project for a New American Century
1150 17th Street, N.W., Suite 510
Washington, D.C. 20036
Voice: 202.293.4983
Facsimile: 202.293.4572
Web page: www.newamericancentury.org

The Project for a New American Century began in 1997 under the leadership of William Kristol, a leading conservative thinker who in the late 1980s and early 1990s served as Vice President Dan Quayle's chief of staff. Joining Kristol were Robert Kagan and Gary Schmitt, with Schmitt serving as executive director of this not-for-profit organization. The project is intent upon promoting U.S. leadership under moral principles around the world based on strong defense, a moral foreign policy, and global leadership out of Washington. To achieve this goal, the project expects a strong defense built upon an adequate U.S. armed forces to accomplish its mission. The project has released two prominent documents: the first in 2000, entitled "Rebuilding America's Defenses," followed up five years later by a "Letter to Congress on Increasing U.S. Ground Forces," both of which supported increasing the size of U.S. forces available to carry out the missions of the United States. In neither case did the project endorse instituting a national service requirement to accomplish this expansion, but the implications are clear that U.S. national security cannot be protected without an increase in the force charged with protecting the country. According to the *Washington Post*, the project closed in 2006.

Triangle Institute for Security Studies
Rubenstein Hall

2204 Erwin Road
Box 90404
Duke University
Durham, North Carolina 27708–0404
Voice: 919.613.9280
Facsimile: 919.684.8749
Electronic mail: tiss@duke.edu or pumphrey@duke.edu
Web page: www.duke.edu/web/tiss

The Triangle Institute for Security Studies (TISS), currently head-quartered at Duke University in Durham, North Carolina, is a multiuniversity scholarly organization aimed at studying the types of questions involved in national military service. Formed in 1984 by faculty in the Research Triangle of North Carolina State University, University of North Carolina at Chapel Hill, and Duke, TISS offers a series of seminars and programs on security issues, with a heavy concentration on basic questions. In 1997, two of the most prominent members of TISS, former chief historian of the Air Force and professor of history at the University of North Carolina Richard Kohn and Duke political scientist Peter Feaver, coauthored an important iteration of the regular TISS study on civil-military relations in the late 1990s to consider whether the believed "gap" between civilians and military in the United States existed. That study was available in the volume *Soldiers and Civilians* and on their Web site through a link button. This project on the gap between military and civilian society received much attention as the country wrestled with the issue of national military service. Dr. Feaver took a leave of absence to work on President George W. Bush's National Security Staff Council on civil-military impacts on strategic thinking in the U.S. public. TISS continues to hold conferences on security issues but is not as prominently involved in national military service topics today.

United for Peace and Justice
322 Eighth Avenue, 9th Floor
New York, New York
Mailing address:
P.O. Box 607
New York, New York 10108
Voice: 212.868.5545

Facsimile: 646.723.0996

Web page: www.unitedforpeace.org

United for Peace and Justice is a coalition of local social activists and not-for-profit organizations that focus on alerting the public to the damage done to both the American and Iraqi public as a result of the war in Iraq.

The groups across the country may be quite small and work within their individual locations on raising public concern about American troops' commitment in Iraq. The coalition holds meetings and protests, and it tries to encourage public debate.

Veterans for Peace

216 South Meramec Avenue

St. Louis, Missouri 63105

Voice: 314.725.6005

Facsimile: 314.725.7103

Web page: www.veteransforpeace.org

Veterans for Peace, a 501 (c) (3) not-for-profit, is headquartered in St. Louis, Missouri, and has actively pursued discussions of national military service commitments since 1985. It is composed of public citizens, but many were U.S. veterans, originally those as far back as from the Spanish Civil War in the late 1930s. Veterans for Peace pledges itself to nonviolent reactions in the interest of preventing war and deaths in national military service.

Veterans of Foreign Wars of the United States

National Headquarters

406 West 34th Street

Kansas City, Missouri 64111

Voice: 816.756.3390

Facsimile: 816.968.1149

Electronic mail: info@vfw.org

Web page: www.vfw.org

Washington Congressional Office

VFW Memorial Building

200 Massachusetts Avenue, N.E.

Washington, D.C. 20002

Voice: 202.543.2239
Facsimile: 202.543.6719
Electronic mail: npomeroy@vfwdc.org

The Veterans of Foreign Wars is an organization that was formed at the end of the nineteenth century when most U.S. involvement in conflicts was relatively close to home, such as in extending the U.S. frontier or defending against nearby threats such as Mexico or the Caribbean. The VFW is a national organization with "posts" in various parts of the country where veterans can come together to share their experiences with other veterans or educate the public that has been left at home. The VFW has shrunk somewhat since, as a result of the end of military conscription, and fewer are serving in the services than was true thirty years ago. The VFW educates local groups but also has a major lobbying function in Washington where it works to improve benefits for those who nobly served their nation or to draw attention to problems of the all-volunteer force, for example, as shown on its Web page in the story "Military Heroism Denied," by Peter Gibbon.

War Resisters' League
339 Lafayette Street
New York, New York 10012
Voice: 212.228.0450
Facsimile: 212.228.6193
Web page: wrl@warresisters.org

Created in 1923 with an eye to ending the carnage that characterized the prior decade through World War I, the War Resisters' League is an activist organization intent on solving world problems through peaceful resolution. Although the league's focus has been on preventing war, the group broadened its concerns to civil rights and disarmament in the last decades. Its Web site notes a commitment to Gandhian nonviolent principles, and the league encourages passive resistance to conflict and government-required action around the world. Embued with the desire to prevent the government from obtaining the opportunity or resources to conduct war, the league emphasizes work against conflict. Of particular interest in national service is the league's Youth and Countermilitarism Program, which concentrates on helping young people in the United States resist national military service recruitment efforts. The War Resisters' League, with e-mail messages sent to youth@warresisters.org, organizes camps to prevent national recruitment efforts and publishes a manual on this topic. Embedded in this project are efforts to build coalitions in the United States among the young men and women of appropriate national service age. The league offers two primary publications: *The Nonviolent Activist*, a bimonthly publication on organizing against military activities, and the 2003 *War Tax Resistance*, which discusses attempts to prevent paying taxes that the league believes goes to fund wars. The league accepts donations but is not a tax-deductible group because it is activist rather than primarily educational. The league has a national office in New York and operates through local chapters across the nation.

For-Profit Research Institutions

The Center for Naval Analyses
4825 Mark Center Drive
Alexandria, Virginia 22311
Voice: 703.824.2004
Electronic mail: inquiries@cna.org
Web page: www.cna.org

The Center for Naval Analyses (CNA), a federally funded research center for the Navy, was created in the late 1940s, along with the RAND Corporation. The center is a major presence in the research field on maritime aspects of national military service. While the center's research activities are well beyond national security within the public policy debate, its most well-known area is national security with three major foci: international affairs, Project Asia, and the Strategy and Concepts Group. Project Asia and international affairs examine specific concerns, developments, and challenges facing the United States around the world. In the Strategy and Concepts Group, the center allows substantial study of military strategy, military transformation, military operations, and resources. The group employs a significant number of retired professionals from the operational Navy and other services. The center provides its analyses through conferences, research papers, and classified studies. Much of its work concentrates on the Navy, but the center is far more involved in questions relating to military service than might appear likely from its title.

Institute for Defense Analyses
4850 Mark Center Drive
Alexandria, Virginia 22311
Voice: 703.845.200
Web page: www.ida.org

Headed by retired Admiral Dennis C. Blair, former combatant commander of the Pacific Command, the Institute for Defense Analyses (IDA) is a vast organization that provides assessments and policy prescriptions for the national military service community. IDA has seven core research areas, which consider all aspects of defense transformation in the United States. Much of the work is highly classified, while other aspects are reported to the public upon completion of studies. Of particular relevance to national service is the field of force and strategy assessments, which include force planning, concept development, national security issues, and plans/processes/organization. IDA does much of its work on classified contracts, but some of it is also self-generated. Much of its work is released through the National Defense Information Center or the National Technical Information Service. The institute is a federally financed research and development center, like the RAND Corporation and the Center for Naval Analyses.

The RAND Corporation
1776 Main Street
Santa Monica, California 90401–3208
Voice: 310.393.0411
Facsimile: 310.393.4818
Web page: www.rand.org

With its inception as Project RAND (Research and Development) within the Douglas Aircraft Company in December 1947, RAND began its prominent role as a public policy research organization. Initially heavily biased toward work on the emerging Air Force of the United States, RAND was originally viewed as a not-for-profit center for scholarly assessment of pressing issues. Today, RAND's headquarters in Santa Monica, California, is also supported by offices in Qatar, Leiden, the Netherlands, Cambridge, United Kingdom, Pittsburgh, Pennsylvania, and Arlington, Virginia. Over its almost seven decades' existence, RAND has evolved to become a broadly concerned institution, writing on topics ranging from obesity to education to international affairs to national security retention problems. Today, RAND is one of the federally financed research and development centers (FFRDCs) providing analysis to the U.S. government. RAND heavily studies a panoply of issues connected to national service, such as *Stretched Thin: Army Forces for Sustained Operations.* National security is a core research function of RAND, containing five further subdivisions: Acquisition and Technology, Force Structure and Employment, Global Security Environment, Logistics and Infrastructure, and Personnel, Training, and Health. RAND's national security studies fall under a series of administrative structures: Project Air Force, Project Arroyo (also known as RAND Army Research Division), and RAND National Security Research Division. Where applicable, RAND also creates special projects to survey a topic, such as Gulf War Illness Studies. RAND has a specific program dedicated to studies by military fellows from the four services. The vast array of RAND publications and products (testimony to Congress, newsletters, op-ed pieces in news outlets, media appearances, and conference materials, as examples), are available online through its catalog at http://www.rand.org/publications/catalogs/RAND_Internat-Mil_05_Cat.pdf and a publication entitled *Recasting National Defense: A Catalog of RAND Research*, available online at http://www.rand.org/natsec_area/products/cp425.pdf. The latter, to illuminate how vast the research ranges, is a fifty-six-page catalog of publications. The RAND Web page is easy to navigate and rather readily leads the user to materials. RAND sells many of its nonclassified products, but some are available to download from the World Wide Web.

U.S. Government

AmeriCorps. *See* **Corporation for National and Community Service**

Corporation for National and Community Service
1201 New York Avenue, N.W.
Washington, D.C. 20525
Voice: 202.606.5000
Facsimile: 202.606.3472
Electronic mail: info@cns.org
Web page: www.nationalservice.org/

The Corporation for National and Community Service is a federal umbrella organization that administers volunteer activities considered as important as national military service. The corporation emphasizes the importance of the commitment to volunteer to help others within the U.S. society. Five of the corporation's programs are Americorps, Senior Corps, Americorps Vista, Americorps NCCC, and Learn and Service America. In addition, the corporation promotes the Martin Luther King, Jr., Day of Service to remind individuals of the importance of sharing with others. President George H. W. Bush created the Commission for National and Community Service in 1990 to bring life to his campaign concept of a thousand points of light to encourage volunteerism. His successor, President Clinton, transformed the commission into the current corporation by the same name. The corporation works with the Department of Education to encourage students to engage in the federal work-study program in community programs. In addition, the corporation provides an interface between volunteer organizations and the federal government, which serves an important national role. The Americorps Project offers state and national grants to promote volunteerism necessary to address local needs. Americorps NCCC, a legacy of the 1930s Civilian Conservation Corps created by President Franklin Delano Roosevelt, is a resident program for individuals between eighteen and twenty-four years of age who seek to work on targeted activities in community service. Americorps VISTA, with roots in President Lyndon B. Johnson's agency of the same name in the 1960s, assists local poverty-prevention and low-income activities with accomplishing their community-service goals. Senior Corps offers a rich linkage between more seasoned volunteers who have much experience to bring to community activities for solving local problems. The corporation's Web page offers scholarship opportunity information and provides access to lists of volunteer needs across the nation.

Military History Institute
22 Ashburn Drive
Carlisle, Pennsylvania 17013–5008
Electronic mail: usamhi@carlisle.army.mil
Web site: www.carlisle.army.mil/usamhi

National Defense University
Fort Lesley J. McNair
Washington, D.C. 20319
Web page: www.ndu.edu

The National Defense University (NDU), founded in 1976 as an umbrella organization for the Industrial College of the Armed Forces and the National War College, now holds several research bodies that consider national military service. The Center for Technology and National Security Policy, created at the start of the twenty-first century, actively examines the cutting issues of technology that will affect national security in the near and longer terms. It focuses primarily on peace operations and their effects on the individual peacekeepers. The transformation of the U.S. military is a key aspect of the center's work. Similarly, the Institute for National Strategic Studies at NDU also examines transformation, with particular emphasis on the strategic environment for national service. Finally, both the National War College and Industrial College of the Armed Forces study strategy but inculcate an appreciation of the effects and challenges of national service in their appraisal of future conflict.

The Peace Corps
Paul D. Coverdell Peace Corps Headquarters
1111 20th Street, N.W.
Washington, D.C. 20526
Voice: 800.424.8580
Web page: www.pc.gov

The Peace Corps, envisioned by President John F. Kennedy in a speech in Ann Arbor, Michigan, in 1961, has endured forty-five years of global change. The Peace Corps was originally seen as a parallel to the Agency for International Development as a governmental arm of development around the world, with the corps having a much more personal, direct, teaching aspect. Others saw the corps as an arm of counterinsurgency as the United States sought to spread its influence in remote areas of the world. The Peace Corps activity revolves around an individual or married couple serving for a fixed term in a location where a particular skill can bring fundamental change to a region and can be replicated by those living there once they have learned the skill. An example might be a fishery expert, often young but increasingly seasoned after another career, living in a remote village of Niger in West Africa teaching the local population how to make the best use of water resources to breed fish, all in the interest of improving the community standard of living. Many young men have chosen service in the Peace Corps over service in the armed forces during the almost six decades of the program, although not without some controversy, as many critics are not convinced that the commitment is equivalent. Almost 200,000 volunteers have served since the program began. Skills in all aspects of development are desirable, but skills are more heavily skewed toward education and health issues. With the gradual rise in world development since the early 1960s, the Peace Corps has taken on a lower profile, but it remains a very active national service organization. The organization's Web page is a simple vehicle for gathering information on activities.

Selective Service System
National Headquarters
Arlington, Virginia 22209–2425
Voice: 703.605.4100
Facsimile: 703.605.4106
Web page: www.sss.gov

President Jimmy Carter created the Selective Service System in 1980 in the wake of the Soviet invasion of Afghanistan in December 1979. Strictly observed as not a return to the draft, the Selective Service System requires all young men between 18 and 25 to register for national military service should the Congress and president call for their use in a conflict. Men register according to their age, not their physical fitness or desire to enter service. The registration is required by law and is not voluntary. Women, however, are specifically excluded from registration. As of September 2003, the service's Web site noted that 13.5 million men had registered under the system. The Web page also indicates the sequence of events that would occur should national service be required, thus activating these Selective Service registrations as active-duty forces. The service is organized into three regional offices, which would administer the program to bring men to active duty if so required. The service has not been without controversy: many groups believe that this registration is an easy move back to a national draft. But President Carter intended to make it possible to re-create a draft mechanism relatively easily when he instituted the Selective Service program, and all four of his successors have continued it.

Strategic Studies Institute
c/o Public Affairs Office
122 Forbes Avenue
Carlisle Barracks, Pennsylvania 17013–5006
Voice: 717.245.4101
Facsimile: 7171.245.4224
Electronic mail: AWCC-CPA@carlisle.army.mil
Web page: www.carlisle.army.mil/banner/index.htm

The Strategic Studies Institute (SSI) at the Army War College, along with the Peacekeeping Institute and the Military History Institute, is housed at the historic Carlisle Barracks in south-central Pennsylvania. The SSI also is active in holding conferences around the nation in conjunction with other organizations to promote public policy debate on appropriate questions. In 2006, for example, SSI joined with Women in International Security to host a daylong conference at Georgetown University entitled "Military Operations and Society: Continuity and Change." The Army War College publishes a prestigious quarterly, *Parameters,* on the range of national security topics, including many relating to national military service. The Army War College itself is the highest portion of professional military education for those in the Army, a ten-month accredited Master's Degree with emphasis on strategy from the Army's perspective. The Peacekeeping Institute, created in the 1990s, concentrates on the role of peacekeeping in solving and creating various difficulties for the nation as it increasingly uses this approach to ending conflicts around the world.

U.S. Navy War College
Strategic Research Department
Center for Naval Warfare Studies
686 Cushing Road
Newport, Rhode Island 02841–1207
Voice: 401.841.6568
Facsimile: 401.841.4161
Web page: www.nwc.mil.gov

The oldest of the service war colleges, the Naval War College has a research arm, the Strategic Research Department of the Center for Naval War Studies, which examines force issues within the Navy. Its work is wide-ranging and well-respected within the service. The Strategic Research Department also considers the economics of the Navy in the national military— hence its effects on military service. The college publishes much of its research through the touted *Naval War College Review.* Other products of the college and its researchers appear through the extensive Web page.

8

Selected Print and Nonprint Resources

Resources available electronically—whether through broadcast media or on the World Wide Web—are increasingly important in our research and reference concerns. As has been true for a decade, radio and television outlets have proliferated with the rise of cable systems around the country. Added to this volume has been the new category web log, known as "blogs"— Internet-based publications on a Web site created by an author to proliferate his or her views while also providing an interactive method by which the reader can respond to a topic. While blogs are highly subjective, they are increasingly important mechanisms for sharing views across the world, outside of the traditional methods such as voting or polling.

I have selected materials with the humble understanding of the enormous volume of materials on U.S. national military service. I have chosen those that focus as directly as possible on military service, not on the political causes that require that service. Some reports or studies have a broader title that appears to focus on national security because analysts link the requirements for national service to national security needs. At the same time, I link national military service to some social issues, such as desegregation or anthrax inoculations, because the U.S. military service has a long history of functioning in the area of social engineering.

Books aimed at a commercial audience are often also available in audio format, albeit they are usually somewhat abridged in length and content. While I do not highlight that aspect in a separate category, I recommend that individuals interested in finding commercially successful titles, such as that of Harold Moore and

Joseph Galloway, *We Were Soldiers Once . . . and Young: Ia Drang—The Battle Which Changed the War in Vietnam*, look at amazon.com or bn.com for the availability of audio copies of these titles.

Articles and Chapters

Jerry Cooper. "Federal Military Intervention in Domestic Disorders." In Richard H. Kohn, editor, *The United States Military under the Constitution of the United States, 1789–1989*. New York: New York University Press, 1991: 120–150.

The tradition of police forces versus using the national military for internal issues is covered in this fine essay. It also discusses *posse comitatus*, a concept periodically revisited in our history as we struggle with the problem of how to address pressing public policy disagreements.

Deborah Funk. "Troops Who Refused to Take the Anthrax Shots in Legal Limbo." *Air Force Times*. 65: 49 (June 27, 2005): 12.

The Department of Defense program to inoculate troops and officers against anthrax has shown the limits of state control over personal behavior since the program began in the late 1990s. The debate about this topic has surprised some and is not yet over.

"G.I. Jane, Again." *National Review*. 57: 10 (June 6, 2005): 22–24.

This is a discussion of the perennial topic of women in combat and their role, in general, in the services. This topic remains highly charged, particularly among those on the "right" of the political system who would appear to want to limit women's role in combat and in national military service.

Richard H. Kohn and Peter Feaver. *Soldiers and Civilians: The Civil-Military Gap and American National Security*. Cambridge, MA: MIT Press, 2001.

This is a long-heralded study of the relationship between the citizens of the United States and those who have volunteered to defend them. This study was based on interviews and surveys of active-duty officers in the United States during the Clinton administration, with comparisons to prior research studies. This volume came several years after Kohn's controversial *National Interest* article concerning his views of the growing gap.

————. "The Crisis in Civil-Military Relations." *The National Interest* 35. (Spring 1994): 3–17.

This highly controversial article charged that the military was becoming increasingly assertive in the traditional balance between civilian-military relations in the country. Kohn's article spun a debate that has lasted more than a decade—longer than the Clinton administration.

————, contributing editor. "The Constitution and National Security: The Intent of the Framers." In *The United States Military under the Constitution of the United States, 1789–1989.* New York: New York University Press, 1991: 61–94.

The former chief historian of the Air Force describes the goals of the Founders as they struggled with the problem of how to construct a document that would frame the United States' future.

Lawrence J. Korb. "Fixing the Mix: How to Update the Army's Reserves." *Foreign Affairs.* 83: 2 (March/April 2004): 2–7.

Korb served in the Reagan administration's Defense Department but has been a constant critic of President Bush's military policies. In this article, he advocates completely changing the Army Reserves to create a more useful force that will complement, not detract from, the all-volunteer force (active duty).

Allan R. Millett. "The Constitution and the Citizen-Soldier." In Richard H. Kohn, editor, *The United States Military under the Constitution of the United States, 1789–1989.* New York: New York University Press, 1991: 97–119.

A highly respected historian, long at Ohio State, describes the model that is most often cited for the U.S. armed forces and how it has survived a 200-year trial.

Richard B. Morris. "The Origin and Framing of the Constitution." In Richard H. Kohn, editor, *The United States Military under the Constitution of the United States, 1789–1989.* New York: New York University Press, 1991: 41–60.

Morris elegantly describes the trade-offs the Founders made in writing the Constitution, including the forces that made them worry about the need for a national army.

Charles C. Moskos. "Making the All-Volunteer Force Work: A National Service Approach." *Foreign Affairs* 60, no. 1 (Fall 1981): 17–34.

An assessment of how the all-volunteer force in the United States needed shifting almost ten years after it was instituted to end domestic turmoil over the Southeast Asian conflict.

———. "Citizen Soldier and National Service." In Gerald Suttles and Mayor N. Zald, editors, *The Challenge of Social Control.* Norwood, NJ: Ablex, 1985: 149–160.

Known as the "military sociologist of his generation," the author considers where the country is in using the citizen-soldier model and national service as a function of social control.

———. "National Service: Needed and American." *Orbis* 34, 3 (1990): 385–391.

Long an advocate of obligatory military service as good for society in general, Moskos makes his case in this relatively brief piece prior to the First Gulf War.

———. "The New Cold War: Confronting Social Issues in the Military." In H. William Brands, editor, *The Use of Force after the Cold War.* College Station: Texas A & M University Press, 2000: 178–199.

When conflicts appear to be subsiding, analysis often turns to the problems confronting the internal dynamics of the armed forces. This piece explores the range that one prominent sociologist sees as crucial to maintaining or preventing an effective force.

———. "What Ails the All-Volunteer Force: An Institutional Perspective." *Parameters* 31, 2 (Summer 2001): 29–47.

Moskos has visited deployed troops in the field for forty years while also spending much time inside the Beltway. His knowledge of the military institution is vast and his analysis acute.

———. "Reviving the Citizen-Soldier." *The Public Interest* (Spring 2002): 76–85.

Moskos firmly advocates putting the citizen-soldier model back to work in the United States. He paints a poignant picture that anticipates the commitment that men and women in uniform faced in the lead-up to the Iraq conflict and in the early months of Afghanistan.

Bernard Nalty. "The Black Serviceman and the Constitution." In Richard H. Kohn, editor, *The United States Military under the Constitution of the United States, 1789–1989*. New York: New York University Press, 1991: 151–172.

One of the least satisfactory portions of U.S. military service has been the treatment of African American service personnel throughout our history. Nalty discusses this topic in detail, showing how African Americans have advanced despite the poor treatment.

Alexander Soussi. "Interview with Israeli Refuseniks." *New Internationalist* 380 (July 2005): 53.

This article describes why some have tried to avoid military service in the Jewish state, even though that service is virtually a universal requirement.

Eric Umansky. "Explainer: Army Reserve vs. National Guard." *Slate Online Magazine,* January 7, 2005 (accessed on August 23, 2005, at http://slate.msn.com/toolbar.aspx?action-print&id-2112001).

In U.S. society where an increasingly smaller percentage of the public ever participates in national military service, this article clarifies the differences between the Army Reserves and the National Guard.

D. Anthony Week. "Serving as a COTR in Iraq." *Contract Management* 45, no. 7 (July 2005): 54–55.

In the era of increasing "outsourcing" of government services, this article discusses what a civilian contractor finds operating in Iraq.

Edited Books and Monographs

The Army and the New National Security Strategy. RB-3040-A. Santa Monica, CA: RAND, 2003.

This work discusses the changes that will affect recruiting and service in view of the Army's position in national security strategy.

Douglas Bandow. *Human Resources and Defense Manpower*. Washington, DC: Institute of Higher Defense Studies, 1989.

This volume covers the range of defense staffing requirements. Bandow now works at the CATO Institute, a Libertarian think tank that generally opposes U.S. interventions abroad, thus requiring a smaller national service base.

Mark Bowden. *Black Hawk Down*. New York: Atlantic Monthly Press, 1999.

This is a gripping discussion of the Sunday in October 1993 when the United States suffered the loss of men and equipment in a botched attempt to capture a Somali warlord in Mogadishu. Turned into a popular movie, this book describes the problems the Army had in getting its needs across to the civilian leadership in Washington, which was haunted by the specter of Vietnam. Instead of avoiding a repeat of the type of problems encountered in Southeast Asia, the entire Somali intervention of November 1992–summer 1994 proved a demoralizing one and undercut the Clinton administration's already shaky relationship with the uniformed officers corps.

Jimmie Briggs. *Innocents Lost: When Child Soldiers Go to War*. New York: Basic Books, 2005.

While the United States has strict limits on the age of its recruits for national service, conflicts in the Third World (especially Africa and Colombia) often see young boys active as soldiers in conflicts. This has long-term ramifications for the social structure of these societies once conflicts end.

Carl Builder, *The Masks of War: American Military Styles in Strategy and Analysis: A RAND Corporation Research Study*. Santa Monica, CA: RAND Corporation, 1989.

Builder's analysis is fascinating because it touches on so many cultural differences that characterize the services. Builder uncovers the basic orientation that soldiers, sailors, and air personnel develop once they begin operating within the hierarchy of each service, arguing that the "service culture" will win out over reform all too often.

James Burk. *The Adaptive Military: Armed Forces in a Turbulent World*. New Brunswick, NJ: Transaction Publishers, 1998.

The author looks at the many issues that confront the military besides its traditional national security concerns. These include social changes to the military's composition as well as the tasks it receives.

John Whiteclay Chambers II. *To Raise an Army: The Draft Comes to Modern America*. New York: Free Press, 1987.

This book describes the needs, trade-offs, and effects of conscription in twentieth-century U.S. affairs. Chambers is an eminently recognized historian on military service in the United States.

————, editor. *The Eagle and the Dove: The American Peace Movement and U.S. Foreign Policy, 1900–1922*. Syracuse, NY: Syracuse University Press, 1991.

Chambers presents a different angle on national service, to include the debate's other effects on overall U.S. strategy and foreign affairs.

John Whiteclay Chambers II, editor in chief, and Fred Anderson, editor. *The Oxford Companion to American Military History*. Oxford: Oxford University Press, 1999.

This handy volume presents essays on the range of important military events in the first two and a quarter centuries of U.S. history, highlighting the recurring questions about the role of the draft and military service.

John Whiteclay Chambers II and G. Kurt Piehler, editors. *Major Problems in American Military History: Documents and Essays*. Boston: Houghton Mifflin, 1999.

This series is often used in classrooms around the country to illustrate the texts that politicians and military officers actually used to instigate policies as well as to have prominent scholars analyze turning points and decisive events.

Carl von Clausewitz. *On War*. Translated by Michael Howard and Peter Paret. Princeton, NJ: Princeton University Press, 1976.

On War is perhaps the most often-quoted book in military affairs. Clausewitz was a Prussian officer who had a deep understanding of war and the strategy beyond the battlefield.

Rhonda Cornum. *She Went to War: The Rhonda Cornum Story*. Novato, CA: Presidio Press, 1993.

Cornum, an Army physician, served in Iraq where she was taken as a prisoner of war by the Iraqis. Her experiences are haunting but foretell the problems and opportunities for women serving their nation in national service in the future.

John Crawford. *The Last True Story I'll Ever Tell: An Accidental Soldier's Account of War in Iraq.* New York: Riverhead Books, 2005.

Crawford was a Florida National Guardsman who, like many current Guard members from across the nation, never expected to face deployment overseas. Crawford describes his frustration with less than adequate equipment, unclear mission statements, and a general loss over what his Guard experience had to do with his expectations when he signed up. This book rings true for many looking to challenge deployment abroad.

Lawrence Delbert Cress. *Citizens in Arms.* Chapel Hill: University of North Carolina Press, 1982.

This is a treatment of the development of the militia versus the standing army in the fledgling United States, focusing on the crucial developments during the War of 1812 period. It is often cited for its comprehensive explanation of the philosophical differences between the two groups, beginning with the various political ideologies being espoused as the colonists arrived in the New World as well as seeing the role of the British Army in political theory and practice, the decisions that created the system we have in place, and the theoretical underpinnings of the past three centuries. It is a superb explanation of trends that remain every bit as important today.

Constantine Danopoulos and Cynthia Watson, editors. *Political Role of the Military.* Westport, CT: Greenwood Publishing, 1996.

This volume includes studies of the military role in the politics of various states, including China, South Korea, Great Britain, Republic of South Africa, Brazil, and several others.

E. J. Dionne, K. M. Drogosz, and R. Litan, editors. *United We Serve.* Washington, DC: The Brookings Institution, 2003.

This edited volume presents a large number of contributions on national service broadly defined by major figures in public policy debate. It is interesting because of its publication *after* September 11, 2001. It considers, among other topics, how the national ethos of public service changed after that event.

Robert Dole. *One Soldier's Story: A Memoir.* New York: HarperCollins, 2005.

Former Senate Majority Leader Robert Dole details one of the more horrifying effects of national service: surviving serious injury. Dole was almost fatally injured during the Italy campaign toward the end of World War II. His memoir describes the effects on him and his family, together with life as a disabled citizen over the past sixty years.

Tod Ensign. *America's Military Today: The Challenge of Militarism.* New York: New Press, 2004.

This volume considers the importance of resurrecting the military draft, among other topics. Its currency allows inclusion of the Afghanistan and Iraq implications for the concerns about militarism.

Williamson M. Evers. *National Service: Pro & Con.* Stanford, CA: Hoover Institution Press, 1990.

Evers presents a wide-ranging series of nine essays, with an advocacy and an opposition position and discussion between the two positions. Topics include whether citizenship requires national service, how important national service is to federal government actions within society, and who within society must bear the burden of costs of national service.

Lorry M. Fenner and Marie de Young. *Women in Combat: Civic Duty or Military Liability.* Washington, DC: Georgetown University Press, 2001.

A consideration of the questions in the public policy debate about the effects that women would have in combat settings. This volume is written by an Air Force intelligence officer, Fenner, who argue that the services should open participation in combat positions as a fulfillment of the societal commitments. De Young, a retired Army chaplain, disputes that the integration of the sexes would have benefits for the services or society as a whole.

Eric B. Gorham. *National Service, Citizenship, and Political Education.* Albany: State University of New York Press, 1992.

This book covers a range of issues on national service as an alternative to national military service. In the period prior to the global war on terrorism and an expanded role for military service, the idea of national service was open to debate within society.

Robert A. Gross. *The Minutemen and Their World.* New York: Hill and Wang, 1980.

Gross uses local history to consider the development of military service in colonial Massachusetts, explaining why the Minutemen represented a social change in the hierarchy of Massachusetts as much as a military threat to Britain's power in the new world.

Don Higginbotham. *The War for American Independence.* Boston: Northeastern University Press, 1983.

This is a study of the independence period struggles and the importance it has to the consolidating of a national force.

Jeanne Holm. *Women in the Military: An Unfinished Revolution.* Novato, CA: Presidio Press, 1993.

A solid study of the history of women serving the nation by donning the uniform.

Samuel C. Huntington. *The Soldier and the State: The Theory and Politics of Civil-Military Relations.* Cambridge, MA: Belknap Press, 1957.

Huntington's book is arguably the most often-cited work on the relationship between military men and women and their government and, by extension, society.

Morris Janowitz. *The Professional Soldier: A Social and Political Portrait.* New York: The Free Press, 1971.

One of the most important monographs in the U.S. field of civil-military relations, this work covers the experiences that men and women have had while serving in the militaries around the world but with a special emphasis on the armed forces of the United States.

Richard H. Kohn. *Eagle and Sword.* New York: The Free Press, 1975.

Kohn presents an absolutely classic discussion of the trends at work in the United States during the initial decades of the newly independent United States, during the Articles of Confederation, Federalist, Jeffersonian, and Republican periods. It is well written and easily accessible for students of all levels of study and with all backgrounds.

Richard H. Kohn, editor. *Anglo-American Antimilitary Tracts, 1697–1830.* New York: Arno Press, 1979.

This is a compilation of the various views presented in the political tracts of the late seventeenth century into the first third of the nineteenth century. All these tracts became important in supporting those who opposed the establishment of a standing army in the newly independent United States.

Richard H. Kohn, editor. *Military Laws of the United States from the Civil War through the War Powers Act of 1973.* New York: Arno Press, 1979.

This thorough compilation of the wide range of national service laws focuses on the powers of the government, pensions, creation of a Coast Guard, and more issues from the past half of the nation's history.

Richard H. Kohn, editor. *The United States Military under the Constitution of the United States, 1789–1989.* New York: New York University Press, 1991.

This superb collection of essays is by the top historians in the country and covers various topics relating to U.S. national military service. The topics are both functional (Allan R. Millett's treatment of the citizen-soldier tradition in the United States under the Constitution) and practical (Arthur Link and John Whiteclay Chambers's contribution on Woodrow Wilson as commander-in-chief).

Douglas Edward Leach. *Flintlock and Tomahawk: New England in King Philip's War.* New York: W. W. Norton, 1966.

This volume examines the development of militia forces in English colonial America. It effectively weaves political, social, and military history while covering one of the events that first brought the colonists into the global conflicts facing Europe in the late seventeenth century.

James R. Locher III. *Victory on the Potomac: The Goldwater-Nichols Act Unifies the Pentagon.* College Station: Texas A & M University Press, 2002.

This is a fundamental exploration of the process whereby the Pentagon has developed a total force out of the various services and National Guard, active-duty, and Reserve portions. It is complex and well-documented.

John McCain and Dave McCurdy. "Forging a Military Youth Corps: A Military-Youth Service Partnership for High School Dropouts." *The Final Report of the CSIS National Community Service for Out-of-School Youth Project.* Washington, DC: Center for Strategic and International Studies, 1992.

This much heralded study by two important congressional leaders from both sides of the aisle argues for national service aimed at high school dropouts through a military youth corps.

Harold Moore and Joe Galloway. *We Were Soldiers Once . . . and Young: Ia Drang—The Battle That Changed the Vietnam War.* New York: Random House, 1992.

This is an extraordinarily powerful description of the 1965 battle at Ia Drang, one of the earliest major battles in the Vietnam War. Fought at a time when there was much optimism as the United States infused a significant number of troops in its effort to liberate South Vietnam, this book not only details the battle but also discusses the lives of the individuals who fought: some survived while others perished. Additionally, it provides superb insight on war's effects, immediate and longer term, on families at home.

Daniel Moran and Arthur Waldron, editors. *The People in Arms: Military Myth and National Mobilization since the French Revolution.* Cambridge, UK: Cambridge University Press, 2003.

Moran and Waldron present a series of analyses of military service in nations around the world since the late eighteenth century.

Charles C. Moskos. *A Call to Civic Service: National Service for Country and Community.* New York: The Free Press, 1988.

Moskos assesses the issues that face the country in trying to maintain an adequate military service for the United States and gives the various perspectives that pervade the public policy debate.

Charles C. Moskos and John Whiteclay Chambers II, editors. *The New Conscientious Objection: From Sacred to Secular Resistance.* New York: Oxford University Press, 1993.

Two highly respected scholars, a sociologist and a historian, edit a volume on a range of views on conscientious objection, twenty years after the end of the draft.

Theodore Nadelson. *Trained to Kill: Soldiers at War.* Baltimore, MD: Johns Hopkins University Press, 2005.

This book examines the controversial topic of what men and women face as their governments ask them to take another human being's life in conflict. It is a difficult topic to explore because its effects on an individual can be so traumatic.

Michael S. Neiberg. *Making Citizen-Soldiers: ROTC and the Ideology of American Military Service.* Cambridge, MA: Harvard University Press, 2000.

This survey of the Reserve Officer Training Corps experience in the United States, considering its antecedents and twentieth-century development, is a primer on some of the controversies and cultural differences between the academic and military goals in implementing and maintaining this program.

Michael E. O'Hanlon. *U.S. Defense Strategy after Saddam.* Carlisle, PA: U.S. Army War College, 2005.

O'Hanlon is a prolific analyst and resident at the Brookings Institution and offers his critique on whether U.S. military strength is adequate for the world that confronts us. He also discusses the advantages and disadvantages of returning to conscription to alter the size of the armed forces.

Bruce R. Orvis and Beth J. Ash. *Military Recruiting: Trends Outlook, and Implications.* Santa Monica, CA: RAND Corporation, 2001. Its contents are available to download as PDF files at http://www.rand.org/publications/MR/MR902/ (accessed on August 27, 2005).

Published before the Afghanistan or Iraq conflicts, this brief book (sixty-eight pages) is a sociological study of the supply and demand of recruits for the United States should a conflict arise, and it also considers the factors affecting recruiting levels.

John McAuley Palmer. *America in Arms.* New York: Arno Press, 1941.

This discussion of the effects of war on the United States as the nation was facing the possibility of entering on the eve of World War II is one of the most thoughtful criticisms of the existing military system.

Ford Risley. *The Civil War: Primary Documents on Events from 1860 to 1865*. Westport, CT: Greenwood Press, 2004.

These primary documents from the nation's most wrenching military conflict in its history provide an important framework for discussions of national service over the years.

Charles Royster. *A Revolutionary People at War: The Continental Army and American Character, 1775–1783*. New York: W. W. Norton, 1981.

This is an excellent study of the changes that the new nation underwent to create a national identity as well as a national character. Royster carefully notes comparisons between the U.S. system and other systems elsewhere. A complex linkage is shown between the social, intellectual, military, and constitutional history of the United States.

Mark I. Satin. *Radical Middle: The Politics We Need Now*. Boulder, CO: Westview Press, 2004.

Satin would like to see more public debate about the range of issues relating to military service and other important topics that he believes have been ignored.

Peter Shapiro, editor. *A History of National Service in America*. New York: Center for Political Leadership and Participation, 1994.

This outstanding book includes chapters on the major building blocks in this field, such as national service and education and the Youth Corps.

Michael Sherraden and Donald Eberly, editors. *National Service: Social, Economic and Military Impacts*. Elmsford, NY: Pergamon Press, 1982.

This collection of analyses from the United States and abroad concerns the variety of impacts of national service on societies.

Peter W. Singer. *Children at War*. New York: Pantheon, 2005.

Rather than focus on the U.S. system, Singer covers the growing global phenomenon of children being forced to participate as combatants in conflicts.

Don M. Snider and Gayle L. Watkins. *The Future of the Army Profession*. New York: McGraw-Hill, 2002.

This volume is an intensive study of how army personnel need to interact to make certain they meet the requirements that the U.S. society increasingly imposes on this body as the concept of and demands on the army are changing dramatically.

Mark A. Stoler. *George C. Marshall: Soldier-Statesman of the American Century.* Boston: Twayne Publishers, 1989.
This is a biography of the archetypical U.S. officer who went from being Army chief of staff to presidents Franklin Delano Roosevelt and Harry S Truman in the 1940s to being secretary of state under Truman. Marshall was a firm believer in strengthening the role of the military in society.

Russell Frank Weigley. *The American Way of War: A History of United States Military Strategy and Policy.* Bloomington: Indiana University Press, 1977.
One of the United States' most respected academic historians tackles the subject of the U.S. experience in warfare. This volume provides a fascinating contrast to many European experiences of war.

Cindy Williams. "Transforming the Rewards for Military Service." *MIT Security Studies Program Occasional Paper,* September 2005.
This study by a member of one of the major security studies programs in the country advocates increasing the incentives for those considering engaging in military service for the nation.

Opinion Pieces

James L. Abrahamson. "Reinstituting the Draft: Antiwar Activism in Disguise." *American Diplomacy* 3, no. 1 (2003) (accessed on August 21, 2005, at http://www.unc.edu/depts/diplomat/archives_roll/2003_01–03/abrahamson_draft/abrahamson_draft.html).
This article is part of the ongoing political debate on whether the draft, ended in 1973, would be a better way to populate the military ranks than the all-volunteer force.

Doug Bandow. "The Volunteer Force: Better Than a Draft," *Cato Foreign Policy Briefing No. 6,* January 8, 1991.

A vice president at the Libertarian CATO Institute, the author opposes returning to a military draft, particularly since he believes that U.S. commitments around the world should be reduced, not increased.

Doug Bandow. "Fighting the War against Terrorism: Elite Forces, Yes; Conscripts, No." *Cato Institute Foreign Policy Analysis No. 430,* April 10, 2002.

This author has long written in opposition to the need for a military draft in the United States. In particular, he believes that U.S. youth would not be particularly helpful in the war against terrorism.

Doug Bandow. "Sliding Towards Vietnam." *Progressive Theology,* November 6, 2003. (accessed at http://www.progressivetheology.org/essays/2003.11.06-Sliding-toward-Vietnam.html).

This analysis argues that the all-volunteer force and reasons being cited for going to war in Iraq and Afghanistan are dragging the United States toward a repeat of the social turmoil at home and prolonged involved in Vietnam.

Doug Bandow. "America Should Dodge Reinstituting the Draft." *Daily Commentary Cato Institute's Townhall.com,* August 15, 2005 (accessed on August 21, 2005, at http://www.cato.org/pub_display.php?pub_id=4247).

CATO Institute's vice president continues his argument against a military draft that would enlarge the military, making more forces available for conflicts that he believes the United States should not pursue.

E. J. Dionne, Jr., and Kayla Meltzer Drogosz. "The Promise of National Service: A (Very) Brief History of an Idea." *Brookings Institution Policy Brief #120,* June 2003.

The authors point out that Republican president George W. Bush agrees with Democratic former president Bill Clinton on the rights and responsibilities of citizenship, including national service in some form. This piece lays out various arguments to support a call for increasing commitment to national service.

Frederick W. Kagan. "The War against Reserves." *National Security Outlook AEI Online,* August 12, 2005.

Kagan believes that the armed forces Reserves are being seriously underestimated by many analysts; Kagen cites the Reserves' ability to act decisively in the Iraq and Afghanistan environments.

Charles Moskos. "Should the Draft Be Reinstated?" Forum, *Time,* December 29, 2002–January 5, 2003, pp. 101–102.

This circulation weekly discusses the major public policy question of whether the United States needs to return to a draft-based military.

Charles Moskos and Paul Glastris. "Now Do You Believe We Need a Draft?" *The Washington Monthly,* November 2001.

The offbeat Washington journal has a piece by one of the most prominent sociologists of his generation on why a draft would have unintended costs for U.S. society.

New America Foundation. "The Big Picture: A Unified National Security Budget." *National Security Event at Center for American Progress,* May 16, 2005 (accessed on August 23, 2005, at http://www.americanprogress.org).

New America Foundation. "The Draft: Inevitable, Avoidable or Preferable?" *National Security Event at Center for American Progress,* March 30, 2005, (transcript accessed on August 23, 2005, at http://www.americanprogress.org).

Daniel M. Smith. "Remembering the Draft." *Weekly Defense Monitor.* Washington, DC: Center for Defense Information, vol. 2, issue 27 (July 9, 1998).

This is a brief reprisal of the history of the military draft during the twentieth century.

Junious Ricardo Stanton. "Reinstituting the Military Draft: Politically Activating America's Youth." *ChickenBones: A Journal for Literary & Artistic African-American Themes,* October 13, 2003 (accessed on August 21, 2005 at http://www.nathanielturner.com/reinstitutingthedraft.htm).

This is an argument, presented seven months after conflict began in Iraq, that the draft is necessary to fill the force for the unpopular conflict. It also lays out the author's experience with the draft during the Vietnam era.

Rachel Stohl. "International Efforts Address Use of Child Soldiers." *Weekly Defense Monitor*. Washington, DC: Center for Defense Information, vol. 2, issue 27 (July 9, 1998).

As international media coverage about conflicts in the Third World grows, concerns about minimum recruitment ages for the military also grow. This piece considers the "Optional Protocol to the Convention of the Rights of the Child" and Amnesty International's push of the International Coalition to Stop the Use of Child Soldiers.

FFRDC Research Studies

As noted in Chapter 6, a number of organizations around the country specialize in research on national military service. The RAND Corporation, the Institute for Defense Analyses, the Center for Naval Analyses, and the Army Research Institute fall under this category. These organizations provide nonpartisan, expertly staffed analyses, often but not exclusively at the classified level. Some of these analyses have become the basis for the services' and the Department of Defense's operational and strategic decisions for the future of national service.

Rather than try to provide an exhaustive list of studies produced through these centers, their Web sites are on the World Wide Web and can be viewed at interest. Representative studies include the following:

Beth Asch and James Hosek. *Looking to the Future: What Does Transformation Mean for Military Manpower and Personnel Policy?* OP-108-OSD. Santa Monica, CA: RAND, 2004.

This topic is at the heart of the military's considerations for national service.

Richard Buddin and Kanika Kapur. *Tuition Assistance Usage and First-Term Military Retention*. MR-1295-OSD. Santa Monica, CA: RAND, 2002.

This study zeroes in on the problems the Marine Corps and Navy face in their attempts to encourage reenlistment.

Brian Chow. *The Peacetime Tempo of Air Mobility Operations: Meeting Demand and Maintaining Readiness.* MR-1506-AF. Santa Monica, CA: RAND, 2003.

The frequency of operational deployments, more colloquially known as "ops tempo," is a constant concern to anyone in national service and remains a continuous source of study.

Lynn E. Davis, J. Michael Polich, William M. Hix, Michael D. Greenberg, Stephen D. Brady, and Ronald E. Sortor. *Stretched Thin: Army Forces for Sustained Operations.* MG-362-A. Santa Monica, CA: RAND, 2005.

This addresses one of the more disturbing developments facing the members of the national service: their decreasing numbers.

Paul K. Davis, David C. Gompert, Richard J. Hillestad, and Stuart Johnson. *Transforming the Force: Suggestions for DoD Strategy.* IP-179. Santa Monica, CA: RAND, 1998.

Marc N. Elliott, Kanika Kapur, and Carole Roan Gresenz. *Modeling the Departure of Military Pilots from the Services.* MR-1327-OSD. Santa Monica, CA: RAND, 2004.

Ronald D. Fricker, Jr. *The Effects of Perstempo on Officer Retention in the U.S. Military.* MR-1556-OSD. Santa Monica, CA: RAND, 2002.

This review specifically considers the personnel deployments for officers in all the services.

With RAND's historic basic in the Air Force, the discussion of fixed-wing (traditional airplanes) aviation in the services is a natural link to national service recruitment and retention.

David C. Gompert and Irving Lachow. *Transforming U.S. Forces: Lessons from the Wider Revolution.* IP-193. Santa Monica, CA: RAND, 2000.

This work addresses the perennial question of what the military needs to do to transform the force.

John M. Halliday, David Oaks, and Jerry M. Sollinger. *Breaking the Mold: A New Paradigm for the Reserve Components.* IP-190. Santa Monica, CA: RAND, 2000.

This report concentrates on the need to create a new type of Reserve in the services. Similarly, the Institute for Defense

Analyses dedicates a significant portion of its work to issues relating to national military service questions. The Force and Strategy Assessments Division includes concentrations on the following tasks: Joint and Combined Force Planning, Operations, and Assessments; Concept Development and Experimentation; Improving DoD Plans, Processes and Organizations; and National Security Strategy Issues.

Margaret C. Harrell, Nelson Lim, Laura Werber Castañeda, and Daniela Golinelli. *Working around the Military: Challenges to Military Spouse Employment and Education.* MG-196-OSD. Santa Monica, CA: RAND, 2004.

The full version of this document, like many of these RAND citations, is available online at http://rand.org/publications/electronic/force.html. This article focuses on the obstacles and inequalities that exist between spouses in the civilian and military realms. It argues for better provision for military families.

James Hosek. *Deployments, Retention, and Compensation.* CT-222. Santa Monica, CA: RAND, 2004.

This is one analyst's testimony to the House Armed Services Committee on Total Force early in 2004.

James Hosek and Mark Totten. *Serving Away from Home: How Deployments Influence Reenlistment.* MR-1594-OSD. Santa Monica, CA: RAND, 2002.

Dina Levy, Joy Moini, Jennifer Sharp and Harry J. Thie. *Expanding Enlisted Lateral Entry: Options and Feasibility.* MG-134-OSD. Santa Monica, CA: RAND, 2004.

In trying to develop all facets necessary for the force, allowing civilians to enter at a later point in their careers must be explored.

Jamison Jo Medby and Russell W. Glenn. *Street Smart: Intelligence Preparation of the Battlefield for Urban Operations.* MR-1287-A. Santa Monica, CA: RAND, 2002.

Medby and Glenn examine the changes being made to members of the intelligence subfield to prepare them better for urban conflict.

Harry J. Thie, Raymond E. Conley, Henry A. Leonard, Megan Abbott, Eric V. Larson, K. Scott McMahon, Michael G. Shaley, Roand E. Sortor, William Taylor, Stephen Dalzell, and Roland J. Yardley. *Past and Future: Insights for Reserve Component Use.* TR-140-OSD. Santa Monica, CA: RAND, 2004.

This study provides a broad discussion of the future for the Reserves in the United States as part of the Department of Defense's strategy.

Gail L. Zellman and Susan M. Gates. *Examining the Cost of Military Child Care.* MR-1415-OSD. Santa Monica, CA: RAND, 2002.

The health and child-care requirements for the all-volunteer force are a major but little studied consideration to keep people enlisted.

Online Resources

Blogs

Undoubtedly, the most rapid growth in online resources has taken place in the realm of "blogs." It would of course be impossible to list all of the blogs that populate the World Wide Web. These sites are personal opinions, available online, with no outside intervention but intended to generate much public debate. A sample of blogs relevant to U.S. military service is named at www.C-Span.org, the Website for C-Span networks. On that Web site, the blogs listed include the following.

A Reservist's blog at www.stevenkiel.blogspot.com, which has a regular update by Staff Sergeant Steven Kiel, an Army Reservist in a maintenance battalion, about his experiences in Iraq and allowing for reactions from readers around the world. Blogs may be the most basic manner of experiencing the national service experience, albeit they are rather anecdotal in nature.

Similarly, www.iraqpictures.blogspot.com states that it is the Web site for "pictures of soldiers, marines, air force, sailors, contractors, and civilians serving in Iraq" (accessed on August 28, 2005). It includes pictures posted by a wide range of individuals serving in the war theater, giving an authentic sense of the human side of war in the Middle East.

Broadcast Resources

National Public Radio

The public radio hour entitled, "Justice Talking: The Stop Loss Policy: Necessary Policy or a Backdoor Draft?" taped on June 7, 2005.

This program covers the national military debate about "stop loss" policies in the current environment, with an emphasis on the legal side of the controversy. It can be heard online, or transcripts can be ordered from the Web site at http://www.justicetalking.org/programarchive.asp.

Other relevant discussions between legal and political analysts as well as interested citizens include:

"Justice Talking: And Justice for Some: The U.S. Battle with the International Criminal Court," recorded on April 28, 2005.
It considers why the United States does not want its military covered under the Court's jurisdiction.

"Justice Talking: Guantanamo Bay: Dealing with an Enemy in an Era of Terror," recorded on May 16, 2005.
This program looked at the difficult conundrum that holding accused terrorists in Guantanamo provided for the United States.

"Justice Talking: Military Tribunals: Secrecy for Security?" taped on November 18, 2003.
This program discussed the controversial military tribunals that the United States is using in the current conflicts.

"Justice Talking: A Just War," recorded on April 7, 2003.
This program raised the question of whether this conflict meets the criteria for Just War Theory.

"Justice Talking: Military Recruiting," taped on February 24, 2003.
This program laid out the legal and political questions on the then-imminent invasion of Iraq.

John Biewen, "Married to the Military," on American Radio Works (no date).

This broadcast considered the nature of life in both the armed forces and in "military towns," in which the armed services play significant economic and cultural roles. It also examined how a military family functions when at least one of its members is gone for long periods of time.

"Fresh Air with Terry Gross." "Fresh Air with Terry Gross: Dr. Francis DuFrague: Father and Son in Iraq," originally aired on National Public Radio on July 11, 2005. Transcripts and compact discs are available from www.npr.org/transcripts/.

Host Terry Gross conducts a long interview with a Philadelphia-based internist who has been in the Navy Reserves for over thirty years. The discussion covers how it affected his education, his life, and his career, and how this Reservist views the medical program of the armed forces during a war when active-duty and Reservists interact to fight wars.

"Fresh Air with Terry Gross: John Crawford: *The Last True Story I'll Ever Tell: An Accidental Soldier's Account of the War in Iraq*," originally aired on National Public Radio on August 3, 2005.

"Morning Edition" and "The Diane Rehm Show." The National Public Radio flagship programs, "Morning Edition" and "All Things Considered," both have regular discussions of recruiting, veterans' issues, and other portions of national service issues. These stories, far too numerous for listing here, are laid out on the Web page for National Public Radio, www.npr.org/templates/archives/rundown_archive_hub.php Topics can be searched on the Web page. Transcripts are available for a fee.

An example from the "Morning Edition" show that aired on March 14, 2005, considering "Critics: National Guard Unprepared for Iraq" argued that U.S. forces from the "weekend experience" (rather than full-time, duty-hardened troops) were not accustomed to the experiences they face in Iraq.

"The Diane Rehm Show: Military Service and the War in Iraq," originally aired on National Public Radio, August 8, 2005. Compact discs and cassettes available from www.WAMU.org.

This nationally syndicated show with call-in participation examines how the conflict in Iraq is affecting the United States' military service.

"The Diane Rehm Show: U.S. Military Personnel and Policies," originally aired on National Public Radio, June 7, 2005. Compact discs and cassettes available from www.WAMU.org.

This edition of a call-in show considered the range of personnel policies, including "stop loss," which is a program instituted during the Iraq and Afghanistan campaigns to maintain force strength by preventing affected personnel from separating from their units as their original commitments indicated.

"The Diane Rehm Show: Andrew Bacevich and *the New American Militarism*," originally aired on National Public Radio, May 26, 2005. Compact discs and cassettes available from www .WAMU.org.

Bacevich is a retired Army colonel who served through the early 1990s and has been a highly respected academic analyst, now at Boston University, who has argued that the United States is becoming overly enamored with using the armed services to solve all problems. He also focuses on how the armed forces themselves are changing as a result of these constant interventions.

"The Diane Rehm Show: Military Base Closings," originally aired on National Public Radio on May 17, 2005. Compact discs and cassettes available at www.WAMU.org.

For some communities, the presence of military bases is fundamental to the fabric of the community. Increasing budget pressures to close those bases are controversial but integral to the public policy debate in the United States as the society figures how to pursue appropriate policies.

"The Diane Rehm Show: Private Interests and Military Policy," originally aired on National Public Radio on March 11, 2003. Compact discs and cassettes available from www.WAMU.org.

This discussion considered whether the increased use of private firms to carry out functions formerly assigned to the military is affecting military policies.

"The Diane Rehm Show: Military Families," originally aired on National Public Radio on November 27, 2002. Compact discs and cassettes available from www.WAMU.org.

This hour-long show considered the current conditions and issues facing military families in the United States in the lead up to the Iraq war as the Afghanistan conflict entered its second year.

Chicago Public Radio's "Odyssey." "Odyssey" is produced by Chicago Public Radio and airs on weekdays on National Public Radio stations. Various editions concentrate on military service as noted.

"Odyssey: The Future of an All-Volunteer Army," January 31, 2005.

Two prominent analysts considered how the United States will evolve to keep an all-volunteer force while facing a shortage of men and women under arms.

"Odyssey: Military Desertion," July 27, 2004.

This show discussed the array of reasons a person leaves military service without finishing his or her term, including religious or political disagreements.

"Odyssey: War and the Body," July 15 2004.

This broadcast discussed the able bodies needed for wars and the medical or veterans' affairs approaches to those who are injured in these conflicts.

"Odyssey: The Politics of Defense Spending," February 25, 2004.

This show described the many variables that politicians consider as they develop defense budgets. A major portion of the budget goes to the force and efforts to attract young, educated individuals to national service.

"Odyssey: Gender and War," May 1, 2003.

This show focused on how women have been involved in past wars and on the two current conflicts in Iraq and Afghanistan.

"Odyssey: Patriotism and the Military," April 9, 2003.

This broadcast considered whether people who oppose the war are antipatriotic and how this question applies to broader issues such as whether one serves in national service.

"Odyssey: Civilians and Warfare," March 24, 2003.

The discussion covered whether conflict can entirely disconnect warfare from civilians. Appearing at the beginning of Operation Iraqi Freedom, this was a seminal discussion about civilians and the nature of national service.

"Odyssey: The Military and Civil Society," December 18, 2001.

The show discussed the way those in military service interact with the rest of U.S society.

"Odyssey: Pacifism," October 1, 2001.

This broadcast outlined the role of pacifism in the U.S. political and social experience, along with how it affects efforts to provide through the all-volunteer force.

"Odyssey: Patriotism," September 14, 2001.

Coming three days after the September 11 attacks, this hour-long show considered how patriotism affects society, including military service.

"Talk of the Nation." "Talk of the Nation: The Span of War: Cindy Sheehan and Families of the Fallen," aired August 29, 2005.

This show discussed the role of antiwar activism by families directly affected by Operations Enduring Freedom and Iraqi Freedom. Transcripts and compact discs available at www .npr.org/transcripts/.

"Talk of the Nation: Parents, Teens and Military Recruiting," originally aired on National Public Radio on July 5, 2005. Transcripts and compact discs available at www.npr.org/transcripts/.

Coming as national debate on U.S. involvement in Afghanistan and Iraq expands, this national call-in program discussed the tensions that have arisen between parents and military recruiters seeking to influence youth to enlist.

"Talk of the Nation: Women in Combat—Rules and Reality," originally aired on National Public Radio on May 19, 2005. Transcripts and compact discs available at www.npr.org/transcripts/.

Much of the period coinciding with the all-volunteer force has also been the time when women's potential role in this force has been discussed. Many women have sought full participation in the armed forces, including combat; many men both in and out of uniform have opposed that position. This show considered both sides of the debate in some detail.

"Talk of the Nation: Tales of War at Home," originally aired on National Public Radio on March 24, 2005. Transcripts and compact discs available at www.npr.org/transcripts/.

Coming on about the second anniversary of the invasion of Iraq, this hour-long call-in radio show looked at how those left at home are affected by their loved ones being sent abroad by national service.

"Talk of the Nation: Women and War," originally aired on National Public Radio on March 22, 2005. Transcripts and compact discs available at www.npr.org/transcripts/.

This was a full-hour appraisal of women in the various aspects of war facing the United States today.

Pacifica Radio

The liberal radio network Pacifica Radio often considers issues focusing on families and individuals affected by conflict. Included in the Pacifica Radio Archives are three noteworthy programs: "War Stories: A Vietnam Retrospective" and "War Stories: The Winter Soldier Investigations" (both considering the Southeast Asian experience between 1960 and 1975) and senator and former presidential candidate John F. Kerry's 1971 testimony before the Senate Foreign Relations Committee, detailing questions and observations by a young Navy lieutenant fulfilling his national service obligation but leaving with many questions. These are available at www.pacificaradioarchives.org/programs under the "War and Peace" category.

Television

"Frontline." "Frontline" is a long-running investigative series on the Public Broadcasting System and has considered many facets of national military service. Descriptions of the individual shows are available at http://www.pbs.org/wgbh/pages/frontline/shows. Each show gives background, a discussion forum, and interviews with the decision makers and individuals involved.

"Frontline: Ambush in Mogadishu" (originally aired September 28, 1998) covered the lead-up to and execution of the October 1993 operation to bring food to Mogadishu, Somalia, in the midst of a violent civil war. Military service is brought to life as those who experienced the mission gone awry are interviewed, giving a much fuller understanding of combat for the increasing percentage of the population which never experienced war.

"Frontline: The Future of War" (no date given) considered the concerns voiced in 2000 by Army Chief of Staff General Eric Shinseki about the choices facing the U.S. Army as it prepared for new conflicts in the new millennium. It included an interview with Department of Defense official Lawrence Korb who talked about how stretched the Army and other services are in addressing the major threat he sees to the United States: instability, a vague but hovering concept. Other interviews were with the former Chief of Staff General Shinseki, Vice President Richard B. Cheney, and others, all putting the question of military service into the context of the issues that war will bring.

"Frontline: Give War a Chance" (no date) focuses on the use of force debate surrounding the intervention in the Balkans to prevent genocide in the 1990s. It lays out all sides of the debate as well as the policy trade-offs that it involved and that bother service personnel the most: are we asking officers and enlisted men who are dedicated to fighting war to sacrifice their training to humanitarian intervention?

"Frontline: The Gulf War" (originally aired January 9, 1996) contains oral histories that illuminate the horrors and oddities of war through the 1990–1991 Gulf War experience, culminating in ousting Saddam Hussein from Kuwait and setting the precursor for the 2003 invasion of Iraq.

"Frontline: The Last Battle of the Gulf War" (no date) zeroes in on the ongoing debate about veterans' long-running health problems, which many believe were caused by chemical warfare toward the end of the 1990–1991 Gulf War. This debate illuminates the nature of the nation's commitment after war to its veterans.

"Frontline: The Long Road to War," aired initially on March 17, 2003, uses shows from the prior twelve years to detail the slow, painful path that led the United States into conflict in Iraq beginning in mid-March 2003. It gives a sense of how the views on using the U.S. military have broadened in the post–Cold War era.

"Frontline: The Navy Blues" (no date) is a series of synopses of problems that plagued the Navy in the 1990s. These included the perceptions of Navy hostility to women evoked by the 1991 Tailhook Association meeting in Las Vegas, the question of how to integrate women into the naval aviator community, and what is involved in flying on and off of the *U.S.S. Enterprise*. It gives a solid understanding of the challenges facing the sea component of the U.S. military.

"Frontline: War in Europe" (no date) addresses the divisive and complex problems that were brought to the fore both inside the U.S. military and in the Western coalition faced with human rights abuses and intransigent foes in the Kosovo conflict of the late 1990s. Especially compelling is the treatment of the moral and ethical issues that this policy disconnect created. This particular feature also gives a fairly detailed view of both U.S. and European sides with military and civilian leadership interviewed.

"Frontline: The War Behind Closed Doors," originally shown on February 20, 2003, gives a sense of why many people believe that President George W. Bush's waging of war against Saddam Hussein was a fundamentally new use of the U.S. military instrument and how that would impact the nation, including those dedicated to national service, in the future.

The NewsHour with Jim Lehrer. The NewsHour with Jim Lehrer is produced by and shown on the Public Broadcasting System on local public television stations. Because it is shown five times weekly, there are almost fifteen hundred shows covering U.S. military service. They will not, of course, all be listed here, but the archives of *The NewsHour* can be found at www.pbs.org/newshour/search. (The Web site for the show, "The Online

NewsHour," itself is an incredible resource on national service, located at www.pbs.org/newshour.) Transcripts are available through the Web site, and videos of the shows can be ordered. A sample of the show's topics relating to national service is listed. The "NewsHour Index," located at www.pbs.org/newshour/ newshour_index.html, gives a list of the segments that have been shown on the program.

"Presidential Debate: Part III," *Newshour with Jim Lehrer Online,* October 8, 2004, accessed August 21, 2005, at http://www .pbs.org/newshour/vote2004/debates/2nddebate/part3.html.

"The NewsHour with Jim Lehrer Online NewsHour: High School Recruiting," first shown on December 13, 2004. This show discussed the challenges that military recruiters find in going into high schools during a conflict whose purpose is being debated.

"The NewsHour with Jim Lehrer Online NewsHour: Generals Speak Out on Iraq," shown on April 13, 2006. This segment highlighted the criticism of several highly visible former senior military officers who believe President Bush should replace his secretary of defense because Donald Rumsfeld, in the view of these officers, had made critical, repeated errors in conducting the war in Iraq.

"The NewsHour with Jim Lehrer Online NewsHour: Extended Service," shown on June 3, 2004. This segment outlined the implications of the newly announced "stop loss" policy, which prevented soldiers from leaving their units if they were within three months' departure for one of the two theaters of conflict.

Also on *The NewsHour with Jim Lehrer* are "Background Reports" on topical concerns that set up the issues but do not have an interview with an analyst or policymaker.

"The NewsHour with Jim Lehrer Background Reports: Military Base Closings," aired on August 24, 2005, describes the implications of bases staying open in Connecticut while the historic Walter Reed Military Hospital has been closed.

"The NewsHour with Jim Lehrer Background Reports: A Mother's Vigil," aired on August 16, 2005, discusses Cindy Sheehan's protest activity outside President George W. Bush's ranch in Crawford, Texas, and why it is attracting so much attention.

"The NewsHour with Jim Lehrer Background Reports: Town Mourns Fallen Marines," August 9, 2005, lays out the torment of an Ohio town that lost almost two dozen Marine Reservists in two days in Iraq.

"The NewsHour with Jim Lehrer Background Reports: Women in Combat," August 3, 2005, describes the challenges and concerns that women meet in trying to be full players in national service.

"The NewsHour with Jim Lehrer Background Reports: Soldiers' Stories," aired on July 1 and 4, 2005, presents narratives from service personnel in the field in Iraq and Afghanistan.

"The NewsHour with Jim Lehrer Background Reports: Going AWOL," May 25, 2005, describes the soldiers who have left their units without permission or without completing their terms of service.

"The NewsHour with Jim Lehrer Background Reports: Wounds of War," April 26, 2005, considers the military medical community available to veterans.

"The NewsHour with Jim Lehrer Background Reports: Gays in the Military," April 13, 2005, covers the ongoing controversy about the armed services tolerating or welcoming gay members.

"The NewsHour with Jim Lehrer Background Reports: Challenging Orders," February 24, 2005, considers the attempts in Oregon to alter the Army's "stop loss" rules to prevent people from separating from their units.

"The NewsHour with Jim Lehrer Background Reports: War Wounds," February 15, 2005, visits an Army field hospital in Landstuhl, Germany, where the wounded from Afghanistan and Iraq receive intensive assistance.

"The NewsHour with Jim Lehrer Background Reports: Court-Martial," January 15, 2005, describes the problems of the Army Specialist Charles Graner's court-martial process at an Army base in Texas.

"The NewsHour with Jim Lehrer Background Reports: Deadly Day," December 21 and 22, 2004, includes an interview with an embedded reporter who witnessed the suicide bombing that hit a mess tent in Mosul, Iraq, severely affecting an engineering battalion from the Maine National Guard.

"The NewsHour with Jim Lehrer Background Reports: Under Armored," December 9, 2004, covers the ongoing debate on whether the protection for the service personnel, especially the ground component, is adequate.

"The NewsHour with Jim Lehrer Background Reports: Target Fallujah," November 16, 2004, lays out the block-by-block battle for the city of Fallujah.

"The NewsHour with Jim Lehrer Background Reports: Coping with War," November 9, 2004, describes the posttraumatic stress syndrome affecting many veterans of the conflict in Iraq.

"The NewsHour with Jim Lehrer Background Reports: Disobeying Orders," October 18, 2004, discusses the realities of a unit from Mississippi deliberately disregarding direct orders.

"The NewsHour with Jim Lehrer Background Reports: Filling the Ranks," July 21, 2004, considers the alleged difficulties the services are finding in filling their billets with new or renewing recruits.

"The NewsHour with Jim Lehrer Background Reports: Military Targets," July 21, 2004, lays out the scam artists increasingly targeting military families.

"The NewsHour with Jim Lehrer Background Reports: Abuse Investigation," May 11, 2004, includes testimony by Major General Anthony Taguba, the Army investigator whose initial public report revealed significant lapses at the Abu Ghraib prison outside Baghdad.

"The NewsHour with Jim Lehrer Background Reports: A Fallen Son," April 20, 2004, gives a look at how the small town of Dubois, Wyoming, reacted to the death of one of its citizens in Iraq.

"The NewsHour with Jim Lehrer Background Reports: Rape in the Ranks," April 6, 2004, describes alleged rape problems within the services in the war theater.

"The NewsHour with Jim Lehrer Background Reports: Training for Danger," April 1, 2004, outlines recent changes in ways of preparing individuals for their deployments.

"The NewsHour with Jim Lehrer Background Reports: Growing the Army," January 13, 2004, talks about a significantly smaller Army from its predecessor in the First Gulf War (1990–1991) and the effects of that change.

"The NewsHour with Jim Lehrer Background Reports: Vaccine Ruling," December 23, 2004, focuses on a federal court ruling that the Department of Defense's mandatory anthrax vaccine was not enforceable.

"The NewsHour with Jim Lehrer Background Reports: Culture Change," October 14, 2003, describes rape allegations and questions about institutional intolerance for women at the U.S. Air Force Academy.

"The NewsHour with Jim Lehrer Background Reports: America As Occupier," July 21, 2003, describes the difficulties that the United States now faces as the rebuilding of Iraq becomes an occupation mission.

"The NewsHour with Jim Lehrer Background Reports: Noncitizen Soldiers," April 21, 2003, considers the 37,000 men and women in uniform who are not U.S. citizens but are in national service.

"The NewsHour with Jim Lehrer Background Reports: War Plans," March 30, 2003, describes the civilian versus military issues in the initial two weeks of the invasion of Iraq.

"The NewsHour with Jim Lehrer Background Reports: The Home Front," March 23 and 24, 2003, describes the feelings of those left behind by the military waging war in Iraq as the conflict accelerates.

"The NewsHour with Jim Lehrer Background Reports: Military Readiness," September 14, 2000, discusses how well prepared the U.S. forces are for potential conflict.

"The NewsHour with Jim Lehrer Background Reports: The G.I. Bill," July 4, 2000, examines the anniversary of the educational benefits for general enlisted personnel, which has been the reason many men and women have signed up for national service.

"The NewsHour with Jim Lehrer Background Reports: Citizen Soldiers," May 17, 2000, looks at the impact of long-term deployments of U.S. peacekeepers in the Balkans.

"The NewsHour with Jim Lehrer Background Reports: Gays in the Military," January 6, 2000, outlines the continuing controversy about the "don't ask, don't tell" policy and its application.

"The NewsHour with Jim Lehrer Background Reports: Division in the Divisions," November 29, 1999, concerns race problems within the armed forces.

"The NewsHour with Jim Lehrer Background Reports: A Sure Shot?" October 21, 1999, describes the troops' ambivalence about the mandatory anthrax vaccines being administered by the Pentagon.

Other Television Broadcasts

The *American Experience* series on public television has produced a number of series on topics related to national military service. One is the 1983 "Vietnam: A Television Experience," which was a thirteen-part series available in eleven hours of broadcast. The series covered the history of the Vietnam conflict by looking at various periods, including the final French experience, the Diem years, the Tet Offensive, and the negotiations that led to U.S. withdrawal. The Web site on the *American Experience* at http://www.pbs.org/wgbh/amex/vietnam/series/fd.html provides additional readings on the Vietnam War. The series is available for purchase from PBS Online at http://www.pbs.org/wgbh/amex/shop.html.

One of the most widely viewed resources available through a broadcast medium in the C-Span system, captured at www.c-span.org, which covers the four C-Span channels available, the programming on subsequent days, and various other portions of the C-Span "family" such as C-Span Radio, C-Span Web sites, and other materials relating to this nonpartisan system created in the early years of national cable service to provide a window into congressional activities.

One of the more useful portions of this vast Web site is the Video Library on a wide range of issues, including Defense/Security. C-Span.org also contains a series of electronic links to various reports from the U.S. and foreign (such as British) governments, congressional hearings, Weblogs from serving military personnel, Pentagon and Central Command news releases, the Walter Reed Army Hospital, the Pentagon television station, the U.S. Embassy in Baghdad, the transitional government in Iraq, the White House, the Iraqi constitution as drafted in August 2005, and various other concerns relevant to those serving in national service. Three curious links at the bottom portion of the C-Span Web site are electronic links to the current body count in Operation Iraqi Freedom, a military death chart, and an Iraqi body count.

C-Span has a unique role in the United States in that its four televised networks and C-Span Radio regularly broadcast events where military service issues arise. These are frequent enough that the Web site does not list individual events, but the Web site C-Span.com does indicate the shows that are on at various times. Much of C-Span's daily broadcasting during the week is dedicated to congressional hearings, but its twenty-four-hour activity allows many events to appear that would otherwise receive little attention.

The History Channel, a cable television channel created in the 1990s, presents a fascinating selection of programs with a significant emphasis on military and national service topics. An example was "The True Story of Blackhawk Down," aired on March 5, 2006. History Channel programs tend to use nationally or internationally known specialists who seek to educate the broadest swath of the public. The History Channel Web site, http://www .historychannel.com, also includes links to the *History Channel Magazine* and an archive of speeches and videos. The Web site also has a secure server to sell many of its shows and series as DVDs and videos. Series include topics such as World War II, Vietnam, and various service capabilities (air craft carriers, fighters, bombers, and such).

Over There is a television series on the FX station that appeared after it became apparent that the Iraq conflict was going to be a more prolonged one than had been originally anticipated. Developed by successful producer Stephen Bochco, this show gives a detailed, often grimy portrait of the nature of military service when on the ground in another land.

U.S. Government Publications

The Congressional Budget Office (CBO) is a relevant source on national military service, particularly in cases of disputes over cost. In May 2005, CBO published *Options for Restructuring the Army* (Washington, DC: Government Printing Office, 2005), which includes a chapter on how the military's force levels can be raised and the effects that would have on reducing support for the armed forces across the country.

The Government Accounting Office (GAO, formerly the General Accounting Office) is the congressionally mandated investigative arm of the federal government. It regularly reviews some programs (usually annually funded activities) while it investigates special requests initiated by representatives and senators. Examples of GAO reports are "Reserve Forces: Actions Needed to Better Prepare the National Guard for Future Overseas and Domestic Missions," GAO-05–21, Washington, DC: 2005; "Military Personnel: Information on Selected National Guard Management Issues," GAO-04–258, Washington, DC: 2004; and "Military and Veterans' Benefits: Enhanced Services Could Improve Transition Assistance for Reserves and National Guard," GAO-05–522, Washington, DC: 2005. Each report has a question posed to the GAO, its research methodology, and its findings and recommendations. GAO reports can be found at www.gpoaccess.gov/ and the GAO material can be found in the Legislative Branch materials by searching within a GAO Report.

The Congressional Research Service, located within the Library of Congress for the purposes of creating immediate studies to meet congressional inquiries, also studies national military service regularly.

Congressional hearings are a regular, vital source of information since the Congress is integral in the process of creating a national service through writing and funding the laws that make it possible. The major committees on national security questions in each branch of the Congress have their own Web sites. The House of Representatives' Committee on Armed Services, for example, is located at www.house.gov/hasc, and the Web site has listings of speakers at various hearings, the transcripts of the hearings, and other information vital to inform the public that their representatives are paying attention to the issues. The House Committee on Veterans Affairs is located at www.veterans.house.gov where the committee can monitor postconflict assistance to eligible personnel and spouses. The House Committee on International Relations may occasionally consider topics of interest to those studying or contemplating military service; the Committee Web site is www.house.gov/international_relations. The funding body in the House of Representatives is the Committee on Appropriations, located at www.appropriations.house.gov. In addition, the House Committee on Ways and Means, which determines the country's spending priorities, covers a range of topics that relate to military service affairs. Ways and Means is found at www.waysandmeans.house.gov. Each of the committees has a variety of subcommittees, which can also be found through these Web sites.

On the Senate side of the Hill, the Senate Foreign Relations Committee, available at www.foreign.senate.gov, is an exceptionally prominent committee, while defense is covered by the Senate Armed Services Committee, www.armed-services.senate.gov on the Web. Veterans' issues are the purview of the Senate Committee on Veterans' Affairs (www.veterans.senate.gov). The Senate committee that considers funding for national service is the Committee on Appropriations at www.appropriations.senate.gov.

The Government Printing Office (GPO) is the federal agency that publishes multitudes of publications on issues relating to national service and everything else that concerns the U.S. government. The easiest way to find the relevant materials is through the GPO Web site at www.gpoaccess.gov. The site is easily navigated and is a treasure trove of reports from the government's vast holdings.

A particularly important Web site is the Department of Defense's (DoD) "Defenselink," found at http://www.defenselink.mil/home, which provides access to a wealth of DoD reports, links, speeches, studies, and other official government information. In addition, www.ntis.gov/products/families/military.asp has extensive publication material aimed at families.

An example of the type of information available through this source is a 2005 study on the growing problem of sexual harassment and violence at the service academies. The "Report of the Defense Task Force on Sexual Harassment and Violence at the

Military Service Academies," published in June 2005, was made available at http://www.defenselink.mil/home/pdf/High_GPO _RRC_tx.pdf (accessed on August 29, 2005).

Testimony

One of the most prominent sources of information on military service is testimony before congressional hearings. All senior members of the services face confirmation hearings prior to assuming their jobs, but the U.S. system of checks and balances acts as a fundamental component of government that requires that Congress ask various individuals for their views at any point.

Testimony on the question of recruiting and retention has been important throughout the postdraft era. Lieutenant General Daniel James III, U.S. Air National Guard, provided such testimony on July 19, 2005, before the House Armed Services Subcommittee on Military Personnel. Many more testimonials exist.

Senator and unsuccessful 2004 presidential candidate John F. Kerry's infamous testimony in 1971 before the Senate Foreign Relations Committee is worth looking at because of the effect it had on the 2004 presidential campaign (both to galvanize and to repel some voters) and for its description of what a young Navy lieutenant faced in carrying out orders in a controversial conflict.

Films

Many movies have discussed national service since the genre first appeared a century ago. A couple of films, however, portray the issues of surviving the horrors of armed conflict or the grind of perpetual life on deployment with special vigor. Many of these shows are available in DVD format for home viewing.

Band of Brothers was created in the early 2000s by movie producer Steven Spielberg and actor Tom Hanks to describe the experiences of so many veterans of World War II.

Platoon, a 1986 release staring Tom Berenger, traces a platoon's experience in Vietnam during the war. Many have praised this film as extraordinarily honest and accurate. It is available on DVD from amazon.com or bn.com.

The film *We Were Soldiers,* based on the 1992 book *We Were Soldiers Once . . . and Young: The Battle of the Ia Drang,* by Harold Moore and Joe Gallaway, opened in 2002 starring Mel Gibson. An exceptionally moving portrayal of one of the earliest bloody battles in Vietnam, the movie gives an acutely accurate sense of how soldiers struggle to survive and save their brethren in combat.

Saving Private Ryan, first shown in 1998, starred Tom Hanks and Matt Damon, and portrayed the story of a squad, following the Normandy invasion in June 1944, sent to find a sole-surviving son of parents who had lost all but one of their sons to the war.

One video of note is the 1999 *War at Home* about the antiwar movement and the bombing of the physics building at the University of Wisconsin in Madison on August 24, 1970. The video is available through Amazon.com.

Many movies have parodied national military service over the decades. Two of the most famous are *M*A*S*H,* starring Elliott Gould and Donald Sutherland in the movie that premiered in 1972, then Alan Alda, MacLean Stevenson and Harry Morgan in a subsequent, long-running television show in the 1970s and 1980s, and the 1964 *Dr. Strangelove or How I learned to Stop Worrying and Love the Bomb,* starring Peter Sellers, George C. Scott, Sterling Hayden, and Slim Pickens. Similarly, highly critical smaller circulation movies, such as *Atomic Café,* have shown the oddities of the civil defense preparation of society in case of a nuclear conflict in the 1950s and have examined the impact that military service and delivering the weapons the armed services are charged with using have affected the United States and, by extension, the world.

Service Web Sites

Each of the services has a Web site that covers aspects relevant to military service as enlisted or commissioned officer personnel. The Air Force has its site at www.af.mil while the Marine Corps is at www.usmc.mil/marines/mcn2000.nsf/frontpagenews. The Army has its site at www.army.mil and the Navy has www.navy.mil. Each of these sites has outreach to its community, links to publications and services of interest, and a range of activities tied to the service.

Other Web Sites

Web sites on the Internet covering national service proliferate, in general, in relationship to the current events of the times. The sites listed here give some focus to the range that relates to the topic of military service, service personnel, policies, and family concerns.

Web sites on the Internet covering national service proliferate, in general, in relationship to the current events of the times. The sites listed here give some focus to the range that relates to the topic of military service, service personnel, policies, and family concerns.

Townhall.com is a conservative activist site that began as an offshoot of the Heritage Foundation. Its national-security Web page, www.townhall.com/issues/NationalSecurity.html, takes an inclusive approach in its examination of security-related issues; the site contains a number of blogs, opinion pieces, and electronic links to other sites that consider the military's changing role in U.S. society.

Another fascinating Web site is the Civilian Public Service (CPS) records held by Swarthmore College, an undergraduate institution in southeastern Pennsylvania with long ties to the Quaker congregations. At www.swarthmore.edu/library/peace/DG051–099/dg056cpspers.htm, the records are online with details on various CPS camps, individuals' records, and various other useful data on this alternative service program.

An extraordinarily useful site for basic information on serving in the armed forces is www.military.com, which gives links, data, enlistment information, and other materials useful to current, retired, or prospective service members. Similarly, the Web site for the GI Bill is a commonly used one at www.gibill.va.gov.

Finally, all of the military services have historical organizations. The Army, however, has a fabulous historical series online through the Center for Military History at Fort Lesley J. McNair in Washington, D.C. This series of publications, which often includes the original documents, can be viewed at www.army.mil/cmg. This allows accessing a long list of histories of the United States and of various parts of the Army, such as the *Soldier-Statesmen of the Constitution*, written by Robert K. Wright, Jr. and Morris J. MacGregor, Jr., at the Center for Military History in 1987.

Glossary

Active duty Beginning with the founding of the Republic, a division in thought occurred on whether the nation needed a force of officers and enlisted personnel who were constantly on guard against threats or were merely called up when threats arose. The active-duty status is that under which forces are serving at a state of readiness to respond to attacks against the nation.

All-volunteer force With the end of the draft lottery in 1973, the United States adopted a military entrance policy of voluntary service. The term adopted for the new military was that of an all-volunteer force to characterize the serving men and women's commitment to their force.

Angel Flight Female Air Force Auxiliary Founded at the University of Omaha, this women's parallel organization to the Air Force ROTC programs started in 1952. By 1955, it had become a national organization with chapters at universities and colleges.

AVF See *All-volunteer force*

Bonuses With the historical tensions about what type of force the United States should adopt, a method for enhancing recruiting levels was to pay those who entered or stayed (depending on the particular force level requirements at any particular moment) a bonus for the individual's service.

Bounties During certain periods, such as the early 1860s as the Civil War broke out, bounties were paid to individuals who provided men to meet the needs of the military, especially the Army. This practice was discontinued in the twentieth century.

Chain of command Within the armed forces, a set, easily identifiable hierarchy of responsibilities that govern the relationship between individuals and ranks. This chain of command governs all interactions in a formal sense and also defines certain relationships.

297

The Citadel Established in Charleston, South Carolina, as a military college to defend the city, the Citadel has been known as the Military College of South Carolina since 1824. Long providing officers to the United States Army, it has also had a more recent history of controversy as it wrestled with whether to admit women to its storied halls.

Citizen-soldier One important strain of political thought in the United States is that the most effective and appropriate, while least dangerous, type of military personnel are those who are regular citizens most of their lives but take up arms only to defend the nation when under threat. That defense requires a minimal expense and level of preparation to be adequate but not overwhelming or likely to involve the armed forces in unnecessary intervention in the affairs of the nation.

Commander-in-chief The president of the United States has a different title and role in the chain of command for military personnel: the president is the most senior ranking command official. Although the president would normally command support by virtue of his or her elected office, the Constitution notes that the commander-in-chief is a position of legal authority.

Draft The draft was a process constituted during the Civil War and reintroduced in World War I to assure there would be adequate manpower to fight the nation's wars. Highly controversial by the late 1960s when many young people questioned why they were being drafted by their nation to fight a war they did not believe in, the draft led to considerable political tensions in the country. Many believed it was a fair system because it was conducted by a lottery system. President Richard Nixon decided to end the draft in 1973.

Holloway Program This was the Navy's plan to begin Navy Reserve Officer Training (Navy ROTC) programs at a few select colleges and universities nationwide. Eventually it was expanded to a greater number of schools.

Marshall Commission Selective Service The Selective Service monitors registration for military service should a president need to raise the number of forces for a conflict. The commission is named for Burke Marshall, assistant attorney general under Presidents Kennedy and Johnson.

Military-industrial complex President Dwight D. Eisenhower used this now famous term for the linkage between the armed forces, industrial producers of military goods, and the supporting cast that he feared would begin to push the nation toward a perpetual military posture, unlike any prior time in U.S. history.

Moderate Whig thought The political philosophy that argued, in the twilight of the seventeenth century in England and the colonies, that the Glorious Revolution of 1688 provided the constitutional balance to prevent the outrageous growth of military power that motivated the Radical Whigs to advocate against a professional, standing army.

My Lai incident   On March 16, 1968, Army troops under Lieutenant William Calley engaging in a search-and-destroy mission committed atrocities in the Vietnamese village of My Lai. This divisive event illustrated, in part, the difficulties of asking young men to engage in a war that fails to set out clear conditions.

National Guard   Originally the militia forces in the individual states, the Dick Act of 1903 converted the militia into the National Guard nationwide. The National Guard is a state-based structure with a direct chain of command to the governor of the state in which the individual resides. The governor can call a person up for emergencies, such as for aid during Hurricane Katrina in 2005, or the governor can release the Guard for national deployment—both abroad and domestically. In that case, the Guard is federalized for service and then is placed under federal government control. The National Guard was built on the state militia systems that served as the basis of the U.S. defense experience and the genesis of the civilian-soldier concept, which is fundamental to the U.S. view of warfare and defense.

Newburgh Conspiracy   This was the 1783 movement led by Alexander Hamilton and Robert Morris to replace Congress with martial law as the War for Independence ended because the troops of the Continental Army, encamped at Newburgh, New York, were growing increasingly frustrated with their treatment by the Continental Congress. Upon hearing of the possible coup d'etat, General George Washington addressed and silenced the movement, largely by virtue of his personal prestige and sacrifice.

Officer Candidates School   This is an alternative induction process for officers who have not attended the service academies or a Reserve Office Training Corps program at a civilian college or university. The thirteen-week Navy course takes place at Pensacola, Florida, while the Marine Corps operates its school at Quantico, Virginia. Fort Benning, Georgia, is the location for the Army Officer Candidates School, while the Air Force locates its school at Maxwell Air Force Base in Alabama.

Officer Training School   This provides a twelve-week training course for noncommissioned officers (NCOs) to learn the leadership and administration skills they will need to lead the forces in their respective services. The Air Force Officer Training School is at Maxwell Air Force Base, while the Marines use Quantico Marine Base in Virginia.

Peace establishment   The type of permanent, standing military in place as the Founders and their immediate successors wrestled with the structure of government.

Radical Whig thought   The most severe critics of government, especially the government of England in the late seventeenth and eighteenth centuries, who used a standing army for the repression and economic exploitation of the citizenry. This school of thought held sway with many in the late colonial and early independence periods of the United States.

Reserve Officer Training Corps (ROTC)   Built similarly to the Morrill Act of 1862, which required military training for students at the land-grant schools of the United States, Reserve Officer Training Corps programs were instituted at civilian universities, which prepared officers for entrance to the services beginning in the middle of the twentieth century.

Reserves   Active-duty personnel are full-time servicemen and -women whose sole day-in and day-out job is national security as part of national service. These people are active regardless of whether the United States is engaged in an ongoing conflict, thus leading to their deployment to points around the world, or keeping them home (where they continue to train) because nothing immediately threatens the nation (or our allies).

The Reserves are individuals in each of the four services (Air Force, Army, Marines, and Navy) who have agreed to be part-timers in their national service. These individuals generally train one weekend monthly and for a two-week period each year, with the goal of keeping up their readiness. The Reservist receives pay for the time he or she puts into the Reserve commitment. The individual has the same rank structure as that of the active-duty force. Anyone with a Reserve position (officer or enlisted) is subject to being called up by the president for active duty in case it is deemed necessary.

Risk rule   This policy statement from the Department of Defense centers on which specialties within the armed services women can participate in, for fear they could be put into harm's way because of conflict.

ROTC   See *Reserve Office Training Program*

Search-and-destroy missions   Military officers are sometimes assigned to root out enemy forces from their hiding spots woven into the fabric of civilian societies and then prevent those forces from returning to the fight against the U.S. military.

Standing army   Early debates within the colonies and the newly independent nation focused on whether the defense of the nation would be better handled by a professional, dedicated army or militia forces. The standing army is what the United States has today.

Stop loss policy   When the United States' troop strength declines to levels unacceptable for accomplishing a stated mission, stop loss policies are instituted to prevent personnel from retiring.

Substitution   Students are allowed to take regular courses at some universities in lieu of strictly military science courses.

Ted Wright   This was a cartoon character used in the 1950s to show a guy in the ROTC program, illustrating what the program required and what a participant was allowed to do in his national service.

Total Force   This is the concept that the services are not divided into active duty, Reserve component, and National Guard but rather constitute a Total Force made and facilitated by all portions of the military working together to create a more effective U.S. military.

Tuskegee Airmen   Beginning in 1941, this Army Air Corps program at Tuskegee, Alabama's Moton Field trained 992 African American pilots for duty (in segregated units) during World War II.

Universal military training   This concept signifies that all students in higher education in the United States receive a measure of military training.

Virginia Military Institute   Established in the early part of the nineteenth century at Lexington, Virginia, the Virginia Military Institute—like the Citadel in Charleston, South Carolina—has a program quite similar to that of the service academies, with emphasis placed on military education and a smaller variety of undergraduate courses in other fields to prepare officer candidates for service to the nation.

WAC   See *Women's Army Corps*

WASP See *Women's Air Force Service Pilots*

WAVES   See *Women Accepted for Voluntary Emergency Service*

Women Accepted for Voluntary Emergency Service   (WAVES) Women serving the Navy in voluntary positions that were important support for the World War II effort were part of this organization.

Women's Air Force Service Pilots   (WASPS) This program was created in 1943 to allow women to fly a variety of aircraft in the final two years of World War II.

Women's Army Corps   (WAC) Before World War II began, the Women's Army Corps was proposed to make certain that women who served in jobs assisting with the Army would not have to replicate the World War I experience of seeking their own quarters and food. Because the Army would not accept women, the Women's auxiliary Army Corps, a parallel organization, represented a compromise allowing 150,000 women to assist in World War II in various functions. When the auxiliary became militarized in 1943, its name reverted to Women's Army Corps.

Women's Auxiliary Army Corps   (WAAC) The Women's Auxiliary Army Corps was the compromise devised to satisfy the Army that women would not actually be allowed into the Army. It provided some structure to the volunteers who supported the Army in World War II and became a military corps in 1943, assuming the name Women's Army Corps.

Women's Auxiliary Ferrying Squadron   (WAFS) Created in 1942, the WAFS supported Army Air Corps efforts during World War II.

Index

About the Author

Cynthia Watson earned a doctorate at Notre Dame and a master's degree at the London School of Economics. She has taught national-security strategy and U.S. strategy in East Asia since 1992 at the National War College, where she is professor of strategy. Dr. Watson has written two prior books in the Contemporary World Issues Series for ABC-CLIO.